The Political Economy of Corporate Raiding in Russia

Corporate raiding – the shocking phenomenon whereby criminals, business rivals, and even state bureaucrats visit business headquarters and force owners or staff to transfer business assets, land, or property – is an increasing problem in Russia. This book, based on extensive original research, provides a comprehensive overview of this activity. It describes the nature of corporate raiding, provides numerous case studies, and discusses the role of the state and government officials. Overall the book argues that the prevailing climate of business and government in Russia leads to a situation where control is closely linked to corruption and coercion.

Ararat L. Osipian is Fellow of the Institute of International Education, United Nations Plaza, New York and Honorary Associate at the University of Wisconsin-Madison College of Letters and Science, Department of Political Science.

Routledge Transnational Crime and Corruption Series

Published in association with the Terrorism, Transnational Crime and Corruption Center, School of Public Policy, George Mason University, USA

Russian Business Power
The role of Russian business in foreign and security relations
Edited by Andreas Wenger, Jeronim Perovic and Robert W. Orttung

Organized Crime and Corruption in Georgia
Edited by Louise Shelley, Erik Scott and Anthony Latta

Russia's Battle with Crime, Corruption and Terrorism
Edited by Robert W. Orttung and Anthony Latta

Human Trafficking and Human Security
Edited by Anna Jonsson

Irregular Migration from the Former Soviet Union to the United States
Saltanat Liebert

Human Security, Transnational Crime and Human Trafficking
Asian and Western perspectives
Edited by Shiro Okubo and Louise Shelley

Labour Migration, Human Trafficking and Multinational Corporations
The commodification of illicit flows
Edited by Ato Quayson and Antonela Arhin

Environmental Crime and Corruption in Russia
Federal and regional perspectives
Edited by Sally Stoecker and Ramziyá Shakirova

Disengaging from Terrorism – Lessons from the Turkish Penitents
Kamil Yilmaz

The Political Economy of Corporate Raiding in Russia
Ararat L. Osipian

The Political Economy of Corporate Raiding in Russia

Ararat Osipian

LONDON AND NEW YORK

First published 2018
by Routledge
2 Park Square, Milton Park, Abingdon, Oxon OX14 4RN

and by Routledge
711 Third Avenue, New York, NY 10017

Routledge is an imprint of the Taylor & Francis Group, an informa business

© 2018 Ararat Osipian

The right of Ararat Osipian to be identified as author of this work has been
asserted by him in accordance with sections 77 and 78 of the Copyright,
Designs and Patents Act 1988.

All rights reserved. No part of this book may be reprinted or reproduced or
utilised in any form or by any electronic, mechanical, or other means, now
known or hereafter invented, including photocopying and recording, or in
any information storage or retrieval system, without permission in writing
from the publishers.

Trademark notice: Product or corporate names may be trademarks or
registered trademarks, and are used only for identification and explanation
without intent to infringe.

British Library Cataloguing-in-Publication Data
A catalogue record for this book is available from the British Library

Library of Congress Cataloging-in-Publication Data
A catalog record has been requested for this book

ISBN: 978-1-138-47793-3 (hbk)
ISBN: 978-1-351-10381-7 (ebk)

Typeset in Times New Roman
by Apex CoVantage, LLC

Contents

List of figures	vii
List of tables	viii
Foreword	ix
Preface	xi
Acronyms and abbreviations	xiii
Note on translation and transliteration	xv

Introduction   1

Raiding Russia 1
Contextualizing raiding 4
The structure 10

1   Corruption, coercion, and control   19

1.1 Theoretical explanation of raiding in a transition
economy 19
    Regime sustainability and raiding 19
    Defining raiding and its place 27
1.2 Alienation-appropriation: the inverted character
of raiding 36
    Appropriation and raiding 36
    Nature, causes, and basis of raiding 42
1.3 Concluding remarks 49

2   State and raider and state-raider   57

2.1 State and raider 57
    Optimization of the state 57
    Economically active bureaucracy 62
2.2 State-raider 67
    Aggressive state 67
    Noneconomic factors of influence 72
2.3 Concluding remarks 76

vi *Contents*

3 Raiding in transition   84

3.1 Problem of raiding in the transition economy 84
   Ways of hostile takeovers 84
   Objects of raiding: risks and victims 91
3.2 Magnitude of raiding 96
   Scale of raiding 96
   Discussion and condemnation of raiding 101
3.3 Concluding remarks 107

4 Corruption and raiding   114

4.1 Links between corruption and raiding 114
   Ties between corruption and raiding 114
   Nepotism and inheritance as a basis of raiding 120
*4.2 Bureaucracy, corruption, raiding, and struggle
   against it 125*
   Russian bureaucracy and corruption 125
   Imitating an anti-corruption campaign 131
4.3 Concluding remarks 136

Conclusion   146

Index   151

Figures

1.1	Relation of raiding to other similar themes	35
2.1	Size of kickbacks on governmental contracts as a percentage of contractual value in Russia, 2012	65
3.1	Number of privatized state unitary enterprises in Russia, 1992–2015	97
3.2	Dynamics of economic crimes and number of individuals who committed economic crimes in the Central Federal District of Russia, 2000–2015	100
3.3	Ranking of the top business environment obstacles for firms in Russia and Europe and Central Asia regions, 2012	103
3.4	Ranking of the top business environment obstacles for firms in Russia and upper middle income group countries, 2012	104
3.5	Ranking of the top business environment obstacles for firms in Russia and the world, 2012	105
3.6	Percent of firms expected to give gifts in meetings with tax officials in Russia and Europe and Central Asia regions, 2012	106
4.1	Dynamics of Corruption Perceptions Index for Russia, the USA, China, and Nigeria, 1995–2016	119

Tables

1.1	Interpretation frames of raiding and their major characteristics: political economy	33
1.2	Interpretation frames of raiding and their major characteristics: business	34
2.1	Number of privatized state unitary enterprises in Russia, 1992–2015	58
2.2	State budget revenues from the oil and gas industry in Russia, 2000–2006	61
3.1	Economic crimes statistics in the Central Federal District of Russia, 2000–2015	99
4.1	Values of Corruption Perceptions Index for Russia, the USA, China, and Nigeria, 1995–2016	118
4.2	Number of employees in the state and municipal government in Russia, 1995–2007, in thousands	125

Foreword

> The great questions of the day will not be settled by means of speeches and majority decisions but by iron and blood.
>
>   –Otto Won Bismarck

One of the founding fathers of modern Germany, German Chancellor and Prime Minister Otto Won Bismarck, said in his famous speech entitled "Blood and Iron" that "The great questions of the day will not be settled by means of speeches and majority decisions but by iron and blood" (Bismarck, 1862).[1] Bismarck unified the German states into one Empire. Russian raiders divide the enormous wealth inherited from the Soviet Empire by iron and bribe and they do it special, Russian style. They bribe judges, buy state bureaucrats, negotiate with law enforcers, kill entrepreneurs, blackmail managers, threaten shareholders with violence, falsify statutory documents, and infiltrate corporate boards in order to expropriate and own or resell someone else's property. Similar to the Iron Chancellor, they do not expect commercial disputes to be settled by means of speeches and majority decisions. Russian raiders do it by iron and blood.

The explosive blend of Russian M&A worries Western investors, for it is not done Western style. Russian raiders rarely use Wall Street type corporate games and court hearings in mergers and acquisitions. Hostile takeovers over enterprises and territories take place through bribery, violence, and fraud. Corporate, property, and land raiding in Russia transforms in one of the most profitable forms of business. Raiding threatens the very institute of private property, which is still very shaky and unstable even after three decades of market reforms. And raiding is here to stay.

George Soros and the frustration over the lost investment in Svyaz'-Invest, Mikhail Khodorkovsky and the ever-lasting Yukos saga, Bill Browder and the endless Hermitage Capital affair, Sergei Magnitsky's death and the untouchables.... These are just a handful of bold cases of alleged raiding and unsuccessful investment that have become known not only to the business community internationally, but the general public as well, mostly with the help of tabloids. How many more lost businesses, broken lives, and dead bodies will it take to understand the essence of Russia's modus operandi?

x *Foreword*

World tabloids are good in reporting the news on raiding in order to boost their readership base, but they are not particularly good at looking into the essence of the raiding phenomenon. And scholars are not eager to investigate this phenomenon. Finally, businessmen do not pay much attention to what the scholars have to say, even if the latter issue "do not invest in Russia" warnings. A clear discontent between businessmen and scholars results in lost investment. In order to understand today's Russia one has to dive deep into the beginning, the late 1980s and early 1990s. Both domestic entrepreneurs and foreign investors have the right to make their educated choice. This book is intended to help them in making such a choice. International investors, transnational corporations, investment bankers have the right to act on informed consent when they decide to invest their money, their time, their effort, and their talent in Russia.

Note

1 Bismarck, Otto Won. Blood and Iron. Speech, 1862. Retrieved June 24, 2009, from http://germanhistorydocs.ghi-dc.org/sub_document.cfm?document_id=250&language=english

Preface

The process realizing this book project commenced a decade ago. An extensive media coverage of a raiding case in one of Russia's regions served as an initial push for this study. A dispute over a TV company in Tula turned into a criminal investigation, when a group of armed people was storming premises of the company located in a basement of an apartment building at 81 Gogolevskaya Street, city of Tula, the Russian Federation, on July 31, 2008. There were around fifty storm troopers involved in the storming. Police did not interfere initially, but called for backup support. More police officers arrived later and stopped the storming, arresting thirty-five perpetrators. This story once again brought the public's attention to the rising tide of corporate, property, and land raiding in Russia.

The initial investigation into the issue of corporate, property, and land raiding resulted in the presentation entitled "Corporate Raiding Russian Style: Hostile Takeovers via Corruption and Fraud," delivered at the Annual Conference of the American Political Science Association in Washington, DC in September 2010. Another presentation, entitled "Predatory Raiding in Russia: Institutions and Property Rights after the Crisis," was delivered at the Annual Conference of the Association for Evolutionary Economics/American Economic Association in Chicago in January 2012. Finally, a paper entitled "From Khodorkovsky to Hermitage Capital: Building the New System of Property Rights in Transition Economies" was presented at the Annual Conference of the Association for Slavic, East European, and Eurasian Studies in New Orleans in November 2012.

As the project has proceeded, a large volume of data has been collected from Russian federal agencies and international organizations, numerous media sources, and results of polls, surveys, and interviews. In addition to laws on property, land, corporate governance, privatization, and several other laws and legal documents, over 3,000 media reports were analyzed, including more than 100 episodes of video footage with actual raiding actions, storming, and storm troopers. Finally, case studies of most notorious hostile takeovers of large companies added to the informative base of the research. As this book manuscript was nearing completion, more data continued to arrive from different sources.

Big cases of alleged corporate raiding have become widely publicized and form a narrative of an unwelcoming business environment. Such narratives largely negate the efforts of the ruling authoritarian regime to encourage domestic entrepreneurship and investment. Nor do foreign direct investment flows in Russia indicate a steady increase. And there are reasons for this. The Bureau of Economic and Business Affairs of the US Department of State warns American companies seeking to invest in Russia that "the Russian investment climate continues to be marked by high levels of uncertainty, corruption, and political risk, making thorough due diligence and good legal counsel essential for any potential investment."[1] Furthermore, the US agency offers a negative prognosis, stating that conditions for foreign investors in Russia are unlikely to improve in the near future. This decline in investment reflects the increased risks that investors continue to face when doing business in Russia. Not surprisingly, Russian officialdom ostensibly denies the state-led corporate raiding of Yukos as well as its role in similar cases with large companies.

Note

1 Russia 2016 Investment Climate Statements Report, Bureau of Economic and Business Affairs, the US Department of State. Washington, DC. July 5, 2016. Retrieved March 1, 2017, from www.state.gov/e/eb/rls/othr/ics/2016/eur/254409.htm

Acronyms and abbreviations

ANH, Akademiya narodnogo hozyajstva [Academy of the National Economy]
Duma, Lower Chamber of the Russian Parliament
FIG, financial-industrial group
FNS, Federal'naya nalogovaya sluzhba [Federal Tax Services]
FSB, Federal'naya sluzhba bezopasnosti [Federal Security Services], former KGB
FSFR, Federal'naya sluzhba po finansovym rynkam [Federal Services on Financial Markets]
FSSP, Federal'naya sluzhba sudebnyh pristavov [Federal Services of Court Bailiffs]
Gosduma, Gosudarstvennaya duma [State Duma, Lower Chamber of the Russian Parliament]
GUEBiPK MVD, Glavnoe upravlenie ekonomicheskoj bezopasnosti i protivodejstviya korruptsii Ministerstva vnutrennikh del [Head Department of Economic Security and Corruption Prevention of the Ministry of the Interior]
ILO, International Labour Organization
IPO, Initial public offering
KPRF, Kommunisticheskaya partiya Rossijskoj Federatsii [Communist Party of the Russian Federation]
LDPR, Liberal'no-demokraticheskaya partiya Rossii [Liberal Democratic Party of Russia]
M&A, Mergers and acquisitions
MP, Member of Parliament
MVD, Ministerstvo vnutrennikh del [Ministry of the Interior]
NAK, Natsional'ny antikorruptsionny komitet [National Anti-Corruption Committee]
NGO, nongovernmental organizations
OBEP, Otdel po bor'be s ekonomicheskimi prestupleniyami [Department for Economic Crime Prevention]
OECD, Organization for Economic Cooperation and Development
RAGS, Rossijskaya akademiya gosudarstvennoj sluzhby [Russian Academy of State Services]

xiv *Acronyms and abbreviations*

RF, Rossijskaya Federatsiya [the Russian Federation]
Rosatom, Russian State Nuclear Energy Corporation
RUBOP, Rajonnoe upravlenie po bor'be s organizovannoj prestupnost'yu
   [District Department for Organized Crime Prevention]
Sberbank, Sberegatel'nyj bank [State Savings Bank]
SK, Sledstvennyj komitet [Investigations Committee]
SVR, Sluzhba vneshnej razvedki [Foreign Intelligence Services]
TPP, Torgovo-promyshlennaya palata Rossijskoj Federatsii [Chamber of Trade
   and Commerce of the Russian Federation]
USSR, the Union of the Soviet Socialist Republics
YUKOS, YUganskneftegaz and KuibyshevOrgSintez

Note on translation and transliteration

I transliterated Russian words using the Library of Congress system, omitting diacritics but using two-letter tie characters. The same system was used for names of well-known people, for whom a certain spelling has become conventional, such as Khodorkovsky or Magnitsky. All translations from Russian original documents and records are my own.

Introduction

Raiding Russia

Every year, property owners in Russia suffer thousands of raiding attacks. Large corporations, medium and small businesses, individual entrepreneurs, and regular property owners become victims of raiders. Some raiding attacks are successfully repealed, while many succeed and go unnoticed by the authorities. In fact, many such attacks are staged and even executed by the state authorities. The massive scale of raiding in Russia and the volume of losses inflicted by raiding to the national economy speak to the importance of the topic of raiding in scholarly research. Moreover, raiding damages the reputation of transition societies, especially as viewed by potential foreign investors. The importance of the issue of raiding may also be explained by the fact that raiding is closely linked to such fundamental topics as the structure of property relations and the transformation of the planned economy into the mixed market type economy.

A new category of property crime – corporate, property, and land raiding – is flourishing in the post-Soviet space. Russian raiders use a wide variety of tools and activities including pressuring minor shareholders; bribing managers and bureaucrats; creating artificial debts; producing fraudulent charter documents, deeds, and titles of property; and violent storming of enterprises with the help of private security firms, freelance storm troopers, and criminal thugs. According to Sakwa (2013), the mechanisms of raiding include "specious legal proceedings, tax audits (often by armed tax police), and judicial rulings that are politically directed in favour of the authorities' corporate allies" (p. 8), which take us back to the then Russian President Dmitry Medvedev's notion of *koshmarit' biznes*,[1] although much reinforced. Above all, some have claimed that the state itself is used as an instrument of corporate raiding. Such voices are especially loud and persistent when it comes to the long-lasting Yukos affair and its virtual personification in the widely publicized prosecution of the company's former chief and owner, Mikhail Khodorkovsky.[2] The state authorities continue legal actions against Khodorkovsky even now, conducting searches and linking the company's assets with money laundering and financing social activists and political opposition.[3]

This is not just a new type of crime, but an entirely new phenomenon that has spilled over from Moscow to other regions in Russia and other former Soviet

2 Introduction

republics. Western media have estimated the total number of raiding attacks in Russia at an astronomical 70,000 cases per year (Harding, 2008). The issue of raiding in Russia and problems directly related to raiding are addressed in the work of Barnes (2003, 2006, 2007a, 2007b); Black, Kraakman, and Tarassova (2000); Firestone (2008); Frye (2000, 2002); Kireev (2007); Volkov (2004, 2005a, b, c); and Woodruff (2004, 2005). Raiding in Russia differs significantly from what is perceived to be raiding in the Western world, primarily by its generous use of corruption and violence. Of most recent works addressing the problem of insecure property and hostile takeovers, the most significant are those by Frye (2014, 2017); Gans-Morse (2017); Hanson (2014); Shelley and Deane (2016); and Yakovlev, Sobolev, and Kazun (2014).

Despite the fact that the problem of corporate raiding has existed in Russia for a long time, there are very few scholarly publications devoted to this issue. The problem of raiding is highlighted mostly on the level of short newspaper articles. Russian scholars have been unable to produce any significant and comprehensive works on raiding. Their publications remind more of journalistic notes, media accounts, and anecdotal evidence mixed with some textbook maxims borrowed from their Western counterparts. Western scholars have produced just a few works on raiding in the post-Soviet space, and these come down to reports on the qualitative sociological investigations or legal reviews. Corporate raiding is not a short-term problem and thus the issue of corporate raiding deserves a much closer attention than it has been allotted until now, including by the scholarly community.

This book presents theoretical and empirical investigation of the politico-economic nature of corporate, property, and land raiding; its link to corruption; and its impact on the process of creation of new economic structures in Russia. This research defines raiding as well as its place and role in the process of transition from plan-directive to market economy. It also addresses major foundations and main forms of raiding. A substantial part of the book is devoted to theoretical aspects of raiding illustrated by case studies. This study develops the corruption, coercion, and control model as a theoretical explanation of raiding in a transition economy. The study argues that this model is used by the ruling authoritarian regime in order to secure the regime's sustainability. A large volume of data has been collected from the websites of the variety of related Russian federal agencies, including commercial arbitration courts, court bailiffs' services, the Ministry of Justice, the Ministry of the Interior, the Prosecutor General's Office, Presidential Administration, and numerous other state bodies. This data is supplemented with the data from other federal and regional agencies, international organizations, numerous media sources, and results of polls, surveys, and interviews.[4] Laws on property, land, corporate governance, privatization, and several other laws and legal documents also add to the informative base of the research. In addition, over 3,000 media reports were analyzed, including more than 100 episodes of video footage with actual raiding actions, storming, and storm troopers. Finally, the most notorious cases of raiding along with cases often interpreted as raiding are added to the work.

Raiding is defined as a relation that emerges between economic actors regarding alienation and appropriation of property, when alienation is done against the will of or without consent of the previous owner and without proper compensation, and where appropriation is covered with layers of legality. This study considers the socioeconomic phenomenon of raiding within the alienation-appropriation frame and points to the inverted character of raiding. This study further highlights the nature, causes, and basis of corporate and property raiding in Russia. In the transition economy, the state has two roles in respect to raiding: it guards from raiding and at the same time it facilitates raiding. The duality of this complex relationship finds its expression in overwhelming corruption and poor protection of property rights. Fundamental economic changes that include mass privatization necessitate optimization of the state and bring to life phenomena such as an economically active bureaucracy. A state-raider is an aggressive state that actively utilizes noneconomic factors of influence.

This study focuses on the problem of raiding in a transition economy by researching ways of hostile takeovers, objects of raiding, its risks and victims. This study tries to reconstruct the true magnitude of the raiding phenomenon through estimating the scale of raiding as well as analyzing the public discussion and condemnation of raiding. This study establishes links between corruption and raiding and considers nepotism and inheritance rights as a firm basis of corporate and property raiding in an authoritarian regime. Suppression of corporate autonomy, the induction of state bureaucrats into corporate governing boards, the imposition of pseudo-accountability under the nontransparent financial regulations, and direct informal control are all manifestations of the corruption, coercion, and control model. Stalinist-type bureaucracy and rampant corruption explain the use of law enforcement agencies and courts in raiding. The struggle against raiding comes down to imitating an anti-corruption campaign.

This book takes into consideration fundamental changes in the structure of property relations that take place in post-Soviet Russia. Legal formalization of private property on the means of production symbolizes not only real but also formal alienation of the worker from the means of production. The voucher or so-called "cheque" privatization[5] was the process of creating a virtual reality focused precisely on alienating a worker from the means of production. In this sense, the entire transition from the planned system to the market one was meant not so much to build a market economy, as to appropriate formally public property by a small group of individuals. Frye (2010a) calls post-Soviet privatization "the rapid giveaway of state assets" (p. 174), and rightly so.

Market reforms were organized with the goal of privatization, rather than privatizing as part of the process of building the market economy. Concentration and centralization of production capacities in the hands of a few, and more specifically, the property rights on the means of production, may be expressed as an attempt to achieve a monopolistic position on particular markets. This process is being realized thanks in part to corporate raiding. Concentration and centralization of production capacities is accomplished by raiders and at the same time serves as the engine of raiding. Processes of decentralization and localization

4 *Introduction*

of the national economy take place along with the processes of concentration and centralization of production. Processes of decentralization and localization, including in the court system, may be considered as anti-raiding, but they also result in fragmentation of the unified economic space. Corruption and noneconomic mechanisms of the distribution of property rights and the produced product as the mechanism of resolving economic problems are the main conditions for raiding. At the same time, corruption as a relation does not constitute the fundamental material basis of raiding.

This book also demonstrates the specifics of Russian raiding and distinguishes it from the classical forms of corporate raiding that take place in Western democracies. The limits of this study are determined by the subject matter of the research itself. This study is not about privatization and market transition. Moreover, it is not dedicated to shadow economy, corruption, or crime. This study discovers the problem of raiding rather than related issues, except to the extent necessary to better understand the phenomenon of raiding. If this study would not hold to this strict line of research, it would grow beyond any reasonable limits in an attempt to include all the issues related to raiding, oftentimes mixed and even confused with corporate raiding in transition economies.

Contextualizing raiding

Placing the issue of raiding into the system of related scholarly topics and themes is important, but it is even more important to place the raiding phenomenon in a proper context. Before this study proceeds with the investigation of the nature, causes, and basis of such socioeconomic phenomenon as raiding, it might be necessary to present a proper context in which raiding in Russia exists and proliferates. Contextualizing raiding requires focusing on a variety of key determinants of socioeconomic and political life in the country. Simply put, what is modern-day Russia?

Corruption is perhaps the single most explicit characteristic of modern Russia. The large scale of corruption and significance of this problem is recognized by all parties, including Russian and Western scholars, state authorities, and the general public. The endemic character of this negative phenomenon imposes rigid institutional brackets on any significant attempted reform. Rose-Ackerman and Søreide (2011) present a comprehensive, detailed, and in-depth analysis of the economics of corruption as well as its economic and policy implications. Corruption is a complex and diverse phenomenon. Corruption varies in its types and forms not only functionally, but even conceptually. Wedeman (2012) suggests that developmental corruption may be considered as parasitical, because the political machine sustains itself and lives off the economy, but does not necessarily intend to destroy its basis, while degenerative corruption may be characterized as predatory, because it feeds directly on the economy. Both types are detrimental to the economy, but "degenerative corruption is much more likely to prove fatal and manifest its worse effects more quickly" (Wedeman, 2012, p. 53). It is the second conceptual type of corruption – the degenerative corruption – that threatens the

Introduction 5

Russian economy. Corporate and property raiding is a strong manifestation of degenerative corruption prevailing in Russia.

There is little argument around the suggestion that corruption is at the core of raiding in Russia, given the predominantly criminal nature of the latter. Seizing benefits of public office combined with the strong sense of lawlessness in the country result in violent raiding campaigns. The meaning of seizing benefits is very broad and can even depart from the classical notion of corruption as abuse of public office for private gain. For instance, Søreide and Williams (2014) suggest that, "Grabbing focuses on the selfish act of seizing benefits, while corruption is typically an illegal trade in decisions, usually with the same motivation as grabbing, and thus, the words are close synonyms" (p. 3). In addition to grabbing, there are other substitutes to the discursive notion of corruption, and these include good governance and public trust. Russia lacks the quality of government, and this deficiency causes suppression of domestic entrepreneurs and scares away international investors. Rothstein (2011) suggests that a key feature of quality of government, based on a specific normative and behavioral criterion, is impartiality in the exercise of public authority.

Through the review and criticism of several key works on the quality of governance, Rothstein (2011) derives the definition of the quality of government and suggests that it cannot be defined solely as the absence of corruption. The author concurs with Kurer (2005, p. 230) in stating that "corruption involves a holder of public office violating the impartiality principle in order to achieve private gain" (p. 15). Rothstein (2011) builds his argument around the concept of impartiality, which is a truly contested concept, and suggests that the quality of government as impartiality can be measured. The absence of good governance causes lack of public trust, weakened social cohesion, and high income inequality. Corruption reinforces economic inequality, but inequality may also support corruption. Uslaner (2008) pinpoints the roots of corruption, saying that it rests "upon economic inequality and low trust in people who are different from yourself. Corruption, in its turn, leads to less trust in other people and more inequality" (p. 4). Remington (2011) argues that, "the fact that corruption is lower and investment is higher in more democratic regions is consistent with the view that more openness and transparency reduces the opportunities for governments to capture rents from enterprises" (p. 169). The author concurs with Uslaner (2008) in that corruption and inequality go hand in hand. Russia, where, according to Aslund (2009), market reform succeeded but democracy failed, demonstrates an increase in income disparities and worsening socioeconomic conditions (Kivinen and Chunling, 2012; Salmenniemi, 2012) and has yet to replicate anything closely reminiscent of a European welfare, presented in Hay and Wincott (2013).

A society that lacks trust and social cohesion is continuously seeking for other bases and forms of economic cooperation. As a result, formal institutions are being substituted by informal ones. Informality complements corruption as a less explicit yet not less dangerous characteristic of a transition society. Russia is distinct with its high level of informal relations that penetrate all segments of social and economic life (Brück and Lehmann, 2012). Commenting on the high level of

6 *Introduction*

informal relations in the post-Soviet space, Morris and Polese (2014) make a bold statement that "[i]nformality is here to stay" (p. 1). The informality approach in researching largely corrupt societies gains popularity. "Informal," "cash-in-hand," "corrupt," "illegal," "criminal," "black," "underground," "hidden," "shadow," and many other adjectives are all to be found in the study by Williams, Round, and Rodgers (2013). Informality finds its expression not only in practices and processes, but formalized structures as well. Although paradoxical, informal practices are formalized in informal networks. These informal networks may even become more powerful than formal institutions (Kononenko and Moshes, 2011).

Scholars writing on the issues of post-Soviet Russian state-building, market reforms, economic transition, informal relations, and corruption extend their work in directions that touch upon issues closely linked to corporate raiding. When it comes to issues of crime, corruption, and corporate raiding, contradictions are aplenty. Some scholars suggest that large-scale property disputes in Russia are anything but over (see, for instance, Sonin, 2003, 2005). At the same time, as early as in the 1990s, Aslund (1997) expected crime levels in Russia to fall. Corruption was aplenty even during the Soviet totalitarian regime (Duhamel, 2010; Ward, 2009), and after its dramatic rise in the 1990s, it is hard to imagine why one would expect crime rates, including economic crimes, to decline. These issues also include the legal system, level of democracy and democratic changes, and the role of courts. Popova (2012) presents a study of courts in Russia focused specifically on two types of cases: electoral registration lawsuits and court cases on defamation and libel. She pays a lot of attention to judicial independence, focusing on institutional, behavioral, and decisional types of judicial independence.

The post-Soviet space and Russia in particular is distinct with its organized crime. Organized crime in Russia has corruption as its immanent component and penetrates all spheres of the national economy. Organized crime becomes a natural part of corporate raiding, including violent hostile takeovers. Kupatadze (2012) suggests that, "Centralization also facilitates the construction of pyramids of corruption. The authorities can dismiss regional and local officials much more easily if they disobey by underpaying the required sums to illicit 'cash desks' or 'feeding' political competitors" (p. 112). Amalgamation of organized crime and the state, characteristic of Russia of the 1990s, transforms into a new form of the ruling political regime. When organized crime becomes one of the essential features of the state and the state apparatus becomes more and more reminiscent of an organized crime machine, the nation-state faces challenges of existential nature. The state-building in Russia is adjusted for the nascent capitalism and widespread corruption. Taylor (2011) researches the gargantuan process of state-building in Russia under Putin and points out that, "federal reforms implemented by Putin during his first term in office were designed to change the terms of the federal bargain that existed under Yeltsin sharply in the direction of the center. The power ministries in general, and law enforcement structures (the MVD, the FSB, and the procuracy) in particular, were key objects in this struggle" (p. 144).[6] Apparently, the major character here is that of Russia's unchallenged ruler of two decades, Vladimir Putin.

Raiding is something more than just a derivative of corruption. A successful large-scale corporate raiding rests on the autocratic nature of the ruling political regime. The regime of this type prevents democratization and creates serious obstacles in the way of eradicating large-scale corruption. Furthermore, the need for reconfiguring the relations between the state, business, and employees raises yet again issues of paternalism and neopatrimonial arrangements. Thus, such terms as "capitalism," "liberalization," "globalization." and "institutional reform" are confronted with "etatism," "patrimonialism," "corruption," and "the rule of law" (see Becker et al., 2013). While investigating autocratic and democratic external influences in post-Soviet Eurasia, Obydenkova and Libman (2015) point out that "various actors influence various levels of regime transition in Eurasia" (p. 15). The role of Russia's economic and political outreach in the post-Soviet space and beyond may be strengthening (see, for instance, Gel'man and Ross, 2010; Vinokurov and Libman, 2012; Libman and Vinokurov, 2012; Wilhelmsen and Wilson Rowe, 2011). Medvedev and Jakobson (2012) point out that, "pragmatism does not sit well with Russia's defensive, nostalgic revisionism and the antagonistic approach of the Russian elite" (p. 213). Nevertheless, Russia is more inclined to pursue realistic foreign policy and pragmatic cooperation than conflicts.

While extending its influence outside its geographic borders, the country also experiences influences from abroad, which the Russian regime largely fears. Stewart et al. (2012) present the extent of external influence in strengthening civil society, placing the emphasis on "grey zones" and "hybrid regimes." This external influence comes into controversy with Putin's notion of "sovereign democracy" (Rose, Mishler, and Munro, 2011). According to Robertson (2011), hybrid regimes, positioned somewhere between closed autocracies and liberal democracies, lack repressive power and thus have to monitor the sociopolitical situation. Mass political protests as well as social activism are perceived as a threat. Bunce and Wolchik (2011) point out that, "There are extremely high stakes attached to launching popular protests in response to fraudulent elections. If the demonstrations succeed, democratic progress is likely to follow. However, if they fail, the regime invariably becomes more repressive" (p. 340). Giuliano (2011) argues that people must develop a group grievance, by which she means "a feeling of resentment about important aspects of their present situation" (p. xi). Pursiainen and Pei (2012) suggest that despite Russia's undergoing a significant change in its political system and clearly departing from its totalitarian past, it remains very distant from pure democracy. The decision-making process is still largely centralized, while the overall system can be characterized as a hybrid regime. According to Jonson and White (2012) the Kremlin is well aware of the fact that its model of governance has nothing to do with modern democracy.

The autocracy of Russia's ruling regime has its limitations. Roberts (2012) suggests that the reconstruction of a single party totalitarian model in post-Soviet Russia is unlikely, due to the strength of pluralism in political and economic life. Bodin, Hedlund, and Namli (2012) are quite critical of the Russian ruling political regime, calling it fake authoritarianism, sham paternalism, a nonexistent vertical structure of authority, and an inherently bankrupt system of governance, all related

8 *Introduction*

directly to Russia's president, Vladimir Putin. Bodin, Hedlund, and Namli (2012) are united in their search for a better understanding of the phenomenon of power and in seeing Russia as a deficient democracy. The emerging authoritarian or state capitalism is a hybrid that forms an alternative to the Western model of societal organization (Pursiainen and Pei, 2012). Sakwa (2011) applies the concept of the dual state to Russia's ongoing transition and change, while the country is caught in a stalemate of a permanent crisis. He argues that "a dual state has emerged in which the legal-normative system based on constitutional order is challenged by shadowy arbitrary arrangements" referred to as the administrative regime, populated by various conflicting factions (Sakwa, 2011, p. viii). The tension between these two pillars is the defining characteristic of modern Russian politics.

Russians are worried about the weak state, the lack of order, and corruption. Treisman (2011) acknowledges that Russia's high level of corruption is undeniable: "Russians saw no decrease in corruption or increase in the effectiveness of the state" (p. 382). Urban (2010) researches Russia's political elites and notes that his interviewees demonstrate almost uniform disregard for the law, even as some of them "lament its absence" (p. 10). Legal nihilism characterizes the very political elites that are in charge of establishing and maintaining the law and order. Dzarasov (2014) points out that "Russian privatization's most significant characteristic, with the long-term consequences, was the strong impetus which it gave to criminality and corruption" (p. 87). Corruption, to a large extent, reflects persisting institutional problems (Sutela, 2012). Easter (2013) suggests that, "While state coercion let loose in the upstairs economy, the government sought to restrain the state revenue agents in the downstairs economy. Putin admonished local officialdom's predations on small businessmen as 'legalized bribery'" (p. 64).

Be it strictly authoritarian or hybrid regime, it turns ugly not only in terms of a clear lack of democracy, but human rights violations and insecure property rights. White (2011) refers to numerous scandals in courts, police, and penitentiary, including that of Sergei Magnitsky's death. Overland (2011) models hierarchies of power and consultation present in Russian policy formulation (p. 149). The author also mentions contradictory law enforcement and court practices, selective justice, and the Yukos affair as a part of the energy business. Continuing on the issue of oil and Russia being a dominating energy superpower, Godzimirski (2011) points out that in 2008 Russia was responsible for 12.8 percent of the oil and 23 percent of the gas produced globally (p. 160). Resource-rich and rent-oriented Russian economy maintains the superstructure of the ruling authoritarian regime.

Despite the authoritarian character of the ruling regime and the image of stability that it attempts to convey, Russian society is still in transition and the national economy has yet to reach its steady state. Robinson et al. (2013) put emphasis on the unfinished search for a new balance between the market and the state, property raiding and deficiencies in the state structure, the demographic crisis and illegal immigration, obstacles for developing private farming in the agricultural sector, dependency on oil and gas revenues, and the political dysfunctions of Russian capitalism. Hass (2012) reconsiders Putin's moral economy of security, formulated as the "dictatorship of law," while considering the financial crisis of 2008 as a test for the new moral economy. Despite its weak, outdated, and resource-dependent economy, Russia survived financial crises of 1998 (Gilman, 2010) and 2008 (Vavilov, 2010). Easter (2012) notes that elites in Russia "were not inclined to compromise personal interest for the public good" (p. 141). Similarly, the ruling regime is not willing to compromise its survivability for distant prospects of economic development. The officially approved and advanced discourse is focused on economic security and external threats, with fears of potential chaos replacing hopes for economic prosperity.

Hass (2011) blends political economy and sociology in search for reasons why there is order in the chaotic reality of post-Soviet transformation. He refers to meaning and knowledge as culture and implementation as power in his exploration of the underlying causes.

> We have made our story more complicated than corrupt state officials, capital hunger or oil wealth, or problematic laws; we must ask why officials are "corrupt," how capital and value are embodied and used, and why laws and implementation are problematic in the first place.
>
> (p. 12)

The endemic corruption, bureaucratic red tape, and high concentration of production assets in the hands of just a few oligarchs did not prevent Russia from constructing a consumerist society with its numerous newly emerged customer oriented firms and stores. Commenting on the widespread informal relations that literally help to maintain the whole societal machine, Fortescue et al. (2010) suggest that, "Patronage existed because the structures of supreme power were always weakly institutionalized, because dictatorships, whether of an individual or an oligarchy, operate without external constraints" (p. 13). At the same time, Holmes (2010) manages to keep a well-balanced view on the legitimacy of the ruling political regime and its leaders. Despite all the criticism that routinely comes from the developed nations, Putin's popularity among Russians is beyond doubt.

The problem of legitimacy and public support of the authorities may be closely tied to the socioeconomic background of the ruling elites and their career paths. When it comes to Russia, meritocratic recruitment and promotion are a weak side of the state bureaucracy. According to Huskey (2010), "self-reproducing of a bureaucratic caste" is far more obvious in Russia than in some East European countries (p. 198). State bureaucracies are largely ineffective and multiply, thanks, in part, to inbreeding and nepotism, with many state offices inherited by the heirs of former office holders. Political elites do not represent the populace but originate from a small stratum of officialdom, and maintain their status not because of their professional skills, but due to their clan affiliations, informal networks, corruption, and loyalty to their leaders. Fortescue (2010) remarks that, "In the end the greatest test not just of the legitimacy of a system but also of commentators' models of legitimation is survivability. Clearly that is a test that with the Soviet

10   *Introduction*

system failed" (p. 206). Putin's authoritarian regime tries to avoid mistakes of its Soviet predecessors and focuses precisely on the sustainability of the regime.

Another essential feature of Russia is the absence of a clear delimitation between the state and business. Such vagueness emerges from the early post-Soviet privatization and necessitates close affiliation between the state bureaucrats and businessmen for the sake of protecting economic assets of the latter. According to Frye (2010b), businesspeople report that

> in recent years the security of property rights has become more contingent on political connections. Investment decisions greatly depend on whether businesspeople believe that they can take the state to court. Moreover, political connections in legal disputes remain a powerful asset.
>
> (p. 80)

Myant and Drahokoupil (2011) point out that the creation of capitalism brought to the fore people with a clear lack of economic knowledge, which they compensated for with "the skills to master a lawless environment and to stay in favor with the holders of political power" (p. 256). As a result, businessmen, who are not really entrepreneurs, form a coalition with state bureaucrats, who are not really civil servants, in order to derive rent from their ownership and their public office, respectively.

The structure

The structure of this book reflects the logic of inquiry into the matter of corporate raiding. This volume is structured in the following way. Chapter 1 departs from the literature surveyed on the context of raiding in the introductory section. This part introduces the corruption, coercion, and control model and suggests that it may serve as an explanatory model for corporate raiding in Russia. Building on previous scholarship, this study conceptualizes the coercive nature of the ruling authoritarian regime. In order to establish the key premise of the proposed research, this study argues that the corruption, coercion, and control model is applied by the ruling authoritarian regime in order to guarantee its sustainability, and the study also asserts that the model is directly related to corporate and property raiding. Chapter 1 also argues that the corruption, coercion, and control model has its manifestations, including those directly related to corporate and property raiding. Suppression of corporate autonomy, the induction of state bureaucrats into corporate governing boards, the imposition of pseudo-accountability under the nontransparent financial regulations, and direct informal control are all manifestations of the corruption, coercion, and control model. These mechanisms are used by the ruling political regime in order to control businessmen and the business activities of the companies through the state authorities and administrations. In market transition, when laws are changing and the rules are unclear or subject to interpretation, state bureaucrats are placed in conditions of financial survival while businessmen find it hard to comply with laws and regulations. Numerous

Introduction 11

violations are registered and those bureaucrats and businessmen become subjected to state-organized blackmail. This type of blackmail comes not from the side of criminals and racketeers, but from the ruling regime. With the help of the Russian political establishment, this mechanism of informal control spreads nationwide and extends to different levels of societal organizations.

Methodology-wise, studies in post-Soviet transitions usually use only Western scholarship in their literature overviews, while omitting works of local scholars. As a result, the picture of a given local phenomenon, such as raiding, remains incomplete. This study overcomes such a limitation by analyzing and quoting well over two dozen works by Russian and post-Soviet scholars, published in the Russian language. Passages translated from Russian that come from both scholarly works and interviews give the reader a flavor of local thoughts, expressions, and perceptions on the phenomenon of corporate and property raiding. Chapter 1 defines raiding and its place in the system of political and economic coordinates. Raiding is correlated to such issues as violent entrepreneurship, economic crime, asset grabbing, property grabbing, privatization, economic transition, the role of the state, and corporate governance. Chapter 1 presents the phenomenon of raiding within the alienation-appropriation frame of property relations' dynamics. It introduces and proves the inverted character of raiding in Russia. Finally, Chapter 1 identifies the nature, causes, and basis of corporate and property raiding. Classifications and major characteristics of raiding lead to interpretation frames, divided on those associated with political economy, institutionalism and law, and those associated with business.

Chapter 2 determines the role of the state in raiding and argues that the state is both a victim of raiding and a raider itself. The process of privatization of socialist property was, in essence, raiding. Accordingly, there is an impression that the state became an object of raiding and a victim of aggression of external forces toward the state property, including all means of production. But, in fact, the object of raiding became the state property while the state was an instrument used by raiders in power to appropriate property. In this case, the state itself is seen as a raider. At the same time, state functions, state authority, and execution of state powers were taken over and "privatized" by the ruling regime and its particular representatives. This study explains why three traditional sources of income for post-Soviet bureaucrats – salary from the state, bribes from the clientele, and kickbacks from state-funded projects – are no longer satisfactory for state officials and civil servants. Economically active bureaucrats are no longer satisfied with their function of protecting businesses against external aggressors and their raiding assaults on businesses, delegated to the civil servants by the state. Bureaucrats offer services to facilitate redistribution of not only access to limited resources, public goods, spheres of influence and market segments, but business assets as well. While helping raiders to capture someone else's business, state bureaucrats, in fact, participate in the redistribution of property, profit-generating assets, and businesses, and expect a reward from this future profit, obtained by the raiders or the new owners. Therefore, bureaucrats reach the stage and the level of profit participation. This is no longer the use of authority delegated by the state for personal

12 *Introduction*

purposes or personal enrichment, but an explicit economic activity. Chapter 2 builds the argument of an aggressive state based on a few case studies of hostile takeovers of businesses through state-authorized blackmail. Noneconomic factors of influence, analyzed in this part, demonstrate how state pressure is associated with corporate raiding.

Based on the analysis of numerous media reports, Chapter 3 shows the perpetrators and victims of raiding campaigns and underlines their major characteristics as well as methods of hostile takeovers and defenses employed against them. Distinct from Western-type corporate raiding, in Russia both entrepreneurs and ordinary people suffer from raiders. Entrepreneurial activities are aimed at receiving profit. However, raiders are often interested not in the profit that a firm receives from its business activities, but in extracting profit from a hostile takeover and sale of certain valuable economic assets, be it an enterprise, real estate, housing unit, or any other asset that has market value. Accordingly, entrepreneurs who do not own any material assets are unlikely to be targeted by raiders. At the same time, those private citizens who own certain assets, such as housing, are potential targets of raiding attacks. It is obvious that corrupt law enforcement agencies cannot fight themselves effectively in an attempt to eradicate unlawful corporate raiding, especially if they profit from it. The solution might be in developing institutions of civil society.

Chapter 3 exploits data on ranking of the top business environment obstacles for firms in Russia from Enterprise Surveys by the World Bank in order to explore the applications of the corruption, coercion, and control model. Concerns about high tax rates differentiates Russian businessmen from their peers in the Europe & Central Asia region, upper middle income group countries and the world. At the same time, their worries about access to finance and corruption are about the same as those of their peers in the region and in their income group, and throughout the world. It may sound confusing at first that in such a highly corrupt country as Russia, businessmen see corruption only as the third most significant obstacle for doing business. The corruption, coercion, and control model serves as a perfect explanation for this seemingly confusing ranking of priorities. High tax rates combined with confusing tax legislation and contradictory provisions make it very difficult or even impossible to comply with tax laws. The noncompliance, in its turn, creates a basis for administrative and criminal responsibility of business owners and managers. This responsibility becomes a powerful tool in hands of corrupt state bureaucrats. By using this leverage, top-ranking state officials exploit large corporations while street-level bureaucrats attack small enterprises. Business vulnerability based on tax violations and selective justice forms the base for extortion and threats of hostile takeovers. In many instances, it is less costly for entrepreneurs to give bribes to state officials than to pay taxes to the state budget.

Chapter 4 shifts the discussion from technicalities of corporate raiding to its base, corruption in the state apparatus. It pays a special attention to nepotism and how it plays in inheriting not the stream of income, illicit revenues, proceeds of corruption, access to graft, right to collect bribes, but the fundamental source of profit, that is, the enterprise, the company, the economic asset, the property itself.

The practice of inheriting a public office is supplemented with the one of inheriting a private enterprise, company, or any piece of private property, including land. This seemingly axiomatic situation creates incentives for corrupt state bureaucrats to appropriate economic assets that they manage and formalize their property rights over these assets. And the best and most effective tool in securing not only the stream of bribes, but also full-scale guaranteed profit participation is precisely raiding. The fact that kinship in power is historically detrimental to economic development is of little concern to the ruling authoritarian regime. Russia finds itself in a stalemate, or a low, steady state equilibrium, where the overwhelming well-being of the elites does not facilitate and in fact prevents an increase in the socioeconomic well-being of the masses. Large state-owned companies have no choice but to accept children of top Russian bureaucrats and politicians for top managerial positions. Jointly owned companies and private ones follow this practice as well. In this way, chief bureaucrats "outsource" their function of receiving illicit revenues, such as bribes, to their offspring and other family members, while companies establish close ties with the ruling political regime. As a result of such a reciprocal arrangement, state bureaucrats amass their wealth while fencing themselves off from state prosecution. Companies rely on their governmental connections in order to secure themselves from possible raiding attacks, including those led by the state. This part provides a comparative perspective on corruption, pointing to similarities between Russia and Nigeria, with the former being very distant from the US and even China. While China indicates a strong economic growth over the last three decades, both Russia and Nigeria rely heavily on the export of oil and raw materials and lack development.

Chapter 4 reflects on some legislative initiatives undertaken by leading Russian politicians and political bodies with the goal of curbing illegal raiding and corruption. These legal initiatives have little to do with such issues as corporate litigation, because in Russia, corporate raiding is done predominantly through corruption. This part also explores the potential for the anti-corruption operation known as provocation by bribe. The idea of provocation by bribe as a testing device for state bureaucrats has a potential to become a valid tool of corruption control. It is possible to test state bureaucrats by provoking them to accept a bribe, but the whole operation should be designed and described by the law. This chapter argues that if legalized, provocation by bribe may be applied not only to high-ranking state officials and street-level bureaucrats, but the law enforcement officers as well. However, as long as the provocation by bribe remains illegal, any attempts of an anti-corruption campaign organized by law enforcement agencies may well result in a criminal case against the law enforcement agencies' officers themselves. The book's formal conclusion generalizes its findings and briefly recapitulates major points of the presented work.

Notes

1 Directly translated, *koshmarit' biznes* means causing nightmares for business. Clifford Levy. Medvedev says Russia should end business "nightmares." *The New York Times*,

14 *Introduction*

August 1, 2008. Retrieved from www.nytimes.com/2008/08/01/world/europe/01iht 01russia.14927480.html; Khvatit koshmarit' biznes. *Forbes*, Retrieved from www.forbes. ru/ekonomika/vlast/32096-hvatit-koshmarit-biznes

2 Sakwa's (2009) work on Khodorkovsky, Putin, and the Yukos affair is the single most comprehensive source of information and analysis of the Yukos case.

3 K pravozashchitnitse Zoe Svetovoy prishli domoj s obyskom po delu Yukosa ot 2003 goda [A search warrant is being executed in the house of human rights activist Zoya Svetova in connection to Yukos criminal case that dates back to 2003]. *Newsru.com*, February 28, 2017. Retrieved from www.newsru.com/russia/28feb2017/svetova.html

4 A substantial part of the media references come from *Newsru.com*. This source is a compilation of media reports that come from such major Russian newspapers as *Argumenty i fakty, Balt-info, Ekho Moskvy, Izvestiya, Kommersant', Komsomol'skaya Pravda, Moskovskie novosti, Moskovsky komsomolets, Nezavisimaya gazeta, Novaya gazeta, Novye izvestiya, Novyj den', RBK, Rosbalt, Rossijskaya gazeta, The Moscow Times*, and *Vedomosti*; news agencies *Ekho Moskvy, Interfax, Radio Svoboda*, and *RIA Novosti*; online news sources *Gazeta.ru, Grani.ru, Inopressa.ru*, and *Zagolovki.ru*; and some other media news outlets, including local media sources. This study uses *Newsru.com* for its convenience – web links to its reports are permanent and open access so the reader is able to follow the original source and the original report on every reference.

5 Chekovaya privatizatsiya.

6 MVD [Ministerstvo vnnutrennikh del] is a Russian abbreviation for the Ministry of the Interior. FSB [Federal'naya sluzhba bezopasnosti] is a Russian abbreviation for the Federal Security Services, a direct descendant of the Soviet KGB.

References

Aslund, Anders. (1997). Economic Causes of Crime in Russia. In Jeffrey Sachs & Katharina Pistor (eds.). *The Rule of Law and Economic Reform in Russia* (pp. 79–94). Boulder, CO: Westview Press.

Aslund, Anders. (2009). *How Ukraine Became a Market Economy and Democracy*. Washington, DC: Peterson Institute for International Economics.

Barnes, Andrew. (2003). Comparative Theft: Context and Choice in the Hungarian, Czech, and Russian Transformations, 1989–2000. *East European Politics and Societies*, 17(3), pp. 533–565.

Barnes, Andrew. (2006). *Owning Russia: The Struggle over Factories, Farms, and Power*. Ithaca: Cornell University Press.

Barnes, Andrew. (2007a). Extricating the State: The Move to Competitive Capture in Post-Communist Bulgaria. *Europe-Asia Studies*, 59(1), pp. 71–95.

Barnes, Andrew. (2007b). Industrial Property in Russia: The Return of the State and a Focus on Oil. *SAIS Review*, 27(2), pp. 47–62.

Becker, Uwe (ed.). (2013). *The BRICs and Emerging Economies in Comparative Perspective: Political Economy, Liberalisation and Institutional Change*. Abingdon: Routledge.

Black, Bernard, Kraakman, Reinier, & Tarassova, Anna. (2000). Russian Privatization and Corporate Governance: What Went Wrong? *Stanford Law Review*, 52, pp. 1731–1808.

Bodin, Per-Arne, Hedlund, Stefan, & Namli, Elena (eds.). (2012). *Power and Legitimacy: Challenges from Russia*. New York: Routledge.

Brück, Tilman & Lehmann, Hartmut (eds.). (2012). *In the Grip of Transition: Economic and Social Consequences of Restructuring in Russia and Ukraine*. New York: Palgrave Macmillan.

Bunce, Valerie & Wolchik, Sharon. (2011). *Defeating Authoritarian Leaders in Postcommunist Countries*. Cambridge: Cambridge University Press.

Duhamel, Luc. (2010). *The KGB Campaign against Corruption in Moscow, 1982–1987.* Pittsburgh: University of Pittsburgh Press.

Dzarasov, Ruslan. (2014). *The Conundrum of Russian Capitalism: The Post-Soviet Economy in the World System.* London: Pluto Press.

Easter, Gerald M. (2012). *Capital, Coercion, and Postcommunist States.* Ithaca & London: Cornell University Press.

Easter, Gerald M. (2013). Revenue Imperatives: State over Market in Postcommunist Russia. In Neil Robinson (ed.). *The Political Economy of Russia* (pp. 51–68). Lanham: Rowman & Littlefield.

Firestone, Thomas. (2008). Criminal Corporate Raiding in Russia. *The International Lawyer*, 42(4), pp. 1207–1230.

Fortescue, Stephen (ed.). (2010). *Russian Politics from Lenin to Putin.* New York: Palgrave Macmillan.

Frye, Timothy. (2000). *Brokers and Bureaucrats: Building Market Institutions in Russia.* Ann Arbor, MI: University of Michigan Press.

Frye, Timothy. (2002). Two Faces of Russian Courts: Evidence from a Survey of Company Managers: Reforming Russia's Courts. *East European Constitutional Review*, pp. 125–129.

Frye, Timothy. (2010a). *Building States and Markets after Communism: The Perils of Polarized Democracy.* New York: Cambridge University Press.

Frye, Timothy. (2010b). Corruption and the Rule of Law. In Anders Aslund, Sergei Guriev, & Andrew C. Kuchins (eds.). *Russia after the Global Economic Crisis* (pp. 79–94). Washington, DC: Peterson Institute for International Economics.

Frye, Timothy. (2014). Legality and Violence in Russia: An Introduction. *Post-Soviet Affairs*, 30(2–3), pp. 87–88.

Frye, Timothy. (2017). *Property Rights and Property Wrongs: How Power, Institutions, and Norms Shape Economic Conflict in Russia.* New York: Cambridge University Press.

Gans-Morse, Jordan. (2017). *Property Rights in Post-Soviet Russia: Violence, Corruption, and the Demand for Law.* New York: Cambridge University Press.

Gel'man, Vladimir & Ross, Cameron (eds.). (2010). *The Politics of Sub-National Authoritarianism in Russia.* Burlington, VT: Ashgate.

Gilman, Martin. (2010). *No Precedent, No Plan: Inside Russia's 1998 Default.* Cambridge, MA: MIT Press.

Giuliano, Elise. (2011). *Constructing Grievance: Ethnic Nationalism in Russia's Republics.* Ithaca, NY: Cornell University Press.

Godzimirski, Jakub. (2011). Nord Stream: Globalization in the Pipeline. In Julie Wilhelmsen & Elana Wilson Rowe (eds.). *Russia's Encounter with Globalization: Actors, Processes and Critical Moments* (pp. 159–184). New York: Palgrave Macmillan.

Hass, Jeffrey. (2012). *Rethinking the Post-Soviet Experience: Markets, Moral Economies and Cultural Contradictions of Post Socialist Russia.* New York: Palgrave Macmillan.

Hanson, Philip. (2014). Reiderstvo: Asset-Grabbing in Russia. Russia and Eurasia PP 2014/03. Chatham House, March 2014. Retrieved from www.chathamhouse.org/sites/default/files/home/chatham/public_html/sites/default/files/20140300AssetGrabbing RussiaHanson1.pdf

Harding, Luke. (2008). Raiders of the Russian Billions. *The Guardian*, June 24, 2008. Retrieved May 9, 2009, from www.guardian.co.uk/world/2008/jun/24/russia.international crime

Hass, Jeffrey. (2011). *Power, Culture, and Economic Change in Russia: To the Undiscovered Country of Post-Socialism, 1988–2008.* New York: Routledge.

16 Introduction

Hass, Jeffrey. (2012). *Rethinking the Post-Soviet Experience: Markets, Moral Economies and Cultural Contradictions of Post Socialist Russia*. New York: Palgrave Macmillan.

Hay, Colin & Wincott, Daniel. (2013). *The Political Economy of European Welfare Capitalism*. London: Palgrave Macmillan.

Holmes, Leslie. (2010). Legitimation and Legitimacy in Russia Revisited. In Stephen Fortescue (ed.). *Russian Politics from Lenin to Putin* (pp. 101–126). New York: Palgrave Macmillan.

Huskey, Eugene. (2010). Pantouflage à la russe. In Stephen Fortescue (ed.). *Russian Politics from Lenin to Putin* (pp. 185–204). New York: Palgrave Macmillan.

Jonson, Lena & White, Stephen (eds.). (2012). *Waiting for Reform under Putin and Medvedev*. Houndmills & New York: Palgrave Macmillan.

Kireev, Aleksei. (2007). Raiding and the Market for Corporate Control: The Evolution of Strong-Arm Entrepreneurship. *Problems of Economic Transition*, 50(8), pp. 29–45.

Kivinen, Markku & Chunling, Li. (2012). The Free-Market State or the Welfare State? In Christer Pursiainen (ed.). *At the Crossroads of Post-Communist Modernisation: Russia and China in Comparative Perspective* (pp. 47–113). New York: Palgrave Macmillan.

Kononenko, Vadim & Moshes, Arkady (eds.). (2011). *Russia as a Network State: What Works in Russia When State Institutions Do Not?* New York: Palgrave Macmillan.

Kupatadze, Alexander. (2012). *Organized Crime, Political Transitions and State Formation in Post-Soviet Eurasia*. Basingstoke: Palgrave Macmillan.

Kurer, Oscar. (2005). Corruption: An Alternative Approach to Its Definition and Measurement. *Political Studies*, 53(2), pp. 222–239.

Libman, Alexander & Vinokurov, Evgeny. (2012). *Holding-Together Regionalism: Twenty Years of Post-Soviet Integration*. New York: Palgrave Macmillan.

Medvedev, Sergei & Jakobson, Linda. (2012). Sovereignty or Interdependency. In Christer Pursiainen (ed.). *At the Crossroads of Post-Communist Modernisation: Russia and China in Comparative Perspective* (pp. 181–223). New York: Palgrave Macmillan.

Morris, Jeremy & Polese, Abel (eds.). (2014). *The Informal Post-Socialist Economy: Embedded Practices and Livelihoods*. London: Routledge.

Myant, Martin & Drahokoupil, Jan. (2011). *Transition Economies: Political Economy in Russia, Eastern Europe, and Central Asia*. San Francisco, CA: Wiley.

Obydenkova, Anastassia & Libman, Alexander (eds.). (2015). *Autocratic and Democratic External Influences in Post-Soviet Eurasia*. Farnham & Burlington, VT: Ashgate.

Overland, Indra. (2011). Close Encounters: Russian Policymaking and International Oil Companies. In Julie Wilhelmsen & Elana Wilson Rowe (eds.). *Russia's Encounter with Globalization: Actors, Processes and Critical Moments* (pp. 135–158). New York: Palgrave Macmillan.

Popova, Maria. (2012). *Politicized Justice in Emerging Democracies: A Study of Courts in Russia and Ukraine*. Cambridge: Cambridge University Press.

Pursiainen, Christer & Pei, Minxin. (2012). Authoritarianism or Democracy? In Christer Pursiainen (ed.). *At the Crossroads of Post-Communist Modernisation: Russia and China in Comparative Perspective* (pp. 114–180). New York: Palgrave Macmillan.

Remington, Thomas F. (2011). *The Politics of Inequality in Russia*. Cambridge: Cambridge University Press.

Roberts, Sean P. (2012). *Putin's United Russia Party*. New York: Routledge.

Robertson, Graeme. (2011). *The Politics of Protest in Hybrid Regimes: Managing Dissent in Post-Communist Russia*. New York: Cambridge University Press.

Robinson, Neil (ed.). (2013). *The Political Economy of Russia*. Lanham: Rowman & Littlefield.

Rose, Richard, Mishler, William, & Munro, Neil. (2011). *Popular Support for an Undemocratic Regime: The Changing Views of Russians*. New York: Cambridge University Press.

Rose-Ackerman, Susan & Søreide, Tina (eds.). (2011). *International Handbook of the Economics of Corruption*, Volume Two. Northampton, MA: Edward Elgar.

Rothstein, Bo. (2011). *The Quality of Government: The Political Economy of Corruption, Social Trust and Inequality in an International Comparative Perspective*. Chicago: University of Chicago Press.

Sakwa, Richard. (2009). *The Quality of Freedom: Khodorkovsky, Putin and the Yukos Affair*. Oxford: Oxford University Press.

Sakwa, Richard. (2011). *The Crisis of Russian Democracy: The Dual State, Factionalism and the Medvedev Succession*. Cambridge: Cambridge University Press.

Sakwa, Richard. (2013). Systemic Stalemate, Reiderstvo, and the Dual State. In Neil Robinson (ed.). *The Political Economy of Russia* (pp. 69–96). Lanham, MD: Rowman & Littlefield.

Salmenniemi, Suvi (ed.). (2012). *Rethinking Class in Russia*. Farnham & Burlington: Ashgate.

Shelley, Louise & Deane, Judy. (2016). *The Rise of Reiderstvo: Implications for Russia and the West*. Washington, DC: Terrorism, Transnational Crime and Corruption Center. Retrieved from www.reiderstvo.org/sites/default/files/The_Rise_of_Reiderstvo.pdf

Sonin, Konstantin. (2003). Why the Rich May Favor Poor Protection of Property Rights. *Journal of Comparative Economics*, 31(4), pp. 715–731.

Sonin, Konstantin. (2005). Institutsional'naya teoriya beskonechnogo peredela [Institutional Theory of Endless Redistribution]. *Voprosy ekonomiki*, 7, pp. 1–15. Retrieved May 9, 2009, from http://fir.nes.ru/~ksonin/VESonin.pdf

Søreide, Tina & Williams, Aled (eds.). (2014). *Corruption, Grabbing and Development: Real World Challenges*. Northampton, MA: Edward Elgar.

Stewart, Susan (ed.). (2012). *Democracy Promotion and the "Colour Revolutions."* Abingdon: Routledge.

Sutela, Pekka. (2012). *The Political Economy of Putin's Russia*. New York: Routledge.

Taylor, Brian D. (2011). *State Building in Putin's Russia: Policing and Coercion after Communism*. Cambridge: Cambridge University Press.

Treisman, Daniel. (2011). *The Return: Russia's Journey from Gorbachev to Medvedev*. New York: Free Press.

Urban, Michael. (2010). *Cultures of Power in Post-Communist Russia*. Cambridge: Cambridge University Press.

Uslaner, Eric. (2008). *Corruption, Inequality, and the Rule of Law: The Bulging Pocket Makes the Easy Life*. New York: Cambridge University Press.

Vavilov, Andrey. (2010). *The Russian Public Debt and Financial Meltdowns*. New York: Palgrave Macmillan.

Vinokurov, Evgeny & Libman, Alexander. (2012). *Eurasian Integration: Challenges of Transcontinental Regionalism*. Basingstoke: Palgrave Macmillan.

Volkov, Vadim. (2004). The Selective Use of State Capacity in Russia's Economy: Property Disputes and Enterprise Takeovers, 1998–2002. In Janos Kornai, Bo Rothstein, & Susan Rose-Ackerman (eds.). *Creating Social Trust in Post-Socialist Transition* (pp. 126–147). New York: Palgrave Macmillan.

Volkov, Vadim. (2005a). Transformation of Russian State after 2000. Public Lecture, April 2, 2009. Retrieved June 10, 2009, from www.polit.ru/lectures/2009/04/02/estado.html

Volkov, Vadim. (2005b). Po tu storonu sudebnoj sistemy, ili Pochemu zakony rabotayut ne tak, kak dolzhny [On the Other Side of the Justice System or Why Don't Laws Work as

18 *Introduction*

They Should]. *Neprikosnovennyj zapas*, 4(42). Retrieved from http://magazines.russ.ru/nz/2005/42/vv6.html

Volkov, Vadim. (2005c). *Silovoe predprinimatel'stvo – ekonomiko-sotsiologicheski analiz* [*Violent Entrepreneurship: Economic and Sociological Analysis*]. Moscow: Izdatelski dom GU VSHE.

Ward, Christopher J. (2009). *Brezhnev's Folly: The Building of BAM and Late Soviet Socialism*. Pittsburgh: University of Pittsburgh Press.

Wedeman, Andrew. (2012). *Double Paradox: Rapid Growth and Rising Corruption in China*. Ithaca & London: Cornell University Press.

White, Stephen. (2011). *Understanding Russian Politics*. New York: Cambridge University Press.

Wilhelmsen, Julie & Wilson Rowe, Elana. (2011). *Russia's Encounter with Globalization: Actors, Processes and Critical Moments*. New York: Palgrave Macmillan.

Williams, Colin C., Round, John, & Rodgers, Peter. (2013). *The Role of Informal Economies in the Post-Soviet World: The End of Transition?* London: Routledge.

Woodruff, David. (2004). Property Rights in Context: Privatization's Legacy for Corporate Legality in Poland and Russia. *Studies in Comparative International Development*, 38(4), pp. 82–108.

Woodruff, David. (2005). Nestabil'nost' chastnoi sobstvennosti v Rossii: ekonomicheskie i politicheskie prichiny [The Instability of Private Property in Russia: Economic and Political Causes]. *Russkie Chteniia*. Vypusk 1. Moskva: "Gruppa Ekspert," 2005, pp. 206–219. Retrieved from http://personal.lse.ac.uk/woodruff/_private/materials/kogdan elzia.pdf

Yakovlev, Andrei, Sobolev, Anton, & Kazun, Anton. (2014). Means of Production versus Means of Coercion: Can Russian Business Limit the Violence of a Predatory State? *Post-Soviet Affairs*, 30(2–3), pp. 171–194.

1 Corruption, coercion, and control

1.1 Theoretical explanation of raiding in a transition economy

Regime sustainability and raiding

A substantial block of scholarly literature considers excessive corruption as an indication of the weakness of government. Policy makers and general public are of similar opinion in regards to this conventional wisdom. However, this does not imply that this notion may not be challenged and that such a challenge will not be productive. When it comes to the link between the state, corruption, and corporate raiding, a thorough scholarly investigation might bear fruit. Sceptics challenge the relevance of good governance and political science approach in general to human well-being. Holmberg and Rothstein (2012) give an excellent response, pointing out that societal ills "are not caused by a lack of technical equipment, effective medicines or other types of knowledge ... but by the fact that a majority of the world's population have to live in societies that are dominated by dysfunctional government institutions" (p. 3). North (1990, 1992, 2006, 2007) and Olson (1982, 1996, 2000) point out the significance of organizational changes for societal development and economic growth. Olson, Sarna, and Swamy (2000) argue that the difference in the rate of economic growth among developing nations is due to differences in the quality of governance. The authors show that productivity growth is higher in better-governed countries. De Haan, Lundstrom, and Sturm (2006) summarize that

> Since the time of Adam Smith, if not before, economists and economic historians have argued that the freedom to choose and supply resources, competition in business, free trade with others and secure property rights are central ingredients for economic progress.
>
> (p. 182)

Thus, more theorizing based on political science research frames is needed in order to explain and improve developing nations.

When it comes to the imaginary or perceived weakness of the state and presence of widespread corruption, the opposite may well be true. In nondemocratic

20 *Corruption, coercion, and control*

societies, corruption, informally approved, imposed, or regulated by public authorities, is an indicator of the power of the state, rather than its weakness. To be more specific, this kind of power is not the type of power generally associated with the state and perceived as a tool for betterment of society. On the contrary, this is a specifically designed coercive power, exercised informally by formal state institutions. Corruption may be used on a systematic basis as a mechanism of direct and indirect administrative control and redistribution of wealth on the state level and down to local authorities and administrations of public and private institutions. Control and redistribution of wealth in this case is based not only on formally approved and justified coercion, but on blackmail and selective justice.

Authoritarian countries often informally approve of corrupt activities in exchange for loyalty and compliance with the ruling political regime. Legal traps are often created by the ruling political regime in order to encourage bureaucrats and entrepreneurs to violate the law and then force them to comply and share revenues with the regime. Vertical and horizontal structures of corrupt control allow ruling regimes to sustain themselves and exercise coercive power over their constituents. Administrations of enterprises and institutions are targeted by central and local governments in pursuit of higher degrees of informal control. Administrators, managers, entire institutions, and regular individuals are much easier to be ruled if corrupt. The same is true for businessmen who operate in authoritarian regimes. In such cases, the ruling political regime extracts its rent not only in the form of direct monetary payments, but in loyalty as well. The alleged tax schemes in the Yukos case is a good example in this regard.

The ruling regime derives its rent through the use of the authoritative powers, regulation, and oversight functions of the state. While state bureaucrats extort their rent from the clientele, including businessmen, in form of bribes and numerous other favors, the ruling political regime extorts its rent from the business community in the form of loyalty and compliance, in addition to payoffs, kickbacks, and shares. This is quite characteristic of the concept of corruption, subversion, and coercion developed over the decades and put into action (Almond and Coleman, 1960; Andreski, 1966, 1968; Anechiarico and Jacobs, 1995; Banfield, 1975; Darden, 2001, 2002, 2008). The rent is derived not only in cash, but also in loyalty and obedience (Osipian, 2012). The ruling political regime needs this obedience not only from civil servants and other public employees, but from businessmen as well.

As far as Russia is concerned, the ruling authoritarian regime focuses on suppressing both entrepreneurial and civil initiatives while forcing businessmen to contribute to selected socially significant projects. The corruption and blackmail scheme used to control businessmen has been put in action more than three decades ago, with the start of Perestroika. Thus far, the ruler of Russia has been doing this quite successfully. There are supporters to this explanatory approach. For instance, Mesquita and Smith (2012) suggest that,

> [A]n ineffective economic system, from the viewpoint of a cynical dictator, turns out very effective politically ... you constantly underpay the law

enforcers which creates corrupt incentives. Although they cannot be jailed for being disloyal, they can be jailed for corruption. Then you tell them: I can forgive you corruption if you remain loyal.... Politically, this is very effective. Besides, he does not need to spend much money on the repressive apparatus: they can collect all necessary resources through bribes.

(as cited in Markus, 2015, p. 8)

Inability of the government to cope with endemic corruption – be it Africa or post-Soviet Eurasia – is attributed to a weak state. This weak state is unable to offer due protection to holders of property rights. Markus (2015) departs from the "absence-dominance" approach to the state's role in weakening the security of property rights. He suggests that it is the state weakness, "conceived as the inadequate control of the sovereign over his bureaucratic apparatus, that constitutes the main threat to property rights" in Russia (Markus, 2015, p. 2). The meaning of the state and the ruling political regime becomes split into two: the ruler, king, or czar, and his agents, bureaucrats, or servants. The blame for predation of property is placed conveniently on the latter. Supposedly they rob the people and thus betray their principal. This approach reminds one of the Russians' belief in the good czar, which creates an impression that the king is good, but his servants are evil. This belief was as naive as it was misleading, but consistently high approval ratings of President Putin indicate that this belief is alive and well in today's Russia.

Vertical and horizontal structures of control distribution may be based on corruption and coercion. These structures allow the ruling regime to survive and execute its authority through mechanisms of coercion of its constituents and electorate. Voters, coerced in casting their vote, and moreover, casting it for a certain candidate or political party, create an illusion of democracy. This illusion adds to the proclaimed legitimacy of the state and is attributed to legitimacy of the ruling regime. These two terms, the state and the ruling regime, are frequently confused in Russia. Similarly, the terms of power and authority are confused or not delineated at all. Local officials, bureaucrats, and businessmen may be targeted by the ruling regime in the process of strengthening both formal and informal control. Corrupt local officials and businessmen coerce their constituents and employees into supporting the regime. In this way, large-scale and widespread corruption helps the regime to skillfully manipulate the masses.

Suppression of corporate autonomy, the induction of state bureaucrats into corporate governing boards, the imposition of pseudo-accountability under the nontransparent financial regulations, and direct informal control are used by the authorities and administrations in order to control businessmen and the business activities of the companies. Under the conditions of market transition, when laws are changing and the rules are unclear or subject to interpretation, state bureaucrats are placed in conditions of financial survival while businessmen find it hard to comply with laws and regulations even if they try their best and in good faith to do so. Numerous violations follow; they are registered and those bureaucrats and businessmen become subjects of blackmail. This type of blackmail comes not from the side of criminals and racketeers, but from the side of the ruling regime.

22   *Corruption, coercion, and control*

The Russian political establishment may either use this mechanism of corruption and subversion, or at least be aware of its use. Nevertheless, this mechanism of informal and potential control spreads nationwide and extends to different levels of social organizations.

A monopolistic position is a basis for rent. In this sense, rent and corruption have similar grounds. A monopolistic position explains the noneconomic nature of rent. A monopolistic position of economic agents is based on limited resources, utilized in societal production. Regulating access to limited resources creates opportunities for corruption. In post-Soviet Russia, corrupt transition and rent-seeking behavior merge to form a specific modus operandi for the system, made distinct by high transaction costs. This merger of corrupt transition and rent-seeking behavior occurs in different sectors of the economy, but because market transition is relatively slow, this merger is sometimes hidden due to unclear new rules and regulations, and sometimes very visible due to a long-lasting exposure without changes. This study will now turn to a more specific analysis of corruption and state control in Russia.

It would be beneficial to start constructing the concept of corruption as the instrument of coercion and the mechanism of administrative control from considering the role of the state in society and its relation to corruption. Specifically, the question is: How does the state relate to corruption? Zhdanov (2002) presents the following view on the relation of state to corruption: "Corruption and government are eternal antagonists. Corruption, as a form of social corrosion, 'eats away' at governmental structures, while governmental authority in turn strives to destroy corruption." This study argues the opposite, based on Darden's (2002, p. 2) definition of the state "as a compulsory rule-making organization that is sustained through the extraction of wealth from within its territorial domain." This definition is particularly convenient in investigating power-wealth relations in nondemocratic regimes.

Darden (2008, p. 37) describes the vulnerability of the assets acquired by illegal ways and the mechanism by which the government officials subordinate their lower-level counterparts:

> Hence, the threat of exposing and enforcing his wrongdoing constitutes an enormously powerful sanction and places lower-level officials in an especially vulnerable position. The severity of this sanction allows the state leadership to practice a systematic form of blackmail, with payment exacted not in cash but in obedience.

Leadership of the state apparatus executes a systematic blackmail of its subordinates or even formally independent entrepreneurs not only with the goal of gaining their loyalty and support, but also redistributing already earned benefits or economic assets and illicit income.

The practice of making people guilty and blackmailing them is not new. The scheme is very simple and may be formulated as follows: "Make people feel guilty and propose them salvage in exchange for obedience." In the era of the dominating Roman Catholic Church, this formula was reinforced with the Inquisition and realized through Papal indulgences. In modern autocratic regimes, this formula is reinforced with selective justice and realized through corrupt state institutions. Wrapped in the multilayered coats of legality and justice, the corruption, coercion, and control scheme sustains the undemocratic regime, but at the same time proliferates and reinforces the destructive processes in the country. This approach to the governance is perhaps as old as the Roman "divide and conquer." A similar approach may be applied to businessmen coping with peculiarities of tax laws and changes in the legal system of property rights. They suddenly discover that in past years they did not pay taxes or did not do it correctly and in full. And now they may face charges of grand scale tax evasion and imprisonment. On this legal ground, businessmen may be blackmailed by the state organs.

Political stability in a country does not necessarily mean there are low levels of corruption but rather well-adjusted mechanisms of functioning at all levels of authority, even if these authorities are corrupt. Shlapentokh (2003) asserts that,

> When life in a country is relatively stable, corruption, like some cancers, destroys a society from the inside without producing symptoms or even pain. This is the case for Putin's Russia, where the political arena is calm in comparison to Yeltsin's turbulent years in office.
>
> (p. 158)

He says that widespread corruption creates a parallel, semi-feudal chain of command that competes with the official hierarchy. In fact, this semi-feudal structure is not parallel, but is of the essence of the system. It is informal, but it does not compete with the official hierarchy. This structure is developed and maintained by the frame of formal state institutions. Waite and Allen (2003, p. 294) support this view of self-sustainability of corrupt regimes:

> Corrupt systems are difficult, if not impossible, to challenge and change from within, especially since the power operant in such systems is self-protective and self-perpetuating. Also, corruption may work in tandem with other forms of repression, such as racism, sexism, and classism.

Payne (1975, p. 53) describes similar mechanisms of subversion and corruption in national systems as well as in international politics in an historical perspective, based on practices of dictatorial regimes.

The same mechanism of state-based corruption and coercion is described by Zhdanov (2002, p. 5), who writes about the selective application of criminal law and other repressive legal measures to governmental officials and politicians: "The use of juridical reprisals against political opponents by means of charging them with corruption (or other illegal acts) when there are no legal grounds to do so." Often the laws or the normative acts are composed post-ante in order to prosecute an activity that took place when it was not illegal. Legal craftsmanship is one of the essential features of the government's use of its authority for the

24   *Corruption, coercion, and control*

purpose of selective justice. Political rhetoric is impressive: corrupt opposition-ists claim that they are prosecuted because they are in opposition to the corrupt regime, while the regime states that it opposes corrupt politicians.

Selective justice as one of the primary instruments of coercion implies the exis-tence externally managed courts. Popova (2012) notes that judicial independence is being commonly attributed to "two main casual variables: structural insulation of the judiciary from the other branches of government and political competition" (p. 6). It turns out that competing political powers are not necessarily comfortable with a high level of political independence of their judiciary. As far as Russia is concerned, it is hard to call the country's legislative, executive, and judiciary branches competing political powers. While the role of courts in provision of free and fair elections is significant and growing in Russia, the pressure on courts and judges may also be growing. Nevertheless, as Popova (2012) suggests, judges act in their self-interest and decide whether they should meet the demands of politi-cians or resist political pressure depending on their own career interests. Indepen-dent judiciary is one of the cornerstones of a democratic society, while dependent courts and controlled judges are intended to preserve the autocracy of the ruling political regime.

Putin was objecting to Colton's argument that the present political model is obsolete, countering that the present model of governance in Russia has not exhausted itself.[1] Similarly, Taylor (2011) argues that the strategy chosen by Putin in order to rebuild the Russian state was "fundamentally flawed" (Taylor, 2011, p. 282). The author focuses on such issues as coercion and the state, centralization and federalism, power ministries, corrupt practices of the law enforcement offi-cers, and relations between the state and society in the process of recreating Rus-sian statehood. He also emphasizes the issue of state coercion in Russia's volatile North Caucasus region, concluding that "Although revolution seems unlikely, the current nature of Russian state coercive organs in the North Caucasus gives little reason for confidence about long-term political order" (p. 282). Hedlund (2011) cautions that "Russia is certainly not alone in exhibiting a track record that may be construed as long-term systemic failure" (p. 246). Aslund, Guriev, and Kuchins (2010) conclude that Russia's current strategy may be productive in the short run, but it lacks perspective in the long run. Perhaps they were talking in essence about two different models. As far as the corruption, coercion, and control model is concerned, its resources for the ruling regime are far from being depleted. Instead, the model has a strong potential at least in the near future, until the resource-based economy will deteriorate so significantly that the need will emerge to reconfigure or replace this model.

The inability of the central authorities to seek sustainability of the regime among its constituents, i.e. broad electorate, urges them to rely on informal mechanisms of control. While formal mechanisms of exercising political power preserve their legality and visibility, the informal ones become of primary importance and slowly replace formal mechanisms of control with corrupt mechanisms. This replacement soon acquires systemic characteristics. One can trace the following sequence: singular – particular – system – unity. While in the first stage corruption as a form of control occurs on a case-by-case basis; in the second stage it is a recognized phenomenon; in the third stage it is broadly used by different branches of authority and acquires systemic characteristics; and in the last, fourth stage it is a norm, not only well established but unavoidable. Along the sequence line the informal first emerges, then develops, becomes predominant, and finally overcomes the formal, while the formal, being absolute in the first stage, declines down to a fiction at the last. The informal becomes real and the formal becomes nominal. The agent becomes accountable to his principal not only on the formal level, but also and mostly on the informal level.

The presence of formal channels of power is explained by two factors: 1) certain social constraints imposed on the members of the central authorities by the voters and 2) by the necessity of legal coercive power to enforce mechanisms of corruption and coercion. At the same time informal channels of power become predominant. Within the principal-agent relations frame, the principal who cannot rely on population as a primary base of his power and formal authority requires from the agent both loyalty and compliance and expects him/her to be helpful in receiving public support. In exchange, the agent receives from the principal both the informal authorization for corrupt activities and cover-up or protection. In this case the principal is more concerned with the personal fidelity of the agent and hiswillingness to share the benefits from corruption rather than with his performance of formal duties.

The positive role of the state in developing and sustaining corruption is often underestimated. Prominent Russian economic reformer, Anatoly Chubais, famous for his liberal economic views and for privatization, remarked that "Corruption depends very little on the authorities. It depends on the people" (Chubais, 2002). Chubais's view appears to be somewhat outdated, since corruption in Russia has been largely institutionalized. Entire corrupt organizational hierarchies develop within state institutions, penetrate public and private sectors, and take over state functions (Osipian, 2010). Shlapentokh (2003, p. 156) criticizes Putin for his declarations about strengthening the state and at the same time avoiding taking serious action against corruption and commenting on the issue of corruption in the media. For us it is not surprising, because according to the concept of corruption and coercion, strengthening the state through vertical administrative hierarchy is exactly what is necessary to advance the policy of coercion through corruption. This policy, in its turn, leads to further strengthening of the state machine. Accordingly, Russian leaders always mention the importance of administrative resources and managed democracy.

Rose, Mishler, and Munro (2011) point to the established and reinforced administrative vertical in both politics and business. In politics, the vertical is federal districts; in business, it is the social responsibility of loyal oligarchs. The authors touch on the issue of the legitimacy of the ruling regime and the legitimacy of property or swiftly accumulated wealth:

> Taking advantage of the fact that no one could have amassed great wealth in Yeltsin's Russia without breaking laws, civil and criminal actions were

26 *Corruption, coercion, and control*

selectively filed against oligarchs such as Boris Berezovsky, Vladimir Gusinsky and Mikhail Khodorkovsky. The first two went into exile; Khodorkovsky went to prison.

(Rose, Mishler, and Munro, 2011, p. 47)

The authors further suggest that a growing number of Russian billionaires no longer possesses an independent power. Instead, the wealthy are subordinated to the ruling political regime. If they will not demonstrate sufficient loyalty to this regime, they may well be deprived of their wealth and business.

The processes of sharing and profiteering create a base for and strengthen the vertical structure of the corruption, coercion, and control mechanism. The degree of sharing of the benefits from corruption is an indicator of the strength of the vertical hierarchy. The formal frame is necessary to enforce sharing and the state is utilized as a formal structure for that matter. Zhdanov (2002, p. 7) suggests the necessity of existence of such formal systems by saying

> The perpetrators of corruption cannot exist without the official subsystem. This subsystem is a necessary prerequisite for them to establish corrupt relations; in order to abuse authority, one must first possess it. One must have been appointed to an appropriate position within the agencies of central governmental authority (or local self-government), and must have both actual powers and the opportunity to use them officially. Besides that, the official subsystem serves as a cover for the unofficial one. In the first place, the perpetrators of corruption use the powers granted them by the law to achieve their unlawful goals. In the second place, they use official status to evade the responsibility provided for by law.

This view on the relations between corruption and the officialdom is applicable to Russia, but it does not capture that intent of corrupted authorities to corrupt their subordinates and independent agents in order to make them dependent on the authorities. The "bad apple" theory that presupposes the existence of the office of official power to be abused by a corrupted bureaucrat ignores the systemic and indeed endemic character of corruption.

The structuralized conclusions of this section, devoted to the corruption, coercion, and control model as applied to Russian politics may be formulated as the following. First, elections as they are conducted, and taking into consideration falsifications and other trickery, are nothing but the raiding and hostile takeover of state power. The distribution of offices of authority based on the results of rigged elections signifies the process of legitimation of otherwise illegitimate appointments and distribution of access to state power. This state power and authority are used to gain further access to economic assets and, moreover, the facilitation of state-led raiding campaigns. Second, the realization of mechanisms of corruption and coercion allows for continued redistribution of property, sanctioned and indeed managed by the state. Redistribution of property, including by raiding, is a managed process and not a chaotic and sporadic movement, as it is often

Corruption, coercion, and control 27

portrayed by officialdom. Third, this model allows for infiltrating businesses by way of the introduction of state bureaucrats into the company management, including trading memberships in the corporate boards of directors in exchange for protection. Fourth, the corruption and coercion model creates the basis for realization of mergers and acquisitions, or more precisely expropriations and transfers of property, based on the Yukos model. The state guarantees its control over some companies and assets through the real threat of a hostile takeover. The continuous attempt to hold every significant and street-level bureaucrat and businessman under control leads to proliferation and encouragement of corruption. This arrangement is considered acceptable as long as the scale and scope of corruption do not threaten the existence of the system and the ruling regime itself. A similar situation may be with raiding, kept within "modest" limits.

Politics being a strong motive for the corruption, coercion, and control scheme, economic interests, such as profiteering, are certainly given priority. Political leaders in corrupt ruling regimes always expect to obtain a share of the illegal income, including income that originates from corrupt activities. Darden (2008) creates an impression that the leaders are only concerned about obedience and the secrecy of bribery and embezzlement, when their primary concern is rather about sharing in profits. The strength of the vertical hierarchy is defined not only by the blackmail-loyalty relation, but also by the share of illicit revenues that subordinates pay to the top, or so-called "roof" [krysha]. This "roof" may be as important for raiders as it is for corrupt subordinates. Two of the most negative phenomena in modern Russia, corruption and raiding, apparently have very close ties. The ruling political regime utilizes both corruption and raiding, the goal being to reach a steady state and stabilize the autocracy. Whether this is the highest possible steady state is another issue. In fact, it may well be true that the regime would settle even for the lowest point of a steady state in order to assure the regime's stability. For instance, as the oil prices drop significantly, the ruler would continue to enjoy high popularity despite the mounting economic problems.

Defining raiding and its place

The application of the corruption, coercion, and control scheme by the ruling political regime may offer some ideas on why raiding exists, polity-wise, but it does not define raiding, nor does it discover the essence of raiding. Thus, this study needs to turn to the key question, the question of definitions: What is raiding? In practically any dictionary one can find the following explanation of the term *raiding* and its accompanying or derivative terms as related to business. A raid is an active phase of a hostile takeover of an enterprise or its assets. A raider is a participant in the hostile takeover. The term *raiding* has more to it: *raiding* denotes either a certain action or a set of operations, or more broadly, a certain phenomenon. Raiding as a distinct phenomenon is a reflection of social and economic causes and effects on various redistributional processes. Raiding is a socio-economic category associated with clear manifestations that include observable events, appearances, and experiences. At the same time, both the legislators and

28 *Corruption, coercion, and control*

law enforcers face the challenge of properly identifying raiding as a phenomenon that has a negative impact on the national economy.

Defining raiding remains one of the major tasks not only for legislators, but also for researchers. Despite the fact that as of today there are several definitions of raiding presented in the scholarly literature, one may note similarities between them as well as complexity and generalist character. These definitions may be too inclusive, with a potential to include not only raiding, but other similar actions that take place in the emerging market economy. Thus far, none of the authors who presented definitions of raiding succeeded in formulating and disclosing the essence of the raiding phenomenon and at the same time underlining its specifics in Russia. Nevertheless, this study will present and discuss some of these definitions offered in scholarly literature.

According to Western views, raiding in the national economy refers to corporate hostile takeovers. In fact, the term raiding is quite rare in relation to corporate processes, and is routinely replaced with a more accommodating term "hostile takeovers." Another rare term that denotes most aggressive raiders is "liquidators" or "liquidator companies." These hostile takeovers are done in accordance with appropriate laws, at least in most of the instances. Corporate hostile takeovers are researched by Atanassov (2013); Auerbach (1988); Bhagat et al. (1990); Coffee, Lowenstein, and Rose-Ackerman (1988); Drucker (1986); Gaughan (1996); McKee (1989); Nelson (1959); and Sinha (2004), to name but a few. These authors investigate such key processes as restructuring, liquidation, change of management and governance, and mergers and acquisitions, all of which are present in the US corporate market.

Corporate hostile takeovers that take place in the US are frequently characterized by the aggressive "American style" tactics used. Those tactics include greenmail, buyouts, stock market manipulations, and endless court litigations. If Western scholars consider "American style" raiding as aggressive, it is only because they are not familiar with corporate raiding Russian style. Also this study uses the term "corporate raiding"; it addresses problems that go far beyond the corporate world. Property that belongs to small businessmen and owners, as well as land, is also being actively targeted by raiders in Russia. Since the post-Soviet society may be considered as one big corporation, as it largely remains since the Soviet era with its collectivism, the generalizing or overarching term "corporate raiding" seems to be appropriate.

Corporate and property raiding in Russia, also referred to as *reiderstvo, rejderstvo,* or *reyderstvo,* differs significantly from corporate raiding in developed Western democracies. Gans-Morse (2012) says that, "While the term is taken from the American usage, it involves far more than buying up a company's shares in order to change management" (p. 281). The author notes that the corrupt judiciary became involved in attacks on property, including those with illegal corporate raiding. For instance,

> One common scheme was to acquire a company's debt and then utilize legal loopholes to initiate forced bankruptcy, despite the firm's sound financial

health. Raiders would then bribe a judge to appoint a loyal bankruptcy trustee, who would facilitate the seizure of the firm's assets.

(Gans-Morse, 2012, pp. 281–282)

This was especially possible prior to changes introduced to the Law on Bankruptcy in 2002. The criminal component is important when it comes to staging a hostile takeover in Russia. And in this criminal component, courts play a significant role.

In the academic discourse of post-Soviet Russia, crime-related corporate raiding clearly dominates over the notion of hostile takeover. Apparently, the notion of raid as a core aggressive action is especially important in this discourse. One can hardly find any Western scholarly publication that uses "corporate raiding" in its title, unless the topic of the paper is precisely on corporate raiding in Russia or other former socialist states. So far, there have been only a handful of publications on this outmost important topic, and, not surprisingly, most of them appear in law reviews (see, for instance, Firestone, 2008, 2010; Rojansky, 2014; Volkov, 2004). The West continues to perceive Russian corporate market processes as a constant legal challenge rather than a part of commonly accepted mergers and acquisitions schemes.

Raiding in the post-Soviet space is quite distinct from basic forms of criminally charged violent extortion and racketeering. Firestone (2008, p. 1207) defines raiding in Russia by delineating it from primitive criminals and standard protection schemes:

In contrast to more primitive criminals, Russian "reideri" rely on court orders, resolutions of shareholders and boards of directors, lawsuits, bankruptcy proceedings, and other ostensibly "legal" means as a cover for their criminal activity. "Reiderstvo" is also more ambitious than classic protection schemes in that it seeks not just a portion of the target business' profits but the entire business itself. Finally, because raiding typically involves the use of documents such as corporate resolutions and judicial orders as covers for threats of physical violence, it is more sophisticated and can be much more difficult to investigate and prosecute than straightforward extortion schemes.

Russian scholars also give definitions of raiding, including both those that are Russia specific, and those of more general nature. Kireev (2008) offers a formalized description of a raiding action as a "set of actions characterized by features common for investment projects, including goals, tasks, terms of completion, budget, and such" (p. 4). Here, raiding is being portrayed as just another investment project. A clear lack of specificity makes this definition too broad and too inclusive to reflect the essence of this controversial phenomenon. Tishchenko (2009) does not offer his own definition of raiding, but relies on the one given by Kireev (2007), saying that raiding "is systematic activity by stable formal or informal groups, aimed at obtaining the ability to use and distribute (control) assets belonging to other economic actors" (p. 5). The author points out that

30 *Corruption, coercion, and control*

specialists and teams in raiding business are referred to as predators, aggressors, raider structures, and raider companies. These terms are part of the raiding discourse that fit the general narrative of aggressively conducted business, so popular in the post-Soviet Russia. Sychev (2011) is even more explicit in regards to the aggressive and indeed violent character of raiding in Russia. He defines raiding as a "violent hostile takeover of an enterprise against the will of its owner or manager" (Sychev, 2011, p. 25).

In Russia, property is regarded as a complex relation. This complexity is also embedded in the legislature that regulates property relations that emerge between economic agents. The full set of property rights includes ownership, use, and management of a certain asset, be it building, equipment, or land. This classification is not original or exceptional and does not distinct Russia from generally accepted views on property rights structure. Referring to Barzel (1997), Markus (2015, p. 18) discloses the meaning of property rights, as these are "a bundle of rights containing: (1) the right to derive income from assets; (2) the right to use and manage assets; (3) and the right to transfer assets to someone else." Markus (2015) holds to the broadly accepted politico-economic approach and views the right to derive income from assets as income rights and the right to use and manage assets and the right to transfer assets to someone else as ownership rights (p. 18).

When it comes to raiding, the division of property rights on income rights and ownership rights may be important. Post-Soviet scholars highlight raiders' interest in acquiring – or rather even hijacking – the full bundle of property rights, calling it the full triade that includes ownership, use, and management rights. Tkachenko and Lobodenko (2007) suggest considering raiding as a "sequence of operations, performed on the basis of imperfect legislation, which allow one to obtain property rights, including the full triad – ownership, use, and management – on a certain asset" (p. 212). Understanding raiding as a sequence of operations anticipates seeing raiding as an action aimed at achieving certain premeditated goals. Such an understanding of raiding is deeply functional.

Raiding unites in itself both violence and property rights issues as two major characterizations. As long as violence used in hostile takeovers is not sanctioned by the state, it is illegal. The state holds monopoly on sanctioning violence. Fedorov (2010, pp. 38–39) studies the etymology of the term "raiding" and offers the following definition:

> Raiding is a socially dangerous, unlawful action, linked to an illegally obtained ownership right, and/or usage right, and/or management right, over the assets or shares of the legal entity in the charter capital of this legal entity and/or voting shares of a joint-stock company, that cause damages to rights and lawful interests of owners and done against their will, threatening their personal safety, as well as the security of the society and the state.

This definition underlines the legal aspects of raiding. While violence is clearly unlawful, the structure of property rights' related issues may not be that straightforward.

Corruption, coercion, and control 31

It is clear that raiding is committed against the will of the legal owner, and nevertheless some definitions simply miss this point. Varnalij and Mazur (2007) offer the following definition of raiding:

> Raiding in a modern understanding is a hostile acquisition of companies and redistribution of property and corporate rights.... Raiding is a hostile takeover of someone else's property in favor of another individual that extends beyond limits of the Civil Code, done against the will of the legal owner, achieving full control over this property both legally and physically with the use of corrupted state bureaucrats and/or use of force.
>
> (p. 129)

This definition may be one of the best definitions of raiding presented in the scholarly literature. It is appealing first of all because it points to such key aspects of raiding as being done against the will of the legal owner, anticipating not only legal but also physical control over the property in dispute, the use of corrupt bureaucrats, and use of violence.

Nongovernmental organizations (NGOs), based in Russia, also take part in studying and discussing the problem of raiding. In 2008, the Moscow-based Center of Political Technologies (CPT) led by Igor Bunin, conducted an investigation into the raiding phenomenon. The major findings of this investigation were presented in the report entitled "Raiding as a Socio-Economic and Political Phenomenon of the Modern Russia: A Report on the Qualitative Sociological Investigation." The research was based on conducting thirty interviews, including thirteen interviews with experts on raiding working in public organizations, NGOs, research institutes and think tanks; nine interviews with journalists who report on raiding; four interviews with lawyers; and four interviews with Members of Parliament (MPs) from the State Duma (Lower Chamber of the Russian Parliament). Experts, lawyers, journalists, and politicians were asked, among other things, to give their definition of raiding. According to the results of this investigation, all respondents tied raiding with terms of illegal alienation of property. One of the definitions was formulated in the following way: "Raiding is a hostile takeover of property, plots of land, and property rights which uses the legal loopholes and corruption in state bureaucracies and law enforcement agencies."[2] Respondents point out property, land, and particular property rights as objects of raiding or targets for raiding companies. They also point to corruption among state bureaucrats and insufficiently developed legislation as means with which raiders achieve their goals.

In the study by the Center of Political Technologies, interviewees offered other definitions of raiding as well. The majority of the respondents think that raiding is an illegal and unlawful alienation of property that lies outside the legal limits. Raiding occurs when one firm takes over another firm with the use of either legal or illegal means and gains a broad control over it. Raiding is a takeover of assets with the help of initiating a business-conflict. Raiding is a way of property redistribution, gangster-type in its essence, but covered in the layers of some legal procedures.[3] In this definition, the term "alienation" comes into play. This definition

32   *Corruption, coercion, and control*

also emphasizes the attempt of raiders to cover their unlawful actions with the layers of legal procedures.

Overall, one can find a good dozen definitions of raiding in the literature, some of which are quite simple and restrictive, while others do a relatively good job in discovering and denoting the essence of raiding. At the same time the problem of defining raiding remains, and as the problem of raiding persists, so does the need for strong definitions. Scholars and experts frequently use such terms as "burial teams," "unethical lawyers," "robber-lawyers," (see, for instance, Sychev, 2011), as well as "gangsters," and "piracy." Some scholars mistakenly identify raiding as merely an object of their research. Raiding is not an object, but a subject matter; raiding is a phenomenon with its own dynamics. Moreover, raiding is not just a phenomenon as an indication of a certain process; raiding signifies a relation and is a relation.

This study defines raiding as a relation that emerges between economic actors regarding alienation and appropriation of property, when alienation is done against the will or without consent of the previous owner and without proper compensation, and where appropriation is covered with layers of legality. In addition to alienation and appropriation, this study would like to turn the reader's attention to three important components of this definition, namely, "against the will or without consent of the previous owner," "absence of proper compensation," and "putting the act of raiding in a proper legal form," giving it a look of legality. Absence of the consent on the side of the previous owner is pointed out by other scholars in defining raiding, particularly with the phrase "against the will," but it makes little sense without the other two parts to which this study is pointing. The question that "against the will" component raises is whether a street robbery or the theft of a valet in a bus by a pickpocket can be qualified as raiding. These types of alienation of personal or private property are also done against the will of their lawful owners, although they can hardly be identified as raiding. That is why this study emphasizes the second component, namely the absence of proper compensation. Under the proper compensation one should understand compensation in accordance with existing market price of a given asset.

Raiding anticipates an economic damage that may exist in the form of a loss of economic assets, or in the form of interruption of a production process, or as damage to business reputation. Covering raiding actions with layers of legality, giving raiding the form of legal action, can be observed through many stages of the hostile takeover: raiders submit proper documentation in courts, even though some of the documents may be nothing but fraud; storm troopers used by raiders to take over the targeted enterprise often dress in a uniform reminiscent of that of the state law enforcement agencies or even the real police uniform with all the insignia, which is clearly illegal. Raiders use the mask of legality with a special level of hypocrisy and at full capacity in order to project an image of state-served justice, and produce some impression of legality, at least at first glance. Even in cases of outright fraud, with the fake court decisions and manipulations of the charter and registration documents, the act of appropriation is dressed in the cloth of pseudo-legality.

Depending on the applied frame, corporate and property raiding may have different interpretations. These interpretations include raiding as a socioeconomic

Corruption, coercion, and control 33

phenomenon, a form of economic relations, property reallocation mechanism, mechanism of realizing state dominance, post-privatization redistribution, institutional arrangement, unlawful activity, merger & acquisition, entrepreneurial activity, segment of services market, occupation, and source of income. Each interpretation frame carries specific major characteristics of raiding. These interpretation frames of raiding may further be divided on those associated with political economy, institutionalism, and law and those associated with business. Classification of raiding interpretation frames and their major characteristics are presented in Tables 1.1 and 1.2.

Table 1.1 Interpretation frames of raiding and their major characteristics: political economy

Interpretation	Major characteristics
Socioeconomic phenomenon	While raiding has yet to be determined legally, economically, and socially, there is little argument about the existence of raiding as a distinct socioeconomic phenomenon. Raiding phenomenon is a reflection of social and economic causes and effects on various redistribution processes. Raiding is a socioeconomic category associated with clear manifestations that include observable events, appearances, and experiences.
A form of economic relations	Raiding is a relation that emerges between economic actors regarding alienation and appropriation of property, when alienation is done against the will or without consent of the previous owner and without proper compensation, and where appropriation is covered with layers of legitimacy and legality.
Property reallocation mechanism	Raiding in its classical understanding facilitates the reallocation of economic assets from less effective to more effective owners and managers. In the post-Soviet context, raiding is used as a mechanism of redistribution of property from less connected to more powerful economic agents acting under the conditions of the existing authoritarian regime.
Mechanism of state dominance	The ruling authoritarian regime uses raiding to achieve its sustainability, including through the use of corruption, coercion, and control schemes. Interests of the ruling regime dominate over economic preferences of the masses.
Post-privatization redistribution	Raiding is seen as a natural continuation of the mass privatization of the 1990s. The post-Soviet privatization was a giveaway of economic assets in the hands of a few. Raiding serves as the tool of "correcting" biases in property distribution during the initial privatization.
Institutional arrangement	Raiding is a vaguely institutionalized phenomenon. The existing institutions that reflect the existence of raiding or facilitate raiding are located on both "legal" and "illegal" ends of the spectrum.
Unlawful activity	Raiding establishes legal and/or physical control over the targeted enterprise or property with the use of legal loopholes and illegal methods, such as bribery and fraud.

Source: Composed by the author

34 *Corruption, coercion, and control*

Table 1.2 Interpretation frames of raiding and their major characteristics: business

Interpretation	*Major characteristics*
Merger & acquisition	Raiding is a part of corporate mergers & acquisitions, many of which have a criminal component. Raiding is a hostile takeover of a company against the will of the original owner at a price below the fair market price.
Entrepreneurial activity	Raiding has formed into a special form of entrepreneurial activity with its division of functions and narrow specialization. Some raiding firms are officially registered. In some other instances, raiders use services of officially registered firms that specialize in raiding-associated activities and operations.
Segment of services market	Raiding is associated with a specific set of very different services. Raiders formed firms that specialize in selling raiding services, necessary for hostile takeovers. These include legal services, managerial services, financial consulting, establishing connections with state agencies and law enforcement services, security services, and services of storm troopers.
Occupation	Raiding is a professional occupation. Lawyers, managers, guards, criminals, hitmen, forgers, and corrupt civil servants find temporary or full-time employment in raiding organizations. Raiding requires many skills and professions.
Source of income	Corporate and property raiding is a type of economic activity that brings a revenue stream through exploitation or sale of a targeted company or economic asset.

Raiding in Russia has a corrupt nature. Thus, it directly relates to corruption as a feature of all economic as well as political relations in the country. But raiding as a phenomenon needs to have its base aside corruption. Raiding finds its fundamental base in property, for if there is no property, then there is nothing to raid. Most hostile takeovers are associated with material assets, while nonmaterial assets, including intellectual property, are of little interest to raiders. Raiding is one of the manifestations of the corruption, coercion, and control model advanced by the ruling regime. Thus, raiding is in need of close ties with the state apparatus. Moreover, in many instances, raiding campaigns are orchestrated or even executed with the help of the state, or with its direct intrusion.

Under the specific conditions of post-Soviet transformation, raiding feeds on privatization. The ruling regime converts state property into private, and raiding is used in this process in both primary and secondary markets. Along with corruption of state organs, law enforcement agencies, and courts, raiding uses violence as its tool for executing hostile takeovers. Thus, raiding is directly related to violent entrepreneurship and in fact the latter may be to a large extent embedded into the former. But raiding is not all corrupt and/or violent. Raiders use civilized schemes of hostile takeovers as part of their strategies, or use them in combination with corruption and violence. That is why corporate management is a necessary – although not necessarily crucial – ingredient of corporate raiding in Russia. Techniques used in corporate management may be useful in giving the flavor of legality and decency to the otherwise criminal activity.

In addition to the problem of defining raiding and categorizing different types and forms of raiding, there is the problem of defining the place of raiding in the system of related topics and themes. Oftentimes different terms and issues are used interchangeably or are being replaced without proper justification or explanation, even though they should not be. Such kinds of mishaps cause some confusion among scholars and readers as well. The theme of raiding is normally linked to such issues as violent entrepreneurship, economic crime, asset grabbing, property grabbing, privatization, economic transition, and corporate governance. Not only it is closely tied to these issues, but frequently it is embedded in them or is being named as such. This study tries to focus specifically on raiding and moreover delineate raiding and other related issues, themes, and blocks of problems and phenomena researched in scholarly literature, especially when it comes to Russia. Such a delineation of topics is demonstrated in Figure 1.1.

While focusing specifically on raiding, this study attempts to correlate raiding with such topics as corruption, the state, and property relations. Topics of violent

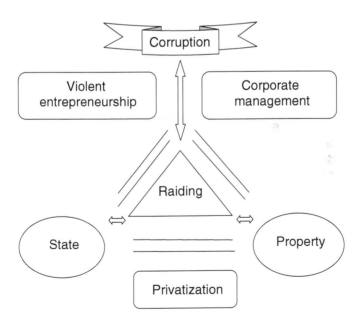

Figure 1.1 Relation of raiding to other similar themes

36 *Corruption, coercion, and control*

entrepreneurship and economic crime are well researched in the works of Volkov (2003) and Ledeneva and Kurkchiyan (2000). Skidanova (2010, p. 18) reports that,

> A comparative analysis of violent entrepreneurship and raiding shows that there are many commonalities between these two phenomena: major characteristics, economic essence, stages of development, and forms of interaction with business. However, while preserving certain characteristics of violent entrepreneurship, raiding has acquired several new characteristics, which allow it to adapt to the changing conditions of the Russian economy. Comparing violent entrepreneurship and raiding one can suggest that the latter is a more complex modification of the former, its new type. A set of determinants of the transition society served as a fertile ground for raiding.

According to this interpretation, the growing complexity of economic relations in the post-Soviet Russian economy and society led to an increase in complexity of violent entrepreneurship, raiding, and raiding-related activities.

In this case, the wide spectrum of problems covers just about everything from racketeering to shadow economies. As far as corporate governance, management, and mergers and acquisitions are concerned, there is plenty of literature on these issues, including some sources in Russia, as well as those produced locally and those translated from English. Finally, the themes of privatization and economic transition are researched so thoroughly by now that there is not much reason to focus on them and spend time and space on these otherwise important issues. This research uses all these themes as starting points and only to the extent necessary to highlight different aspects of raiding. This study finds much more productive correlation of the raiding phenomenon with the themes of corruption, role of the state, and property relations, in discovering the raiding phenomenon and putting together this socioeconomic puzzle.

1.2 Alienation-appropriation: the inverted character of raiding

Appropriation and raiding

Appropriation plays a key role in raiding. The meaning of appropriation in modern economy goes far beyond the usage of previously unowned land or access to natural resources and registration of property rights on such land and resources. Appropriation is not to be confused with such categories as eminent domain, compulsory purchase, resumption, compulsory acquisition, or expropriation. For instance, expropriation denotes the power of the state to take private property for public use. It is true that the state can delegate the expropriation function to private firms, but only for a specific case and for public purpose, if authorized by the law. Raiding is an economic phenomenon that has no direct legal authorization. The process of expropriation occurs when a government agency takes private property on a compensatory, partially compensatory, or noncompensatory basis to realize the project that will serve public interest. And again, expropriation is not limited to taking over private land in public construction projects. Also, raiding has little to do with appropriation known as the usage of money previously allocated by the legislatures for certain purpose.

Raiding may be classified based on the type of targeted objects. Tarkhanova (2008) offers a remarkable classification of raiding, greenmail, and violent entrepreneurship based on the criterion of the nature of the targeted objects of raiding. She notes the following:

> Specifics of the appropriation process of the non-market component of corporative control over the process of appropriation of managerial rent/quasi-rent indicates itself in the following: the dominating object of raiding is appropriation of the conditions of production (financial capital, particular elements of the material base of an enterprise, and such), in greenmail the dominating process is appropriation of the production itself (firm strategy, organizational and managerial innovations), while violent entrepreneurship specializes in the appropriation of the results of production (currency flows, parts of profit, kickbacks).
> (Tarkhanova, 2008, p. 8)

By conditions of production, the author means financial and physical components necessary for production. This classification mentions violent entrepreneurship with the meaning of racketeering rather than storming enterprises. The classification underlines the multiplicity of forms found within the raiding phenomenon.

Appropriation is close-coupled with alienation. Logically, alienation precedes appropriation. But this is only in cases when the object already has its lawful owner. And when it does not, appropriation may precede alienation in the form of initial or original appropriation. In legal terms, alienation presupposes the legal transfer of title of ownership to another party. Marx sees alienation in much broader terms.[4] In Marx's theory of alienation, the central idea is the alienation of the worker from the means of production. Alienation is thus perceived as the intentional separation of individuals and things that naturally belong together. Such an intentional separation, and especially a forceful one, signifies the antagonism between those who own the property and those who use it in the process of production.

Raiding appears situational and indeed insignificant as compared to Marx's grand theory of alienation. But this is only at first glance. In essence, raiding not only raises fundamental questions, but may be itself a fundamentally important phenomenon, especially in transition societies. One such fundamental question may be formulated as the following: Is it possible to define raiding as a process of alienation of lawful property from a lawful owner and its lawful (or is it lawful?) appropriation by another individual or an entity? Furthermore, would that be a lawful appropriation? The answer to this question is: Yes, it is possible, if one is to consider a court decision as an absolution of lawfulness or justice. Moreover, it is possible independently from the chance that the decision was bought and the judge was bribed. Either an individual or a legal entity may play the role of an owner. Here an emphasis is placed on lawfulness of property and lawfulness of the owner. If, for instance, a house was built unlawfully, then it does not make sense for raiders to take over it, because this house is a high risk asset. It can be demolished at the initiative of the state oversight agency and by a court decision.

38   *Corruption, coercion, and control*

The lawfulness of the owner is beyond doubt; otherwise it is by definition impossible to take over the property if it does not belong to him/her. A hostile takeover of a property that does not belong to its would-be owner or unlawful owner will unavoidably make raiders eventually face a lawful owner, no matter who this is. This lawful owner will demand his property back from either the unlawful owner or the raiders.

Raiding in Russia has an inverted character: appropriation precedes alienation. The term inverted, from the verb to invert, meaning to reverse in position, order, or relationship, originates from the Latin *invertere, in-* and *vertere-* to turn.[5] In the case of Russian raiding, certain key processes and actions take place in a reversed order, and this is not by accident. At first, court decisions are made and documents for the change of ownership are legalized. This initial stage symbolizes appropriation. Then comes the second stage, the alienation. Alienation can materialize in a violent form as a storming of the property, or in a nonviolent form. The latter is what the public sees on mass media reports, while the former is much less visible. As a result of this kind of inversion, many objects and much property have two or more owners at once. These owners claim exclusive ownership rights over the property, not that they share the property. Each type of owner waives court decisions with big round seals and the right to manage and make decisions about the property. There is a time lag between the final realization of the acts of alienation and appropriation.

The inverted character of raiding is preserved in its essence even in cases when a property is first alienated and only then appropriated. It happens because formally the alienation is done with a hidden intent and a clearly designed plan of the consequent appropriation. This means that de facto appropriation precedes alienation. Here one can observe a clear delineation of the formal and the real: the formality of the initial stage of alienation is based on the real existing and preceding stage of appropriation. For instance, when state bureaucrats alienate state property, move it out from under state control, they a priori know exactly how they will pass the property rights to themselves or the client, who paid for the whole operation. It means that there is a clearly designed plan and basis for such an appropriation.

Transition to a market economy in Russia has a nonevolutionary character. The inverted character of raiding in Russia has its root in the institutional diffusion and unclear and changing property rights as well as the prevalence of noneconomic determinants. Kolganov (1995, p. 57) puts an emphasis on institutional diffusion as a characteristic of the transition economy. This notion of institutional diffusion includes legal vacuums, unclear and changing property rights, and broken connections between different civil, economic, and regulatory institutions. The continuous redistribution of property rights takes place along with the process of legalization of criminal capital and shadow or unofficial economy, as well as money laundering. Redistribution of property rights during the exogenous transformation is also influenced by local and corporate regulation and noneconomic determinants.

Forms of property and property rights embedded in legislation are often inadequate to the realities of transition. Around 70 percent of large privatized enterprises were open-membership joint-stock companies under the control of the state and the workers. This meant de facto concentration of property rights in hands of the plant administration and the state bureaucrats. Zadorozhny (1996, p. 134) points out that the existing forms of property are not supported by the necessary legal mechanisms. The process of distribution and redistribution of property rights is often oversimplified and viewed as a development of private property. For instance, Sachs and Pivovarsky (1994, p. 48) say that former state property is distributed for free among workers and the population. This view is based exclusively on the legislation and does not take into account real processes in the economy.

According to the definition given by Buzgalin (1995, p. 48), a vital characteristic of a transition economy is a dual process of property rights transformation. On the one hand, there is a decomposition and elimination of the state-bureaucratic system of property rights, legalization of criminal property, and spontaneous growth of private property on the basis of the primary accumulation of capital. On the other hand, there is a parallel transformation of this formally private and mixed property into state nomenclatural and capitalist property. The latter causes proliferation of the process of alienation of workers from the means of production and property and slows down the use of workers' economic incentives for productive labor. This process creates obstacles for the socialization of property. Buzgalin (1995) arrives at the conclusion that the transition economy is characterized by a process of integration of principles and features of the totalitarian state property of the past, in conjunction with a trend of property corporatization, typical for a modern market economy.

In the Soviet system, the alienation of workers from the means of production was hidden behind the fact of virtually absent unemployment and so-called state and collective forms of property. Private property during the Soviet era simply did not exist, at least in legal terms. The economic transition of the 1990s included the process of transformation and conversion of the state property into monopolistic property that belonged to newly emerged corporations, where private capital shared property rights with the state nomenklatura, i.e. former and present state bureaucrats. Alienation of workers from the means of productions on both levels – process of production and property rights – led to a dramatic increase in unemployment. Gritsenko (1997, p. 7) points out that under the inversion-type transition, alienation of workers from the means of production was formalized in legal terms or within the legal framework.

The nonlinear trends in development, mosaic structures, and confusing and contradictory old and new rules of the economic game are all characteristics of Russian economic transition that has lasted for three decades. Buzgalin (1995, p. 40) says that economic transition is a change of economic relations, including allocation of the scarce resources, property rights, mode of production, incentives, goals, and means of economic development, institutions, and legal conditions. He sees noneconomic determinants as dominant in the transition process and points out the mosaic of the transition economy that consists of many pieces of the new and the old. Corporate, property, and land raiding is a part of this Russian transformational mosaic.

40 *Corruption, coercion, and control*

Due to the dramatic changes in the balance of public and private property rights in favor of the latter, scholars have become more favorable toward the notion of the mutually divided character of property. Skidanova (2010) essentially discovers the mutually divided character of the property-power and the dualistic character of interpretation of private property in Russia by pointing out the following:

> The major characteristic of Russia's social system is the absence of a clear demarcation, separation or division between power and property. The considered concepts present Russian history as a sequence of periods of tight centralization and authoritarian power and periods of relative democratization and attempts to implement market institutions. Privatization, which was formally designed with the goal of moving away from state dominance in the economy, in practice simply reinforced already existing old systems of power and property. In this context state-led raiding may be considered not as a lawful alienation of property from individuals, but a certain form of returning property given away earlier.
>
> (p. 15)

During the period of transition, characterized by attempts to implement market reforms and introduce private property, the state made an attempt to form a certain kind of quasi-private property. One of the most important features of this quasi-private property is that it can be expropriated by the state at any time. Under such circumstances, the sensitivity of the phenomenon of private property is that the general public perceives this property as truly private, while in fact it is just quasi-private. Such a duality in perceptions and reality creates a negative reaction to raiding as an unlawful alienation or expropriation of property. Here, private property in Russia is labeled as being de facto quasi-private and poorly protected by the state.

Raiding anticipates the act of alienation-appropriation. Victims of the raiding attacks are, no doubt, concerned only with the phase of alienation, not appropriation. For instance, if raiders take over a stock of commodities but fail to sell it before it reaches the expiration date, the previous owners have no concern with it for they already lost it. Their entire attention is focused on the moment of alienation, with no concern about the moment of appropriation. Accordingly, a principal question emerges: is appropriation without alienation possible at all? Is it possible to lead the situation to the point where it will be fair to say both that the wolves have eaten much and the sheep have not been touched? Figuratively speaking, can one make an omelet without breaking eggs?

Appropriation without alienation is possible in case of artificial or produced public goods. For economists, a public good is a good that is nonrival and nonexcludable. Nonrivalry means that consumption of the good by one individual does not reduce the availability of the good for consumption by other individuals; nonexcludability means that no one can be effectively excluded from consuming this good. Sunlight is a natural public good, but when it comes to a spot under the sun, let us say on a public beach, it is only a public good as long as there are

Corruption, coercion, and control 41

enough places for all those who wish to take sunbaths. An example of artificial or produced public goods would be free roads, although this can hardly be the case with Moscow's congested roads and their lengthy traffic jams.

The logical question that may follow the discussion on alienation-appropriation of privately owned objects is: Is raiding possible with regard to public goods? It is generally considered impossible to set a price for the consumption of public goods due to their two key characteristics, nonrivalry and nonexcludability. That is why private companies are not interested in the production of public goods. However, such an approach anticipates consumption only and thus is somewhat limited. It is obvious that it is nearly impossible to impose a price on sunlight. Nevertheless, it is quite possible to take over a public road, a highway, or a bridge and set a toll. In reality, public parks and public beaches become the targets of raiders. Fallen victim to a hostile takeover, the territory of public parks may then be sold to developers for their construction projects. Thus, the park itself is of no value to raiders, but the territory of this park is. Raiders can be interested in taking over artificial or produced public goods.

State, public, collective, or so-called whole-people property presents yet another challenge for potential raiders. The key question to estimate this challenge would be: Is it possible to take over a whole-people property, as it was known in the Soviet era? The answer is "yes"; it may be possible if one is to restrict access to it. However, such a restriction by an individual would be impossible, because the private property did not exist and was outlawed, indeed. Perhaps it is exactly for this reason that there was no raiding in the USSR. In principle, it was possible to de facto take over particular objects, but only for personal use and not for resale. Moreover, private consumption during the Soviet era was so limited, restricted, and subjected to state control that a takeover of any significant objects, property, or any other kind of material assets simply did not make any sense. In case of conspicuous consumption, the perpetrator would be exposed immediately.

Corruption is frequently referred to as the necessary basis for raiding in Russia to exist. At the same time, corruption is often called a hostile takeover of the state functions, also known as state capture. In order to sell something, one has to possess it, take it over, steal it, and own it, i.e. appropriate it by any means. It is impossible for an economic agent to sell something that does not belong to him/her, for he/she will be held liable for the supply of the good or service in question later. In legal terms, this is called fraud. Whether this property belongs to this economic agent lawfully or not is another issue. A state bureaucrat openly takes over, secretly steals, or de facto appropriates a state function, and then sells it to the interested private party in exchange for a bribe, doing it again either secretly or openly. This process signifies the abuse of discretionary power committed by a civil servant. Such a process is sometimes referred to in the literature as the privatization of the state, done by state bureaucrats in order to serve their clientele and derive illicit benefits privately.

A particular bureaucrat or even a bureaucratic organization represents a unit of micro-level analysis. Rent and rent-based relations in particular, as a characteristic of the basis for the raiding phenomenon, equally refer to the macro-level

42 *Corruption, coercion, and control*

analysis. Lenin's thesis that all wars under capitalism occur due to the struggle for resources and markets equally applies to the raiding movement, but indirectly. Resources in an abstract economic sense mean rent derived from their use, while markets mean a monopolistic position achieved with the help of noneconomic means. The result of a hostile takeover is a monopolistic rent.

Certain progressive forms of economic organization slowly become outdated and backward, transforming into a barrier or an obstacle for further economic development. Raiding in Russia, which in principle had the potential to become a symbol of a certain kind of progress, in particular in redistributing ownership rights on the means of production to the benefit of more effective owners or producers, such as businessmen and entrepreneurs, in fact turned into yet another obstacle for normal market-based economic development. In the transition economy, it is hard even to distinguish between raiders as either organizers of hostile takeovers or corporate managers able to increase the effectiveness of ineffective enterprises. Moscow's former Mayor, Yuri Luzhkov, commented in this regard that,

> In fact raiders are out of the reach of criminal legislation for the simple reason of the practical absence of an evidentiary base. It is necessary to delineate lawful and honest takeovers from unlawful and dishonest ones. We need to define such terms as "hostile takeover of an enterprise" and introduce them into our legal language. Today such a term is formally absent.[6]

An increase in raiding in Moscow does not facilitate the development of small businesses.[7] To the contrary, small businesses present easy targets for raiders. While legislators struggle with the new terminology that would make raiding more difficult, raiders struggle with lawful owners to make a living.

Nature, causes, and basis of raiding

Raiding in economic segments with preindustrial characteristics goes as far as small and medium-size businesses are concerned. The question that comes next is about the vulnerability of large enterprises, which also become targets and victims of raiding. Certainly, large industrial enterprises are a part of industrialized society, not a component of an improvised productive medieval settlement. They operate under a different model. Moreover, many of these large enterprises already reach a level at which they are ready to become or have already been converted into joint-stock companies. Historically, the process of forming joint-stock companies was always connected to all kinds of fraud and manipulations, and other problems in property relations. One such example is dealings during the construction of the Panama Canal in the late 19th century. In this gigantic (for its time) construction project the joint-stock company was used for personal enrichment by fraud and taking over the investment made by stockholders. The term "Panama" was used for many years after as an analog to the terms "fraud," "manipulation," and such. Today, as a hundred years ago, the term "Panama" remains associated with large-scale fraud, now through the so-called Panama Papers scandal.[8]

The diversity of sectors of the national economy leaves its print on the phenomenon of raiding, including the actors, the methods they use, and the forms of hostile takeovers. That is why the ways of hostile takeovers differ depending on the sector of the economy. In raiding that occurs on farmers markets or flea markets one can see storm troopers, often with criminal pasts, as analogous to warlord fighters or trade road robbers. In the corporate world of large companies, one can observe intellectual raiding, acquiring stocks and debt restructuring done by the white-collar workers. The unifying feature in both of these segments is an obvious presence of the state with its attributes: institutes and institutions, bureaucrats, police, court decisions, court bailiffs, etc. Where does this unifying feature come from? It comes from the specifics of Russia's market transition, where the state not only remains in the economy, but persists with its attempts to stay there and strengthen its position instead of exiting the economy.

In Russia, a mix of production relations and their existence on different levels at the same time exists as a result of the mix of different levels of development of production forces. For instance, in Moscow, one can observe elements of a postindustrial information society, while on the periphery one can see a semi-feudal type of capitalism with the mix of emerging market relations and agrarian society. Moscow attempts living according to the high standards of Western capital, while just a 100 miles away one can observe some elements of natural production, or subsistence farming, not so widespread even during the late Soviet era, that have reemerged due to the closure of local industrial enterprises. Some stagnant regions in Russia are especially telling in this regard. The mixture of different levels here is obvious. As a consequence, there is an attempt to equalize the stunning inequalities and disparities. Raiding is a result of such an attempt at equalization.

Modern Russia is characterized by the process of forming a class society with the capitalist mode of production. This process has not been completed; it continues along the vectors of nonlinear development. In class societies, including capitalist societies, the state represents the interest of the ruling class within the limits of its territorial domain. In a capitalist society the ruling class is represented by the owners of the means of production. In Russia, the class society continues its formation, and thus the state cannot fully represent and protect the interests of the owners of the means of production. One of the results of such incompleteness is the phenomenon of raiding, including violent raiding. The transition to the new basis and the change of superstructure demand the emergence of a new hegemonic class. The old pseudo-hegemonic class – the working class – served its purpose and is now being successfully decomposed, while the new hegemonic class – the class of capitalists – continues its formation. The absence of the new well-shaped hegemon is now being shamefully covered by a fig leaf of a mirage-like but strongly and persistently cultivated image of the middle class.

While Russia experiences the process of forming a class society with the capitalist mode of production, advanced market-based democracies enter the era of postindustrial production in the streamline of globalization. Thus, it is hard to call the changes that Russia undergoes as particularly progressive. One can only hope that with the formation of the class society and its move to the capitalist stage of

44   *Corruption, coercion, and control*

development, the interests of the ruling class will be protected much better and raiding will eventually start declining. This statement is concerned primarily with large enterprises, which form the basis of Russia's national economy as they did during the Soviet era. This is quite natural, because the level of development of production forces of society is at the stage of large machine production.

As far as small producers and protection of their property are concerned, here the key role may belong to a different factor in relations of society and the state, namely, the level of democracy. The electivity of the nation's leaders – real electivity, not only nominal or procedural – will force those aspiring for the leading state offices to take care not only of the representatives of the ruling class, but also the interests of the majority of the population. Of course, it is hard to find an example of a truly developed democracy anywhere in the world and thus it would be too naive to expect such a development in Russia. Nevertheless, the majority of the population has some weight in political battles and some say during the elections, including presidential elections. The development of this determinant will counterbalance the raiding of small owners, including, among others, such phenomena as the raiding of apartments and raiding of small plots of land.

To finalize this discussion, one may conclude that the raiding of large enterprises will eventually be limited by the structure of state authority and power, when the state will develop a better system and mechanisms for protecting the interests of the ruling class, consisting of owners of the means of production. This will also imply that oligarchs will capture the state directly, eliminating such middlemen as popular politicians. Raiding of small businesses and personal property may decline thanks to the state's efforts to attract the support of significant strata of the population, if such efforts will ever materialize. These broad social strata of population do not have more or less significant private property or means of production, but hold a stake in influencing the political situation in the country.

There is a clear need for more analysis on correlations between raiding, violent crimes, racketeering, protection, and violent entrepreneurship. Raiding is frequently considered a direct descendant of violent entrepreneurship. According to Skidanova (2010), the economy of a racket, being an institutional form of Russian business in the second half of the 1990s, brought to life raiding as a more sophisticated and intellectually developed mode of extortion and attempts on property rights of others. As the author points out, "Today raiding is a new type of informal (shadow) economy that grew from violent entrepreneurship as a type of 'black' shadow economy" (Skidanova, 2010, p. 18).

The next stage of analysis may be the question of whether the process of privatization was a raiding type or raiding itself; i.e. was raiding in this case a phenomenon or a characteristic of the process? Was the Russian privatization done raiding-style or was it raiding in its essence? Barnes (2006) offers perhaps the most comprehensive and thoughtful analysis of Russian privatization of the 1990s. He disagrees with the notion that all privatization essentially came down to de jure legalization of de facto existing property rights of top managers over their enterprises. Barnes (2006, p. 67) notes that,

Many individual enterprises remained at least partially embedded in their ministerial hierarchies. It is a mistake, therefore, to see the post-Soviet Russian struggle for property simply as a matter of converting de facto ownership developed in the late Soviet period into de jure property rights. Enterprise managers represented a powerful force in asset redistribution in Russia, but they competed with other potent interests, and the property at stake extended far beyond what managers had claimed in the last years of the USSR.

Directors of Soviet enterprises, including factories, plants, collective farms, and many other types of state firms were not completely independent. The state did not recall completely its property rights over former state enterprises. Moreover, directors of Soviet enterprises were certainly not the only pretenders on these enterprises. Woodruff (1999, 2004, 2005) also offers a good conceptual frame and a comprehensive analysis of the property rights in the context of the post-Soviet privatization.

The issue of completed formation of private property as a dominant form in the system of property relations in Russia remains contested. Furthermore, the proper institutionalization of private property is also an open question. Tarkhanova (2008, p. 8) points out that the research of the evolution of the institution of property has shown that the initial institutionalization of private property in Russia has been completed. However, the nonmarket character of the processes of privatization predetermined the unequal insider structure of the joint-stock property, lack of transparency, and the absence of a clear delineation of functions between owners and hired managers. Tarkhanova (2008) further suggests that "This inequality allowed for branch and structural inequalities in the development of the Russian market for corporate control and the development of its non-market component" (p. 8). Apparently, raiders use this nonmarket component of the Russian market for corporate control as a basis for their hostile takeovers and related activities.

Among the major causes of raiding in Russia scholars normally point out the following: large-scale corruption, including in the court system, weakness of the legislative base, increase in well-being, growth in production assets, increase in the value of real estate and land, ineffective use of property, low level of entrepreneurial culture, weakness of market institutions, negative perceptions of the public regarding businessmen and their businesses, disrespect toward the institution of private property, weakness of the state institutions, absence of the institutionalized protection of stockholders' rights, and use of insider information (see, for instance, Fedorov, 2010, pp. 59–63). Such causes characterize Russian transitional society in general. It is obvious that its distinction from Western market-based societies points to the existing difference between raiding in its classical understanding and raiding Russian style.

Western scholars also discuss the causes of Russian raiding. Firestone (2008) names four causes of raiding in Russia. First, there is the general uncertainty of property rights resulting from the privatization of state assets in the early 1990s. Because the legal basis for so much of the privatization of state assets after the collapse of the Soviet Union was so vague, almost any property is subject to a

46 *Corruption, coercion, and control*

challenge that it was illegally acquired. This situation, in turn, creates the possibility for allegations of other improprieties regarding the business and its holdings. These all provide a basis for the lawsuits and criminal investigations that play such an important role in raiding schemes. Second, corruption in law enforcement and the judicial system helps raiders to achieve their goals, because raids often depend on commissioned criminal investigations and inspections of the targeted business and purchased judicial orders. Third, there is poor corporate governance and many raiding schemes grow out of shareholder disputes and rely on illegal access to internal corporate records and manipulation of the targeted company's stock and internal regulations. Current Russian legislation does not provide sufficient defenses for minority shareholders in cases where majority shareholders render minority shares worthless through a corporate reorganization. Minority shareholders are left with no option but to employ the services of professional raiders to get their property back. Fourth, the legal system is simply not yet equipped to deal with this novel form of crime. Legal gaps, particularly in criminal law and the structure of the court system, facilitate criminal raiding (Firestone, 2008, pp. 1218–1219). The author regards corporate and property raiding in Russia as a new form of sophisticated organized crime.

Let us turn to major distinctions between Western types of raiding and raiding in Russia. Tarkhanova (2008) underlines the national specifics of Russian raiding and points out that,

> In distinction from foreign models, the Russian model of raiding features the following: a more frequent use of courts and administrative resources; specialization and outsourcing of raiding based on types of economic activities and branches of the economy; a characteristic low information transparency of transactions; absence of regular market valuation of high liquidity assets of enterprises; a high level of conflict and contradictions in contracts and commercial transactions.
>
> (p. 7)

Given the overall high level of corruption found in the Russian justice system and economic arbitration courts in particular, it appears surprising that raiding in Russia is distinct by a relatively frequent use of courts and administrative resources. However, it is precisely the corruptness of courts that makes raiders – not rightful owners – turn to courts in search of unjust but favorable decisions. Moreover, it is at least as much about criminal courts as it is about commercial arbitration courts. By using the administrative resource, raiders pressure rightful owners with criminal investigations and unlawful prosecution. Historically absent contractual culture combined with legal nihilism complicates the issue of peaceful resolution in commercial disputes.

Distinct from other authors, who place emphasis on the violent character of raiding, Tarkhanova (2008) points to a frequent use of courts and bureaucratic resources by Russian raiders. The author also emphasizes the illegal and criminal character of raiding. Fedorov (2010, p. 47) also points out speculative incentives of Russian predatory raiding and its criminal character as major distinctions from Western raiding. At the same time one should not idealize Western raiding practices. In the West, speculative interest also serves as one of the incentives for raiders and hostile takeovers. In Russia, raiding is not limited within the sphere of traditional M&A. It goes far beyond corporate raiding, extending and reaching out to property and land raiding. Moreover, these latter forms continue to acquire more weight and significance in the overall mainstream of the Russian raiding movement.

Overall, the authors are united in their opinion that raiding in Russia has negative consequences for the national economy and the process of societal development. Scholars normally point out the following consequences of Russian raiding: negative impact on the business climate, destabilization of the normal functioning of domestic enterprises, destruction of workers' collectives and social conflicts, poor investment climate, and damage to the international image of the country overall (Varnalij and Mazur, 2007). However, raiding has more serious negative consequences as well. Raiding facilitates further concentration and centralization of production, monopolization, amalgamation of business and the state, development of corruption in courts and other organs of the state authority, and formal and real alienation of workers from the means of production.

Raiding has a negative impact not only on owners of targeted enterprises, but on managers and employees as well. Tkachenko and Lobodenko (2007) point out such negative consequences of raiding for workers collectives: "raiding attacks bring damage to owners of enterprises, but frequently their victims and even hostages are employees" (p. 212). Other scholars point out similar negative characteristics of the impact of raiding on enterprises. In some instances, employees find themselves locked inside premises of enterprises stormed by raiders. They are locked against their will. In other instances, workers are banned from entering the raided enterprise by the storm troopers.

According to the defensive organization theory, developed by Duvanova (2013), a high regulatory burden coupled with affordable unofficial or informal ways to avoid regulatory compliance should suppress the process of business organization. Furthermore, "Relatively low costs of bribery, together with a legal system that cannot prosecute corruption effectively, may in fact make participation in business associations a less attractive option for post-communist businesses" Duvanova (2013, p. 51).

Russian scholars tend to ascribe large national corporations with anti-raiding defense strategies reliant on economic methods. The latter includes mechanisms met on financial markets and characteristic of large Western corporations. At the same time, anti-raiding defense strategies associated with small and medium businesses come down to administrative and legal methods. For instance, Tarkhanova (2008) suggests that specifics of the Russian institution of raiding are determined by the use of both market- and nonmarket-based methods of defense from raiders. She further suggests that large enterprises may use market mechanisms of financial markets, including IPOs (initial public offerings), poison pills, and converting stock and shares into obligations. According to the author, the dominant methods

48 *Corruption, coercion, and control*

of defense for small and medium-size businesses are nonmarket methods, such as "administrative and legal methods, including transparency in the structure of property rights, proper documentation and registration of shareholders, proper legalization of a firm's assets, abolishing double accountancy, good relations with the local authorities, and such" (Tarkhanova, 2008, p. 7).

In the West, raiding is expensive, because it anticipates the buying of a company or any business or enterprise at a price that normally significantly exceeds its current market value. Raiding only makes sense in situations when the raiders or their clients expect significant returns in the future. Otherwise, the hostile takeover may turn out to be an economic failure, which is often the case. This is the situation with raiding in the developed market economies. Corporate raiders take economic risks of losses. They try to calculate the costs of the takeover and its future expected benefits. As is the case with any economic calculations, however sophisticated they may be, the cost can exceed the expected gain and the raiding company itself can suffer bankruptcy. In most of the instances, a hostile takeover of some company or property is economically senseless.

The situation with raiding in Russia is quite different. Here, a hostile takeover is normally planned at a targeted price well below the market value of the targeted company or any other object. The reason for such a distinction in prices of the hostile takeover in the two systems, the market system and the transition economies, is that in the former the targeted company is bought through economic, normally market mechanisms, while in the latter the targeted company is being taken over with the help of noneconomic, or at least nonmarket mechanisms with the use of corruption.

Corporate raiding may have a positive face too, but not in Russia. Despite the ongoing discussions about the positive role of raiding in washing ineffective enterprises away from the market and transferring property to more effective owners, the image of raiders remains negative. In this regard, the opinion expressed by German Gref, the former Minister of Economic Development and Trade of Russia from 2000 to 2007, who currently serves as the CEO and Chairman of the Executive Board of the largest Russian bank, Sberbank, is of value. Gref points out that, "raiding is not that homogeneous. Legal raiding, which facilitates redistribution of property on the market in legal ways, is a normal activity." Gref calls the raiding companies that stay within legal limits "market cleaners" because they help to redistribute ineffectively used property. Such redistribution leads to a higher rate of return on capital. The problem is that in Russia raiding oftentimes has a criminal character: "As soon as an attractive piece of property appears on the market, everyone starts looking at it." Raiding in Russia should not have a criminal character, concludes Gref.[9] The targets of hostile takeovers are not ineffective enterprises, but economically attractive and highly profitable firms.

Let us turn once again to causes of hostile takeovers of enterprises. There is no doubt that enterprises are taken over by raiders in pursuit of immediate profits. Raiders can extract profit by selling machinery and equipment, especially if raiders are in a hurry to get rid of the property they took over and to receive some fast cash. But who will be interested in buying machinery and equipment, if they will

Corruption, coercion, and control 49

bring no profit? Simply put, why would one want a piece of machinery, if one can't eat it? It is natural that one would need it in order to make profit on this piece of machinery by putting it to work, using it in production. Accordingly, if certain machinery and equipment bring no profit, then there is no need to take them over by raiding an enterprise. Let us assume that a hostile takeover is done in order to eliminate the competitors. But what kind of competitors are they, if they cannot make a profit? Yet another option is a hostile takeover of an enterprise in order to use its territory for construction and development projects. But this is a part of the general trend of changing the structure of the national economy, including prioritization of consumption over production. Such a process is hard to identify as raiding.

In general, corporate mergers and acquisitions are necessary and beneficial not only for some participating companies, but for the national economy overall. They can have a positive impact on socioeconomic development. A member of the Security Committee of the State Duma, Gennady Rajkov, says that society should differentiate normal economic processes and criminalize hostile takeovers. Rajkov thinks that in Russia businesses lead the process of consolidation and attempts to restore economic ties, torn apart by the process of privatization in the early 1990s. Accordingly, "society should consider mergers and acquisitions of enterprises as normal." Processes of consolidation through mergers and acquisitions have a positive economic impact while the forms in which they occur have become more and more civilized. The MP claims that "the Russian economy becomes more and more civilized." Rajkov says that mergers and acquisitions, conducted in a legal manner, facilitate market competition and the modernization of production lines, and help industry to develop according to modern market realities.[10] In people's minds, however, the differentiation between normal economic processes and criminalized hostile takeovers is not that easy to establish, especially after the robber-type privatization of the 1990s.

1.3 Concluding remarks

Concluding remarks will highlight once again the major points presented in this chapter. First of all, this study offers the following definition of raiding: Raiding is a relation that emerges between economic actors regarding alienation and appropriation of property, when alienation is done against the will or without consent of the previous owner and without proper compensation, while appropriation occurs within the layers of legality. In addition to alienation and appropriation, the study would like to turn readers' attention to three important components of this definition, namely, raiding happens against the will or without consent of the previous owner, in absence of the proper compensation, and in a proper legal form, giving it a look of legality. Absence of the consent on the side of the previous owner is pointed out by other scholars in defining raiding, particularly with the phrase "against the will," but it makes little sense without other two parts, to which this study is pointing. This study emphasizes the second component, the absence of the proper compensation. This study understands compensation in accordance

50   *Corruption, coercion, and control*

with existing market prices on a given asset. Raiding anticipates an economic damage that may exist in the form of a loss of economic asset, or in the form of interruption of a production process, or as damage to business reputation.

Raiding is the art of taking over someone else's asset in such a way that the whole operation would create an impression of legitimacy and legality. Russian mass media openly points to the fact that raiding cannot exist without corruption. A substantial block of literature considers excessive corruption as an indication of the weakness of the government. However, the opposite may well be true. In nondemocratic societies, corruption, informally approved, imposed, or regulated by public authorities, is an indicator of the power of the state, rather than its weakness. Corruption may be used on a systematic basis as a mechanism of direct and indirect administrative control and redistribution of wealth on the state level and down to local authorities and administrations of public and private institutions. Control and redistribution of wealth in this case are based on blackmail and selective justice.

Informal approval of corrupt activities in exchange for loyalty and compliance with the regime is broadly used in many countries. Legal traps are often created by the regime in order to encourage bureaucrats and entrepreneurs to violate the law and then force them to comply and share revenues with the regime. Vertical and horizontal structures of corrupt control allow ruling regimes to sustain themselves and exercise coercive power over their constituents. Administrations of enterprises and institutions are targeted by the central and local governments in pursuit of higher degrees of state control. Corrupt administrators, managers, entire institutions, and regular individuals are much easier to be ruled if corrupt. The same is true for businessmen. The ruling regime extracts its rent not only in the form of illicit payments, but in loyalty as well. The example of tax schemes in the Yukos case is a good example in this regard.

The ruling regime derives its rent through the use of authoritative powers, regulation, and oversight functions of the state. While state bureaucrats extort their rent from clientele, including businessmen, in the form of bribes and numerous other favors, the ruling political regime extorts its rent from the business community in the form of loyalty and compliance. This is quite characteristic of the concept of corruption coercion and control, developed over the decades and put into action. The rent is derived not only in cash, but in obedience. The ruling political regime needs this obedience not only from public employees, but from businessmen as well. Vertical and horizontal structures of control distribution may be based on corruption and coercion. These structures allow the ruling regime to survive and execute its authority through mechanisms of coercion of its constituents and broader electorate. Voters, coerced in casting their vote, and moreover, casting it for a certain candidate or political party, create an illusion of democracy. This illusion adds to the proclaimed legitimacy of the state and contributes to legitimacy of the ruling regime. These two terms, the state and the ruling regime, are frequently confused in Russia. Similarly, the terms of power and authority are confused as well, or not delineated at all. Local officials, bureaucrats, and businessmen may be targeted by the ruling regime in the process of strengthening both formal and informal control. Corrupt local officials and businessmen coerce their constituents and employees into supporting the regime. In this way, large-scale and widespread corruption helps the regime to skillfully manipulate the masses.

Suppression of corporate autonomy, the induction of state bureaucrats into corporate governing boards, the imposition of pseudo-accountability under the nontransparent financial regulations, and direct informal control are used by the authorities and administrations in order to control businessmen and business activities of their companies. Under the conditions of market transition, when laws are changing and rules are unclear and subject to interpretation, state bureaucrats are placed in conditions of financial survival while businessmen find it hard to comply with laws and regulations even if they try their best and in good faith to do so. Numerous violations follow; they are registered and those bureaucrats and businessmen become subjects of blackmail. This type of blackmail comes not from the side of criminals and racketeers, but from the side of the ruling regime. The Russian political establishment may either use this mechanism of corruption and subversion, or at least be aware of its use. Nevertheless, this mechanism of informal and potential control spreads nationwide and extends to different levels of social organizations.

Covering raiding actions with layers of legality, giving raiding a form of legal action, can be observed through many stages of the hostile takeover: raiders submit proper documentation in courts, even though some documents may be nothing else but fraud; storm troopers used by raiders to take over the targeted enterprise often dress in a uniform reminiscent of that of the state law enforcement agencies or even the real police uniform with all the insignia, which is clearly illegal. Raiders use the mask of legality with a special level of hypocrisy and at full capacity in order to project an image of the state-served justice, produce some impression of legality, at least at a first glance. Even in cases of outright fraud with the fake court decisions and manipulations with the charter and registration documents the act of appropriation is dressed in the cloth of pseudo-legality.

This study suggests that raiding in Russia has an inverted character: appropriation precedes alienation. At first, court decisions are made and documents for the change of owner are legalized. This initial stage symbolizes appropriation. Then comes the second stage, the alienation. Alienation can materialize in a violent form as a storming of the property, or a nonviolent form. The latter is what is seen on media reports, while the former is much less visible. As a result of this king of inversion, many objects and property have two or more owners at once. These owners claim exclusive ownership rights over the property, not the shared property. Each type of owner waves court decisions with big round seals and the right to manage and decide the property.

There is a time lag between the final realization of the acts of alienation and appropriation. The inverted character of raiding is preserved in its essence even in cases when a property is first alienated and only then appropriated. It happens because formally the alienation is done with a hidden intent and a clearly designed plan of the consequent appropriation. This means that de facto appropriation precedes alienation. Here one can observe a clear delineation between the formal and

52 *Corruption, coercion, and control*

the real: the formality of the initial stage of alienation is based on the real existing and preceding stage of appropriation. For instance, when state bureaucrats alienate state property, move it out from under the state control, they a priori know how exactly they will pass the property rights to themselves or the client, who paid for the whole operation. It means that there is a clearly designed plan and the basis for such an appropriation.

Among the major causes of raiding in Russia, scholars normally point out the following: large-scale corruption, including in the court system, weakness of the legislative base, increase in well-being, growth in production assets, increase in value of real estate and land, ineffective use of property, low level of entrepreneurial culture, weakness of market institutions, negative perceptions of the public regarding businessmen and their businesses, disrespect toward the institute of private property, weakness of the state institutions, absence of the institutionalized protection of stockholders' rights, and use of insider information. Such features characterize Russian transition society in general.

Raiding in Russia has negative consequences for the national economy and the process of societal development. Scholars normally point out the following negative consequences of Russian raiding: negative impact on the business climate, destabilization of the normal functioning of domestic enterprises, destruction of workers' collectives and social conflicts, poor investment climate, and damage to international image of the country overall. However, raiding has more serious negative consequences as well. Raiding facilitates further concentration and centralization of production, monopolization, amalgamation of business and the state, development of corruption in courts and other organs of the state authority, and formal and real alienation of workers from the means of production.

Notes

1 Nyneshnyaya model' upravleniya Rossiej sebya ne ischerpala, dokazyvaet Putin dekanu iz Garvarda [Present model of governance in Russia has not exhausted itself, proves Putin to Harvard's Dean]. *Newsru.com*, November 11, 2011. Retrieved November 11, 2011, from www.newsru.com/russia/11nov2011/valday.html
2 Reiderstvo kak sotsial'no-ekonomicheskij i politicheskij fenomen sovremennoj Rossii: otchet o kachestvennom sotsiologicheskom issledovanii. Issledovanie "Tsentra politicheskih tehnologij" pod rukovodstvom Bunina. Moskva, 2008. [Raiding as a socioeconomic and political phenomenon of the modern Russia: A report on the qualitative sociological investigation. An investigation conducted by the Center of Political Technologies led by Bunin]. Moscow, May 2008. Retrieved June 12, 2009, from www.politcom.ru/; www.compromat.ru/main/mix1/raiderycpt.htm
3 Ibid.
4 See, for instance, Marx, Karl. (2012). *Economic and Philosophic Manuscripts of 1844*. New York: Courier Corporation.
5 Merriam-Webster Dictionary. Retrieved from www.merriam-webster.com/dictionary/invert
6 Yuri Luzhkov: "Malyj biznes vo mnogom obespechivaet zhiznedeyatel'nost' finansovoj sistemy stolitsy" [Yuriy Luzhkov: "Small business to a large extent maintains the proper functioning of the financial system of the capital"]. *Moskovskij Komsomolets*, September 2, 2007. Retrieved May 9, 2009, from www.mk.ru/daily/83784.html

Corruption, coercion, and control   53

7 Mer Moskvy Yuri Luzhkov predlagaet vnesti v UK stat'yu, karayushchuju za reider-stvo [The Mayor of Moscow, Yuri Luzhkov, suggests to introduce a special paragraph about the punishment for raiding in the Criminal Code]. *Newsru.com*, September 3, 2007. Retrieved May 9, 2009, from www.newsru.com/russia/03sep2007/noreider.html
8 The Panama Papers: Politicians, Criminals and the Rogue Industry that Hides Their Cash. The International Consortium of Investigative Journalists. Retrieved January 27, 2017, from https://panamapapers.icij.org/
9 Reiderstvo v Rossii ne dolzhno nosit' kriminal'nyj kharakter – G. Gref. [Raiding in Russia should not have a criminal character – G. Gref]. *Prime-TASS*, May 18, 2006. Retrieved May 9, 2009, from www.prime-tass.ru/news/show.asp?id=593347&ct=news
10 Gennadiy Rajkov: pogloshcheniya v otlichie ot reiderstva – pozitivnyj ekonomicheskij protsess [Gennadiy Rajkov: Compared with raiding, acquisitions mean a positive economic process]. *Newsru.com*, July 26, 2006. Retrieved April 3, 2009, from www.newsru.com/finance/26jul2006/raikov.html

References

Almond, George & Coleman, James. (1960). *The Politics of the Developing Areas*. Princeton, NJ: Princeton University Press.
Andreski, Stanislav. (1966). *Parasitism and Subversion: The Case of Latin America*. London: Weidenfeld and Nicholson.
Andreski, Stanislav. (1968). Kleptocracy or Corruption as a System of Government. In Stanislav Andreski (ed.). *The African Predicament: A Study in the Pathology of Modernization*. New York: Atherton.
Anechiarico, Frank & Jacobs, James. (1995). *The Pursuit of Absolute Integrity: How Corruption Control Makes Government Ineffective*. Chicago: University of Chicago Press.
Aslund, Anders, Guriev, Sergei, & Kuchins, Andrew C. (eds.). (2010). *Russia after the Global Economic Crisis*. Washington, DC: Peterson Institute for International Economics.
Atanassov, Julian. (2013). Do Hostile Takeovers Stifle Innovation? Evidence from Antitakeover Legislation and Corporate Patenting. *The Journal of Finance*, 68(3), pp. 1097–1131.
Auerbach, Alan. (1988). *Corporate Takeovers: Causes and Consequences*. Chicago: University of Chicago Press.
Banfield, Edward. (1975). Corruption as a Feature of Government Organization. *Journal of Law and Economics*, 18(3), pp. 587–605.
Barnes, Andrew. (2006). *Owning Russia: The Struggle over Factories, Farms, and Power*. Ithaca: Cornell University Press.
Barzel, Yoram. (1997). *Economic Analysis of Property Rights: Political Economy of Institutions and Decisions*. 2nd Edition. New York: Cambridge University Press.
Bhagat, Sanjai, Shleifer, Andrei, Vishny, Robert, Jarrel, Gregg, & Summers, Lawrence. (1990). Hostile Takeovers in the 1980s: The Return to Corporate Specialization. *Brookings Papers on Economic Activity: Microeconomics*, pp. 1–84.
Buzgalin, Alexander. (1995). Zakonomernosti perehodnoj ekonomiki: teorija i metodologija [Laws of the Transition Economy: Theory and Methodology]. *Voprosy ekonomiki*, 2, pp. 32–44.
Chubais, Anatoly. (ed.). (2000). *Privatizatsiya po-rossijski* [*Privatization a la Russe*]. Moscow: Vagrius. Retrieved from www.chubais.ru/show_prn.cgi?/current/public/publik_1.htm
Coffee, John C., Jr., Lowenstein, Louis, & Rose-Ackerman, Susan (eds.). (1988). *Knights, Raiders, and Targets: The Impact of the Hostile Takeover*. New York: Oxford University Press.

54 Corruption, coercion, and control

Darden, Keith. (2001). Blackmail as a Tool of State Domination. *East European Constitutional Review*, 10(2–3).

Darden, Keith. (2002). *Graft and Governance: Corruption as an Informal Mechanism of State Control*. New Haven, CT: Yale University Working Paper.

Darden, Keith. (2008). The Integrity of Corrupt States: Graft as an Informal State Institution. *Politics & Society*, 36(1), pp. 35–59.

De Haan, Jakob, Lundstrom, Susanna, & Sturm, Jan-Egbert. (2006). Market-Oriented Institutions and Policies and Economic Growth: A Critical Survey. *Journal of Economic Surveys*, 20(2), pp. 157–191.

Drucker, Peter. (1986). Corporate Takeovers: What Is to Be Done? *Public Interest*, 82, pp. 3–24.

Duvanova, Dinissa. (2013). *Building Business in Post-Communist Russia, Eastern Europe and Eurasia: Collective Goods, Selective Incentives, and Predatory States*. New York: Cambridge University Press.

Fedorov, A. Yu. (2010). *Reiderstvo i korporativny shantazh (organizatsionno-pravovye mery protivodejstviya* [Raiding and Corporate Blackmail (Organizational and Legal Counter-Measures)]. Moscow: Volters-Kluver, p. 480.

Firestone, Thomas. (2008). Criminal Corporate Raiding in Russia. *The International Lawyer*, 42(4), pp. 1207–1230.

Firestone, Thomas. (2010). Armed Injustice: Abuse of the Law and Complex Crime in Post-Soviet Russia. *Denver International Law & Policy Review*, 38(4), pp. 555–580.

Gans-Morse, Jordan. (2012). Threats to Property Rights in Russia: From Private Coercion to State Aggression. *Post-Soviet Affairs*, 28(3), pp. 263–295.

Gaughan, Patrick. (1996). *Mergers, Acquisitions, and Corporate Restructurings*. New York: John Wiley & Sons.

Gritsenko, Andrei. (1997). Struktura rynochnoj transformacii inversionnogo tipa [The Structure of the Inversion-Type Market Transformation]. *Ekonomika Ukrainy*, 1, pp. 4–10.

Hedlund, Stefan. (2011). *Invisible Hands, Russian Experience, and Social Science Approaches to Understanding Systemic Failure*. New York: Cambridge University Press.

Holmberg, Sören & Rothstein, Bo (eds.). (2012). *Good Government: The Relevance of Political Science*. Cheltenham, UK & Northampton, MA: Edward Elgar.

Kireev, Aleksei. (2007). Raiding and the Market for Corporate Control: The Evolution of Strong-Arm Entrepreneurship. *Problems of Economic Transition*, 50(8), pp. 29–45.

Kireev, Aleksei. (2008). Reiderstvo v rossijskoj ekonomike: sushchnost', tendentsii i vozmozhnosti protivodejstviya [Raiding in the Russian Economy: Essence, Trends, and Possibilities for Resistance]. Doctoral dissertation. Moscow: Institute of Economics and Mathematics RAN (TsEMI).

Kolganov, Andrei. (1995). Zakonomernosti perehodnoj ekonomiki: ekonomicheskie tendencii i modeli [Laws of the Transition Economy: Economic Tendencies and Models]. *Voprosy ekonomiki*, 2, pp. 50–60.

Ledeneva, Alena & Kurkchiyan, Marina. (2000). *Economic Crime in Russia*. London: Kluwer Law.

Markus, Stanislav. (2015). *Property, Predation, and Protection: Piranha Capitalism in Russia and Ukraine*. New York: Cambridge University Press.

McKee, David L. (1989). *Hostile Takeovers: Issues in Public and Corporate Policy*. New York: Praeger.

Mesquita, Bruce Bueno de & Smith, Alastair. (2012). *The Dictator's Handbook: Why Bad Behavior Is Almost Always Good Politics*. New York: Public Affairs.

Nelson, Ralph L. (1959). *Merger Movements in American History, 1895–1956*. Princeton, NJ: Princeton University Press.

North, Douglass. (1990). *Institutions, Institutional Change, and Economic Performance*. New York: Cambridge University Press.

North, Douglass. (1992). *Transaction Costs, Institutions, and Economic Performance*. San Francisco, CA: ICS Press.

North, Douglass. (2006). *Understanding the Process of Economic Change*. Princeton, NJ: Princeton University Press.

North, Douglass. (2007). Institutions, Transaction Costs and Economic Growth. *Economic Inquiry*, 25(3), pp. 419–428.

Olson, Mancur. (1982). *The Rise and Decline of Nations: Economic Growth, Stagflation, and Social Rigidities*. New Haven, CT: Yale University Press.

Olson, Mancur. (1996). Big Bills Left on the Sidewalk: Why Some Nations Are Rich, and Others Poor. *Journal of Economic Perspectives*, 10(2), pp. 3–24.

Olson, Mancur. (2000). *Power and Prosperity: Outgrowing Communist and Capitalist Dictatorships*. New York: Basic Books.

Olson, Mancur, Sarna, Naveen, & Swamy, Anand. (2000). Governance and Growth: A Simple Hypothesis Explaining Cross-Country Differences in Productivity Growth. *Public Choice*, 102(3–4), pp. 341–364.

Osipian, Ararat. (2010). Corrupt Organizational Hierarchies in the Former Soviet Bloc. *Transition Studies Review*, 17(4), pp. 822–836.

Osipian, Ararat. (2012). Loyalty as Rent: Corruption and Politicization of Russian Universities. *International Journal of Sociology and Social Policy*, 32(3/4), pp. 153–167.

Payne, Robert. (1975). *The Corrupt Society: From Ancient Greece to Present-Day America*. New York: Praeger Publishers.

Popova, Maria. (2012). *Politicized Justice in Emerging Democracies: A Study of Courts in Russia and Ukraine*. Cambridge: Cambridge University Press.

Rojansky, Matthew A. (2014). Corporate Raiding in Ukraine: Prevention, Defense, and Policy Reform. *Review of Central and East European Law*, 39(3–4), pp. 245–289.

Rose, Richard, Mishler, William, & Munro, Neil. (2011). *Popular Support for an Undemocratic Regime: The Changing Views of Russians*. New York: Cambridge University Press.

Sachs, Jeffrey, & Pivovarsky, Alexander. (1994). *Ekonomika perehidnogo periodu* [The transition economy]. Kyiv: Osnova.

Shlapentokh, Vladimir. (2003). Russia's Acquiescence to Corruption Makes the State Machine Inept. *Communist and Post-Communist Studies*, 36, pp. 151–161.

Sinha, Rajeeva. (2004). The Role of Hostile Takeovers in Corporate Governance. *Applied Financial Economics*, 14(18), pp. 1291–1305.

Skidanova, Lilia. (2010). Raiding as a Socio-Economic Phenomenon. PhD dissertation. Moscow: Moscow State University.

Sychev, Pavel. (2011). *Khishchniki. Teoriya i praktika reiderskih zakhvatov* [*Predators: Theory and Practices of Hostile Takeovers*]. Moskva: Alpina Publisherz.

Tarkhanova, Zarina. (2008). Funktsionirovanie instituta reiderstva v RF [Functioning of the Institute of Raiding in the RF]. Dissertation. Vladikavkaz: Severo-Osetinsky State University.

Taylor, Brian D. (2011). *State Building in Putin's Russia: Policing and Coercion after Communism*. Cambridge: Cambridge University Press.

Tishchenko, Kirill. (2009). Effective Defense Methods against Hostile Takeovers and Raiders in Russia. Master's Thesis. Helsinki: Helsinki School of Economics.

Tkachenko, N.I. & Lobodenko, M.U. (2007). Mekhanizm provedennya rejders'kyh atak ta shemy zahoplennya biznesu yak chinnyk ekonomichnoji nebezpeky diyal'nosti sub'yektiv

56   *Corruption, coercion, and control*

gospodaryuvannya [Mechanism of Conducting Raiding Attacks and Schemes of Taking over Business as a Factor of Economic Insecurity for Economic Agents and Firms]. *Nauchnye trudy DonNTU. Ekonomicheskie nauki*, 31(3), pp. 211–215.

Varnalij, Zakharij & Mazur, Irina. (2007). Reiderstvo v Ukraini: peredumovy ta shlyahi podolannya. *Strategichni Pryoritety*, 2(3), pp. 129–136. Retrieved April 2, 2009, from www.niss.gov.ua/book/StrPryor/3/17.pdf

Volkov, Vadim. (2003). Silovoe predprinimatel'stvo: ekonomiko-sotsiologicheski analiz [Violent Entrepreneurship: Economic and Sociological Analysis]. *Ekonomicheskaya sotsiologiya*, 4(1–3).

Volkov, Vadim. (2004). The Selective Use of State Capacity in Russia's Economy: Property Disputes and Enterprise Takeovers, 1998–2002. In Janos Kornai, Bo Rothstein, & Susan Rose-Ackerman (eds.). *Creating Social Trust in Post-Socialist Transition* (pp. 126–147). New York: Palgrave Macmillan.

Waite, Duncan & Allen, David. (2003). Corruption and Abuse of Power in Educational Administration. *The Urban Review*, 35(4), pp. 281–296.

Woodruff, David. (1999). *Money Unmade: Barter and the Fate of Russian Capitalism*. Ithaca, NY: Cornell University Press.

Woodruff, David. (2004). Property Rights in Context: Privatization's Legacy for Corporate Legality in Poland and Russia. *Studies in Comparative International Development*, 38(4), pp. 82–108. Retrieved from http://personal.lse.ac.uk/woodruff/_private/materials/property_rights_in_context_scid.pdf

Woodruff, David. (2005). Nestabil'nost' chastnoi sobstvennosti v Rossii: ekonomicheskie i politicheskie prichiny [The Instability of Private Property in Russia: Economic and Political Causes]. *Russkie Chteniia*. Vypusk 1. Moskva: "Gruppa Ekspert," 2005, pp. 206–219. Retrieved from http://personal.lse.ac.uk/woodruff/_private/materials/kogdanelzia.pdf

Zadorozhny, Grigory V. (1996). *Sobstvennost' i ekonomicheskaja vlast' [Property and Economic Power]*. Kharkiv: Osnova.

Zhdanov, Igor. (2002). Corruption in Ukraine: Essence, Scale, and Influence. *Connections*, 1(2). Retrieved May 20, 2004, from www.ciaonet.org/olj/co/co_apr02d.pdf

2 State and raider and state-raider

2.1 State and raider

Optimization of the state

During Russia's market transition, the state was both a victim of raiding and a raider itself. The process of privatization of socialist property was, in essence, raiding. Accordingly, there is an impression that the state became an object of raiding and a victim of aggression of external forces toward the state property, including all means of production. But, in fact, the object of raiding became the state property while the state was an instrument used by raiders in power to appropriate property. In this case, the state itself is seen as a raider. At the same time, state functions, state authority, and execution of state powers were taken over and "privatized" by the ruling regime and its particular representatives, including both state officials and street-level bureaucrats.

For further consideration of raiding, one should define what the state is. Different groups of scholars interpret the meaning of the state differently. For some, the state is an apparatus of violence, which grew to a police state; for others, the state is an achievement of civilization, the highest degree of societal organization. The state can be viewed as a ruling regime or as a way to build democracy and open society. It can be considered as an equal player on the free market, an economic agent; but it is also considered as an arbiter on the market, a gate keeper, a night watchman in the economy. For some, the state is the authoritative bureaucratic hierarchy, a monopoly that distributes permissions; a discrete machine, which creates opportunities for collecting illegal payments. For others, it is a stock-house of material assets, which have yet to be privatized.

The dualistic approach to the state's position in relation to privatization has a direct relevance to the issue of nationalization and reprivatization. Dualism in the position of the modern post-Soviet Russian state is both interested in the transfer of the means of production and other economic assets into private hands, and in maintaining economic control, monitoring, and economic power. And this economic power is only possible while maintaining significant economic assets because without them the controls will be based only on noneconomic mechanisms, coercive power, and dictatorial coercion. Simply put, in order to have

58 *State and raider and state-raider*

economic power, the state should have economic weight. Possible options include the presence of the state in the private sector and/or the presence of a significant public sector in the national economy. The data on the number of privatized state unitary enterprises in Russia during the entire period of post-Soviet transition, from 1992 to 2015, is presented in Table 2.1. These include enterprises of federal, regional, and municipal forms of property, as reported by the Federal Statistics Services.

Dualism of the position of the post-Soviet state is determined by the trajectory of the inverted development. The inversion in this case is due to the fact that the state, which owned everything, now refuses the part of a whole instead of gaining control over it. As a result, images are formed inevitably of the state that gives, the state that takes, and the state that preserves. The state continues facing the issue of optimizing its presence in the economy. The state has yet to decide how much of the national economy should be given into private hands and how much to retain in state or public ownership. The state as a subject of economic activity or an acting economic agent tends to attract more funds into the budget, obtain more funds to maintain the political regime and implementation of national projects

Table 2.1 Number of privatized state unitary enterprises in Russia, 1992–2015

	Number of privatized state unitary enterprises			
	Federal	*Regional*	*Municipal*	*Total*
1992	22684	3560	20571	46815
1993	7063	9521	26340	42924
1994	5685	5112	11108	21905
1995	1875	1317	6960	10152
1996	928	715	3354	4997
1997	374	548	1821	2743
1998	264	321	1544	2129
1999	104	298	1134	1536
2000	170	274	1830	2274
2001	125	231	1931	2287
2002	86	226	2245	2557
2003	161	152	121	434
2004	121	246	135	502
2005	112	226	153	491
2006	98	254	92	444
2007	73	115	114	302
2008	26	135	99	260
2009	140	87	139	366
2010	97	56	64	217
2011	119	80	77	276
2012	69	102	57	228
2013	20	58	58	136
2014	15	50	42	107
2015	27	46	34	107

Source: Composed by the author[1]

State and raider and state-raider   59

funded by the state. In this case, it does not make sense at all for the state to give something away and into private hands, abandon any property, especially for free, with no compensation, on a pro bono basis. However, if this study accepts the suggestion that the private sector as a whole works better than does the state or public sector as a basis, then the starting point will be the statement on the maximization of revenues flowing into the state budget by optimizing the structure of ownership on the means of production and their distribution between the state and private companies. The state as a conveyor of the people's will, acting in their interests, aims to increase production, employment, economic growth, and economic efficiency rather than simply filling the state budget as a goal in itself. In this case, it may be rational for the state to give up ownership of a significant part of economic assets, including on a compensable basis in order to optimize the structure of ownership of productive assets in the national economy.

Property relations are more fundamental than political problems. However, when the question is raised about nationalization or reprivatization, the policy can play a certain functional role. Moreover, the politicians themselves may raise questions about the nationalization of certain assets. For example, Medvedev was asked to nationalize Norilsk Nickel. State Duma's Deputy Viktor Il'yukhin asked the president of Russia to consider the possibility of nationalization of Norilsk Nickel:

> the flared up conflict between groups of shareholders facing a total loss of its controllability, and the traditional scheme of informal participation of the Russian Federation to monitor the activities of the Norilsk Nickel is completely broken. There is a real danger that the company will become non-transparent for the state and its representatives. "It is proposed to consider measures of "responsible government response" to the situation, including the "compensable nationalization under the existing federal law."[2]

Such suggestions are not new for the State Duma, when they are presented by the members of the Russian Communist Party (KPRF).[3] Even though leaders of the KPRF support all forms of property, including private property, nationalization remains high on their agenda, especially when it comes to elections and populist campaigns.

In general, nationalization of large companies, especially those based on rent, i.e. making profit based on exploitation of natural resources, is not a new business and has plenty of precedents and examples in history, including in modern history. For instance, Venezuela's President Hugo Chavez nationalized oil and gas companies with the help of troops. President Chavez nationalized the oil wealth of the country in 2007 and intended to nationalize smaller companies that serve the state-owned company, to which the government owes billions of dollars. The US oil company ExxonMobil withdrew from all Venezuelan projects and the court has demanded compensation for the expropriation of the rights to develop oil fields in the Orinoco River basin. A British court froze the overseas assets of the Venezuelan state oil company worth $12 billion based on the lawsuit filed by

60 *State and raider and state-raider*

ExxonMobil, but a month later reversed this decision. President Chavez continued to nationalize other industries.[4] Nevertheless, the Yukos case and Ivan the Terrible[5] phenomenon of Oprichnina call for certain parallels and analogies.

Yukos appears to be a victim of corporate raiding done with the use of the state apparatus. An assumption that Yukos was sold out in pieces due to the fact that Khodorkovsky was allegedly behind the scenes and had his sights on the Russian presidency is likely not well justified. The former head of Yukos himself assesses the situation with much more sobriety and objectivity, pointing to the predominance of economic interests over the political ones:

> In 2003, when the attack on Yukos began, some observers have interpreted it the way that we – I and my partners – supposedly developed some secret plans to transform the Russian Federation into a parliamentary republic thereby limiting power of Vladimir Putin. In fact, the scenario with the parliamentary republic had nothing to do with the seizure of Yukos. Those who designed the criminal case against me and my colleagues simply wanted to take the most prosperous oil company with the market value of about $40 billion for free. Everything else could be a triggering point, but not the true cause of the attack.[6]

At the heart of the rise and fall of Yukos is a huge need for restructuring the oil and gas industry, which used to bring a major flow of foreign currency earnings into the USSR. Changing the system of industrial relations requires a corresponding restructuring of the industry. The share of the oil export revenue in the total Russian export is now much larger than it was during the Soviet era. Compared with the Soviet Union, Russia's main export is raw materials: by some estimates, 15 and 75 percent, respectively. In addition, the interests of foreign capital in this sector are particularly significant, which also has an impact on the history of the company producer of oil and gas.

There is no such country or state which would voluntarily renounce its right to economically valuable natural resources, and in this sense a recently popular topic of the so-called resource curse sounds quite comic. Here the whole power of the rent character of economic relations manifests itself. Russia is not going to give up its holdings of valuable natural resources. Moreover, it also claims ownership over the resources not yet developed or even explored, including Arctic oil and gas reserves. That is why the Russian "Bear" nuclear bomber planes continue to torment the British pilots.[7] This action is not a threat and not a show of force in the style of the Cold War. It is a demonstrative circling of the sovereign domain, aimed at indicating that "we will explore the Arctic" or the "Arctic will be developed only with our permission." As a practical matter, this means redistribution of oil shelves of the Arctic Ocean. It would be sufficient to refer to the vicissitudes of BP and Exxon in Russia in order to understand the basis for ongoing military and political debates and demonstrations of force.

The question of optimization of the post-Soviet state presence in the Russian economy is in many ways highlighted by the high revenues from resource

State and raider and state-raider   61

extraction and processing companies. Rent as a guarantee of profitability of these companies and the state as a monopolist within its territorial domain determine the inevitability of a high degree of state involvement in the oil and gas sector. The dynamics of the state budget revenues from the oil and gas industry in Russia in 2000–2006 is presented in Table 2.2. The data provided supports the thesis of the dependence of the Russian economy on the markets for hydrocarbons.

The former head of Yukos also comments on the prices of oil and their importance for the state budget and for maintaining political stability in the country:

> Oil and gas directly and indirectly determine over 30 percent of Russian budget revenues. An increase in oil prices, adjusted for inflation, below 12 percent a year cannot provide, without turning to reserves, the 4 percent increase in revenues necessary for public satisfaction and peace. This is if there are no new sources that cover the costs of inflation, and it is not less than 8 percent. Thus, the increase in oil prices in nominal dollar prices of less than 20 percent per year will require the engagement of reserves, or otherwise it will negatively impact the credibility of the government. Poor-quality public administration will not allow balancing the economy with the revenue growth below 4 percent. The main danger to the system in this case is the emergence of multiple local foci of instability, such as those in Pikalevo in 2008. In manual mode, all these problems cannot be solved. The reform of the whole system is needed.

Khodorkovsky also points out that,

> Oil production in Russia, excluding the Arctic shelf, is possible for many years at the level of 450 to 500 million tons a year, when appropriate investments and technology are in place. The extraction of 600 to 650 million tons per year is possible, but economically unjustified, because then there will be the need for excessive infrastructure, which will be built and then taken out of service due to the depletion of deposits in the region.[8]

Table 2.2 State budget revenues from the oil and gas industry in Russia, 2000–2006

	2000	2001	2002	2003	2004	2005	2006
State budget revenue as percent of GDP	37.3	37.5	37.1	36.5	37.0	40.1	39.7
State budget revenue from the oil and gas industry as percent of GDP*	8.6	9.1	8.0	8.2	9.8	13.3	13.7
Share of revenue from the oil and gas industry in the state budget, percent	23.1	24.2	21.6	22.5	26.6	33.2	34.6

*This indicator includes production, refinery, and pipeline transportation of oil and gas

Source: Completed by the author[9]

62 *State and raider and state-raider*

Rich natural resources and high world prices on oil guarantee a relative stability of the current political regime.

While then Russian President Dmitry Medvedev advised not to confuse gas with politics, the importance of oil and gas for the Russian state and its relations with its neighbors can hardly be overestimated. Economic radicals even recommend assigning the gas supply with a status of an important geopolitical instrument for Russia:

> We need to give the gas supply the status of a major geopolitical tool for Russia. Gazprom should not be viewed as an economic or industrial phenomenon, but as a major political and geo-political institution and resource of the Russian government, the Russian authorities.
>
> (Dugin, 2010, p. 293)

This suggestion sounds more in line with a Pan-Russian chauvinism and imperialistic ambitions of the former superpower.

Economically active bureaucracy

The modern world is trading guarantees more than it is trading products. Every businessman wants to buy a guarantee that he/she will not become a victim of the raid and that his/her company will not be raided. The product of today is not a bag of cement, a service, or even information, but the guarantee. This guarantee is not the promised coverage offered for sale by a shifty insurance agent. This is a guarantee to do business for decades, and with high comfort, and pass it to heirs with the rights of inheritance. Anyone who sells such a guarantee controls the market. This fact is especially true of the investment market. This concept of guarantees is well understood by traders and statesmen in both the US and Russia. At the same time, the very notion of guarantee comes into contradiction with the principles of the market, including competition and risks. The challenges to consistency and stability in doing business that come from the market are acceptable as they serve for the betterment of the entire business environment and effectiveness of the economy. However, when such challenges come from the side of the state, and state bureaucrats in particular, they become a matter of concern. This is clearly the case with Russia.

In modern Russia, neither a small business entrepreneur nor a corporate mogul can receive such a guarantee. No one, including the state, can reliably offer or provide such a guarantee. First, the state as a nonprofit organization by definition cannot trade guarantees with profit. Second, many blame the very state in undermining the foundations for such guarantees. At the same time, the personified state, that is, each state officer individually, or bureaucratic factions and clans offer and trade such guarantees, and sometimes do this quite successfully. Accordingly, in addition to running their businesses, businessmen have to work more and establish contacts with government officials in order to secure or preserve their business and personal wealth. Such contacts are nothing but acts of sale of state guarantees. However, these guarantees as business safeguards are temporary.

State and raider and state-raider 63

Their duration and, figuratively speaking "half-life" is defined by the duration of tenure of the necessary state official in his/her office. This official is the seller of guarantees minted at the governmental office. The duration of guarantees also depends on changes in market conditions, legislation, and, finally, the level of raiding activity. No one can give, or even sell, a long-term guarantee to a Russian or foreign businessman in the post-Soviet space.

Failure to provide guarantees either for a fee or free of charge may potentially result in the following things: the readiness of many businessmen to close their business in the short period of time, the systematic outflow of earned profits abroad, opening of bank accounts, subsidiaries and branches abroad, often at an economic disadvantage, and also acquiring citizenship or permanent residency abroad. This "sitting on their suitcases," or standing "one foot in Russia and the other foot abroad" has a negative impact on conducting business and the results of economic activities in general. In this case, the state does not perform the function of the major guarantor of a welcoming business environment, protector of property rights, and enforcer of the rule of law.

Whether Russian bureaucrats prefer to deal with domestic or foreign businessmen when it comes to collecting benefits, including both legally and illegally, remains an open question. However, one can say with confidence that here, as in all other respects, transcending national borders, there is an element of national identity and self-identification. Similarly to the case of Marx's national currencies dropping the "national uniforms" when entering the international market, the business is doing the same. But the money is the highest degree of economic abstraction while businesses retain a lot of national characteristics and features even when entering the world market. Transnational, or rather even international businessmen have to deal with national bureaucrats, and nationalism is being deliberately cultivated among the latter. In this regard, Russian bureaucrats are no different from American, French, or Indonesian bureaucrats. The days when Russian bureaucrats were willing to "sell themselves for a bubble-gum" or "to sell the country for chewing gum" as opposed to businessmen, who demanded the fair market price, are all gone. Modern Russian bureaucrats are no different from businessmen and are well aware of the market prices set for state services they render to their still growing clientele. And because there is a constant competition going on between those companies and businessmen who are in need of such state services, the "selling for chewing gum" no longer makes any sense.

According to Weber (1990, p. 249), modern bureaucracy is a type of bureaucracy where jurisdictional areas are clearly specified, activities are distributed as official duties, the organization follows hierarchical principle, written and clear rules govern decisions and actions, officials are selected on the basis of technical qualifications, continuous records are maintained, rewards are distributed according to the rank, and all bureaucrats are subordinate to one systemic discipline. Here is how Weber's understanding of bureaucracy is viewed in Russia and related to modern Russian bureaucracy:

> According to Max Weber, bureaucracy consists of technocrats, i.e. managers who manage a certain sphere of activity in a relatively strict frame. Such a

64 *State and raider and state-raider*

type of rational bureaucracy is present in many highly developed countries with their well-trained and polished bureaucracy. This type of bureaucracy facilitated the rapid post-war economic development in Germany and Japan. This type of bureaucracy would be good for Russia. However, many features of the Weberian bureaucracy do not work there, or work with a certain twist. Rewards transform into privileges for the bureaucratic apparatus, strict record-keeping transforms into the goal function of the bureaucratic production, written notes turn into papermaking, etc. Max Weber divided all bureaucracy on the rational and the irrational, while here the meaning of bureaucracy became a synonym to irrational bureaucracy. The type of rational bureaucrat is rare, atypical in the USSR (Russia).

(Karatuev, 1998)

Kononenko and Moshes (2011) confront the Weberian notion of the state as an institutionalized authority with the notion of the network state. The authors claim that this analytical approach both challenges the existing scholarly literature on the post-Soviet Russia and adds to it by way of having explanatory power over the issues and trends that would otherwise be overlooked or missed. The network state perspective brings to the fore forms and functions of governance far beyond those conventionally researched within the frame of vertical hierarchy and national sovereignty. It also allows for considering the links between state institutions and networks, which are obviously not synonymous categories.

In Karatuev's (1998) view, bureaucracy in Russia may be understood as a form of irrational organization, characterized with a detachment of the executive authority from the real demands and interests of the society and its individual members. This form of organization is characterized as bureaucracy in a narrow sense. The degree of such a detachment or a gap varies from different manifestations of usually observed bureaucratic delays to persistent domination of one group of the society over the other. In the latter case, the reference is to bureaucracy in a broad sense, understood as a system of politico-economic dominance of the state bureaucracy in society.

Modern Russian bureaucracy considered in terms of relationships with private capital and business in general demonstrates the transition from the security and protection function to the redistribution function. Participation of the bureaucracy in the process of raiding marks this transition. In this regard, this study introduces a new term: the economically active bureaucracy. The term "economically active" is normally used in regard to a given country's population. According to the International Labour Organization (ILO), an economically active population comprises all persons of either sex who furnish the supply of labor for the production of economic goods and services.[10] For bureaucrats, being economically active means something more than that. Bureaucrats are already economically active by default, since they work for the government, and being fully employed, they fall under the definition used by the ILO and Organization for Economic Cooperation and Development (OECD). However, the notion of economically active bureaucracy offered in this study places emphasis on bureaucrats as a special category of economic players.

The bureaucratic caste is traditionally considered as the community of civil servants working for a certain salary and benefits determined and paid by the state. Accordingly, bureaucrats as a rule have no special financial incentives to work more efficiently and effectively. In addition, bureaucrats collect bribes and other illicit private benefits to the extent possible while being cautious and weighing the possible risks of losing their "bread and butter" places and facing criminal prosecution. Economically active bureaucracy means something more than this usual arrangement. The post-Soviet bureaucracy in Russia is not satisfied with its salary received from the state budget and illicit benefits collected from businesses and other clients in form of bribes, gifts, payoffs, and kickbacks. The three traditional sources of income for post-Soviet bureaucrats – salary from the state, bribes from the clientele, and kickbacks from state-funded projects – are no longer satisfactory for state officials and civil servants.

As the data presented by the World Bank's Enterprise Survey indicates, the value of gifts expected to secure governmental contracts in Russia in 2012, also known as kickbacks, is insignificant and constitutes just a small percentage of contractual value. It varies from no kickbacks in the Hotels and Restaurants industry to 4.8 percent in the Transport, Storage, and Communications industry and 7.4 percent in the Wood Products and Furniture industry.[11] The data on the size of kickbacks on governmental contracts as a percentage of contractual value in Russia in 2012, classified by industry, is presented in Figure 2.1. Other data, collected from the Ministry of the Interior and from media reports, indicates similar figures. A good example of a combination of corrupt law enforcement and size of kickbacks

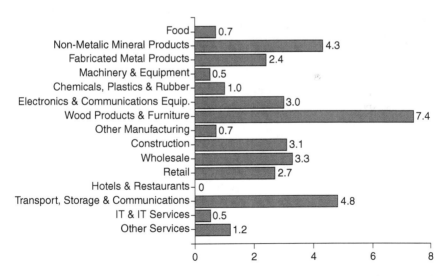

Figure 2.1 Size of kickbacks on governmental contracts as a percentage of contractual value in Russia, 2012

66 *State and raider and state-raider*

would be a bribe of two hydro-cycles and a motorboat given in exchange for a state construction contract. The Head of the Head Department of Economic Security and Corruption Prevention of the Ministry of the Interior, Major General Andrey Kurnosenko, reported that a high-ranking police officer in the Ministry of the Interior received a kickback of 2.6 million rubles for the state contract of over 2 billion rubles, i.e. slightly more than 0.1 percent.[12] Economically active bureaucracy as a newly formed class does not want cash; it wants to co-own property, economic assets that would guarantee a continuous stream of cash.

Russian bureaucrats want to share in the profits, and this is known to be a function of the business owner, the one who owns at least a part of the production. And it is not that civil servants are forbidden to engage in private business – all those who have a business use well-known schemes to circumvent this restriction set by the state. The fact is that not all bureaucrats have their own businesses, including not only street-level bureaucrats, but also high-ranking bureaucrats with strong "resolution" capacity. By resolution capacity, this study means the capability of high-ranking and well-positioned state bureaucrats to resolve problems based on official authority delegated to them by the state. In Russia it is called *reshat' voprosy*; this phrase has a direct idiomatic translation "to solve the questions."

Economically active bureaucrats are no longer satisfied with their function of protecting businesses against external aggressors and their raiding assaults on businesses, delegated to the civil servants by the state. Bureaucrats offer services to facilitate redistribution of not only access to limited resources, public goods, spheres of influence and market segments, but business assets as well. While helping raiders to capture someone else's business, state bureaucrats, in fact, participate in the redistribution of property, profit-generating assets and businesses, and expect a reward from this future profit, obtained by the raiders or the new owners. Therefore, bureaucrats reach the stage and the level of profit participation. This is no longer the use of authority delegated by the state for personal purposes or personal enrichment, but an explicit economic activity. Similarly, Markus (2015, p. 2) argues that, "the low-level bureaucrats jeopardize not only the income rights of entrepreneurs, as per the literature on corruption, but the ownership itself."

In Russia, there are economically active bureaucrats, unlike in the US or the EU, where bureaucrats rarely take bribes, but rarely have direct economic incentives to work effectively. Russian bureaucrats are economically active, acting with a high level of economic or even entrepreneurial initiative, seeking personal benefits, and collecting bribes. Economically active bureaucrats sell access to natural resources and state-granted economic privileges at the prices prevailing on the black market. And if foreign businessmen and investors demonstrate inability to negotiate with local Russian bureaucrats, the former place themselves in a disadvantageous position.

The lawsuit of two Russian oligarchs, Boris Berezovsky and Roman Abramovich, that took place in London in the mid-2000s, may be a good demonstration of different interpretations of the meaning of economically active bureaucracy.[13] The plaintiff and the defendant were fighting over some assets they owned in Russia, deciding who paid who and for what. According to the notion of economically

State and raider and state-raider   67

active bureaucracy, offered by this study, Berezovsky tried to prove precisely that he was an economically active bureaucrat receiving share in profit based on his partial ownership of the company. The court ruled otherwise, specifically that Berezovsky was a corrupt bureaucrat receiving regular payoffs from businessman Abramovich. In either case, Berezovsky may be portrayed as a representative of economically active bureaucracy. This lengthy, exhaustive, and costly civil litigation and the decision made by the court served as an embarrassment for Russia's reformers.

2.2 State-raider

Aggressive state

The state in Russia is quite an aggressive body. Attacks on small and large businesses are initiated not only by criminal groups, but first and foremost by the state. It is no secret that the Court Bailiff Services Office, also known as Federal Bailiff Services, formed in 2008, is being considered by many as an instrument of raiding used by the state itself. At the same time state bureaucrats are also being considered as a backup force in hostile takeovers and sometimes even as the leading force of modern Russian raiding. Skidanova (2010) even brought the statement on state bureaucrats as the main type of raider to her dissertation's finding: "Functioning of the institute of authority-property leads to state raiding as a certain way of returning state property. A state bureaucrat is the main raider today" (p. 12). Furthermore, "Today, the major players on the market of hostile takeovers are state bureaucrats, while the state is the main raider" (p. 15). Nevertheless, it remains unclear whether the state bureaucrat is the major raider or is it the state in its entirety.

A strong feature of research on policing and corruption in Russia, presented by Taylor (2011), is that it mentions corporate raiding and the role that law enforcement agencies play in this unlawful business. Taylor (2011) describes forced hostile takeovers and notes that

> Law enforcement personnel are frequently involved in so-called "commissioned cases" (zakaznye dela), in which a company secures law enforcement support for an attack on a business rival. The phenomenon of commissioned cases is one among multiple tactics used by "corporate raiders" in Russia.
>
> (p. 165)

However, a much stronger emphasis should have been placed on the problem of corporate raiding and in what specific ways the police take part in hostile takeovers. In doing so, corrupt law enforcement agencies accelerate the process of unlawful redistribution of property in post-Soviet Russia.

Kazun (2014) investigates violent corporate raiding in Russia by using a database of 543 cases of raiding that took place during the period of 2011 to 2013, assembled by the Center of Public Procedures "Business against Corruption." The author tests

68 *State and raider and state-raider*

several hypotheses including that violent corporate raiding is widespread not only in Moscow, but in other regions as well, and that it is most widespread in those regions that feature well-developed industrial, construction, and trade sectors. Kazun (2014) suggests that rent-oriented law enforcement agencies cooperate with raiders while low numbers of NGOs are insufficient for successful anti-raiding campaigns.

Baev (2011) mentions the corruption scandal with the VDV[14] general Shamanov while describing the shortcomings of the reform aimed at modernizing and reorganizing the Russian military. The scandal was about Shamanov's order to move a small detachment of paratroopers in order to protect a business controlled by Shamanov's son-in-law against some police and court bailiffs involved in a criminal investigation. Baev (2011) points out that "this high-resonance case reminded the top authorities that combat troops could easily be deployed in pursuit of any kind of agenda of their commanders, including political ones" (p. 70). The scandal with Shamanov's use of the military in resolving corporate conflicts, in fact, points to the aggressive role of the state in corporate raiding.

As far as the role of the state is concerned, Shvartsman offers the following idea:

> We have resources which are currently not in demand, including the council of veterans of the MVD [Ministry of the Interior], former officers of OBEP [Department for Economic Crime Prevention], RUBOP [District Department for Organized Crime Prevention]. Six hundred people around the country! They conduct thorough analytical work, watching which enterprises in each region are at what stage of corporate relations. Where are the possibilities to force out owners, who are not loyal to state authorities, with the help of greenmail or through co-operation with minority stock holders, etc.? By the way, we are now building a collector agency with them, which, according to our plans, will occupy 30 to 40 percent of the entire market in all regions of the country. This agency will act as a prophylactic to financial violations, i.e. the problem of non-repayment of credits.... When it is clear that someone does not pay back their credit, and that we should go and settle, then there will be people not with big clubs, but former law enforcement officers with substantial experiences of investigation and communication, which will help.[15]

This suggestion is reminiscent of the practice of out-of-court arbitrage, which was done by gangs in the 1990s and is now turning in a more sophisticated business. The essence of this business, however, remains largely the same, especially if former law enforcement agency officers are actively involved in it.

Opinions of the respondents of the Center of Political Technologies in Moscow were grouped around two major views regarding the role of the state in raiding. About half of the respondents believe that the state does not take part in raiding. Another half is certain in the opposite, suggesting that the state is the main raider in the country. Experts share a view that the time of raiding done by private

State and raider and state-raider   69

companies is over. Instead, today the public observes state raiding. Modern raiding comes from the state and originates in the state institutions. One respondent, an MP in the State Duma, says that

> State raiding is a very dangerous phenomenon. Istlajn [East-Line] company faces attempts to take over its business at the plain view of the astonished public. What we see today is the state racket and, honestly, I feel ashamed for the state. Our state bureaucrats became aggressive to the extent that their brains are no longer functioning properly due to their immunity from the law.[16]

The Federal Court Bailiff Services organization executes court orders and, hence, carries on the state authority. Court bailiffs, in fact, have to fulfill the plan in executing court orders. To be precise, they normally interfere when the defendants do not follow court orders. This area of law enforcement is quite new and somewhat unusual for the post-Soviet Russian state. As a result, actions of court bailiffs in executing court orders sometimes do not wait on proper legal provisions that would regulate such actions, instead taking initiative in their own hands. Simply put, court bailiffs sometimes interpret laws in their favor as they strive to meet the quota on the number of court orders executed and debts collected. Furthermore, they fill the existing gaps in the still-developing legislation in order to justify their actions. For instance, court bailiffs ban debtors from leaving the country. In Russia, in the first half of 2009, over 50,000 people lost the right to leave the country and travel abroad. The practice of expropriating cars in compensation for unpaid bank loans or tax debts becomes more and more widespread.[17]

There was a case of expropriating a Land Rover of a famous showman and producer of the TV-6 Channel, Evgeny Kiselev, right near the Kremlin. This case received wide publicity and drew attention to the issue of the possible limits to which the hand of court bailiffs can reach and beyond which it cannot go. Sometimes court bailiffs extend their jurisdiction and exceed their authority. Court bailiffs could not gain access to Kiselev's apartment in order to expropriate some of his property and cover his debt on a court order in the sum of only 5,000 rubles (less than $200). As a result, bailiffs reported his car as being searched by the traffic police. Once the car was spotted, it was impounded. Court bailiffs intended to take a few of its parts and then return the car to its owner, unless he paid the debt first. Court bailiffs said that the plan was to take away and sell the spare tire and the radio and CD player.[18] Maybe it would be easier to proceed as traffic police do in the farmers' market. They take away the license plate with the help of a screwdriver and then wait until the car owner comes to retrieve his plate and pays the fine for parking in the wrong place.

There were times when court bailiffs in Russia had to spy for debtors and try to catch them in their houses in order to seize some of their property. Facing locked doors with no one inside or facing unwilling owners was not a very effective way of doing the debts collection business. Now the authority delegated to court bailiffs expanded significantly. Court bailiffs are allowed to enter the premises

70   *State and raider and state-raider*

and seize property without asking the owner first, because now they are allowed to break in.[19] Court bailiffs are not the only debt collectors. The collectors' business in Russia is flourishing. A rapid growth of collectors' firms is explained by the phenomenal growth of consumer credit and mortgages over the last decade, followed by economic decline.[20] The state collects, businesses collect, and businesses collect with the help of the state.

Raiding is not only done by the state, but by some state representatives on their own. For instance, former Vice Chair of the Russian Chamber of Trade and Commerce, Maxim Biryukov, was sentenced to seven years in prison for fraudulent dealings with real estate priced at over 210 million rubles (around $7 million). In addition, Biryukov is due to pay a fine of 50,000 (around $1,700). Biryukov and his accomplice formed an organized criminal group in order to take over two buildings in downtown Moscow that cost over 210.8 billion rubles. When the victims of fraud and hostile takeover learned about the raiding, Biryukov tried to convince them to increase the capitalization of the two buildings, sell them, and split the money. Then he offered lawful owners to pay him 53 million rubles in order to return their property.[21] This case of raiding turned into an extortion, orchestrated by a former high-ranking state bureaucrat.

Street-level or lower-level bureaucrats, identified by Markus (2015) as piranhas, attack small businesses and property owners in search for extra benefits:

> The threat of expropriation by lower-level bureaucrats is the rule in weak states. Such threats may include a municipal court issuing an injunction paid for by a competitor; a policeman shutting down some retailers to intimidate others; a local official pressuring a firm to give a job to his relative lest the company lose its operation license; and so forth.
>
> (Markus, 2015, p. 22)

However, these "piranhas" are only secondary in their capacity to raid to the top establishment of the ruling political regime. Street-level bureaucrats are not capable of attacking large, well-protected and well-connected companies.

Raiding attacks are supported by state-bureaucratic organizations and institutions. The mechanisms used in these raiding attacks vary and are likely to increase in variety and become more sophisticated. One of the classical mechanisms is licensing. Minor violations in numerous codes and regulations may be used in order to suspend the license of the firm and stop its economic activity. The heavy involvement of the state in the raiding schemes is now confirmed by the legal cases where defendants are state officials.[22] The sentences, however, are handled by the court not on the basis of anti-raiding legislation, which is simply nonexistent, but for fraud, falsifications, blackmail, extortion, bribery, and other related criminal activities.

The Head of "Finansgrup" financial-industrial group (FIG), Oleg Shvartsman, spoke about the business group he leads. He said that relatives of the members of the presidential administration take part in the business, which essentially point to a blunt nepotism. Shvartsman also spoke about a possibility of creating a state corporation titled "Social investment," and about the idea of "velvet re-privatization": "we are very closely affiliated with some political figures and manage their assets. We have relations with the presidential administration and its law enforcement and military bloc." As far as the structure of real owners is concerned, "these are not members of the leadership of the presidential adminis-tration, but their relatives and well-positioned state officials. There are also indi-viduals, including members of the FSB and SVR [Sluzhba vneshnej razvedki, i.e. Foreign Intelligence Services]."[23] Involvement of relatives implies nepotism, while presence of the power ministries means a threat of state-sanctioned and indeed state-exercised violence.

Shvartsman shares the ideas of the developed concept of creating partnership with businessmen in order to facilitate their participation in social programs, affil-iation with the state, and also acquisition of strategically important enterprises by the state. He points out, in particular, that,

> We created the concept which anticipates building partnerships with objects which we initially thought to violate [idiomatic expression]. We started visiting them with different offers and propositions, which resulted in co-operation.... We are now developing a structure which will soon transform into a state cor-poration called "Social investments." It is based on the concept of "velvet re-privatization," which we developed together with RAGS (Russian Academy of State Services) and the Academy of the National Economy (ANH). We do this also in the interest of "Rosoboronexport." This is a market-based form of acquisition of strategically important assets located in the subsidized regions. We are talking about budget-forming or city-forming assets, which are cur-rently located in incorrect tax regimes.[24]

Mentioning "incorrect" tax regimes can carry a meaning of exercising pressure on private businesses with the help of the tax administration. First thing that comes to mind in this regard is the Yukos case.

Referring to Volkov (2005), Zon (2008) writes that

> Under President Putin, the courts started to be used for economic conflict regulation. Until 2000 the kryshi (roofs), i.e. protection provided by mafia/ private security services and violence were used to settle conflicts. During the 1990s 70 per cent of conflicts were regulated outside the courts. As the governors became more powerful, judges and police became more impor-tant power instruments. The new liberal bankruptcy law of 1998 gave local bureaucrats more power over enterprises, not only to enforce tax payment but also to appropriate enterprises. It is telling that 79 per cent of bankruptcy cases in 2001 were initiated by the state, not by private debtors.

(p. 59)

Volkov (2005, p. 329) points out that law enforcement agencies were hired to raid firms and enforce the bankruptcy laws.

72 State and raider and state-raider

The state is capable of closing entire industries in the services sector. In Russia, the laws banning gambling businesses were signed and enacted on July 1, 2009.[25] All casinos, gambling machine halls, and other gambling facilities were closed. According to some estimates, the ban on gambling in Russia deprived anywhere from 300,000 to one million people employed in this business of jobs. The gambling business in Russia had annual revenues of $2 billion to $3.77 billion, and paid $24 million in taxes. There were 5,170 gambling tables and 350,000 gambling machines in 2006. There were over 60,000 employees in this business, according to the official data of the Federal Tax Services (FNS) [Federal'naya nalogovaya sluzhba]. The more liberal estimates were at least 350,000. The rate of return in the gambling business could have reached up to 50 percent.[26] The gambling business had been pushed into the shadow sector of the economy and was made illegal.

Such nonprofit sectors as art and culture – remnants of the Soviet system – have become targets of raiding campaigns. The entities in the nonprofit sector face criminal investigations, fabricated charges, and pressure aimed at taking away state property they own or operate.[27] It seems as though the state is already fighting itself by pursuing interests of raiders and de facto working to their benefit. Further proliferation of the raiding movement anticipates not only the activation of raiders in less developed or less explored sectors of production and material assets, but also the involvement of new actors, including law enforcement agencies and the military [silovye vedomstva].[28] These ministries and detachments have a great potential on the raiding scene.

One can observe an increase in state pressure in the process of streamlining and putting in proper order property relations in the new, pseudo-market system of economic coordinates. There are governmental agencies acting based on principles of private economic agents, and private economic agents acting under the guise of the state. Instead of offering systemic solutions for systemic problems, the state offers semi-coercive and semi-legal methods, which do not contribute to the formation of a new integrated system of relations between citizens, business, and the state.

Noneconomic factors of influence

Noneconomic factors of influence play a significant role in Russian economy. These factors include laws and regulations enforced by the state. Some of these laws and regulations are intended to address the growing problem of raiding. Russian legislators offer and consider amendments that, in their view, will help curb corporate and property raiding in the country. Amendments to the Criminal Code, included in the "anti-raiding" package of laws, will allow law enforcement agencies to interfere in corporate conflicts on the side of certain stockholders. The Criminal Code can be amended with Article 201.1 "Unlawful appropriation of the duties of the managing body of a legal entity" and Article 201.2 "Abuse of a right of stock holder of a legal entity." The maximum sentence for each of these crimes is ten years in prison. The article "Abuse of a right of stockholder of a legal entity" considers intentional actions of a shareholder to damage the company a crime. This article also considers forcing the management of a joint-stock company to make decisions that would damage the company.[29] These two articles are intended to stop corporate raiders from taking over the company's management directly or by buying out a minority package of shares and interfering in the company's normal production process and business operations.

The Federal Services on Financial Markets (FSFR) also suggests suing top managers for negligence if they poorly represent the interests of the company or cooperate with raiders.[30] The cases of claiming damages from managers are extremely rare in Russia. In 2010, the Deposits Insurance Agency sued top managers of sixteen banks that went bankrupt. The largest damages, 953.2 million rubles (around $32 million) are being sought from the ex-CEO of Vneshtorgbank, Victor Bukato. There is only one case of claiming damages on subsidiary or fiduciary responsibility from a nonbanking sector manager. In April of 2009, the Moscow City Court ordered Director General of International Foreign Trade Agency, Svetlana Sukhorukova, to pay 15.44 million rubles ($500,000) in damages for breach of fiduciary responsibility. The FSFR suggests introducing presumption of guilt for negligent managers. Managers would have to prove that they acted properly in cases of significant damage to the company. Managers who voted against the decision that turned out to be damaging are released from responsibility. A lawsuit can be filed by holders of at least 1 percent of the stock.

Depending on the interpretation of the newly introduced amendments and each particular situation, just about any approval or disapproval of a company's decision may turn out to be a law violation. The same problem concerns appointment or dismissal of top managers and members of the board. But each shareholder has the right to vote according to his/her own beliefs and in his/her best interest. Corporate lawyers are wary that law enforcement agencies will be able to interfere in corporate conflicts on the side of a certain group of shareholders, and thus the state will receive one more tool for influencing business. The police already take part in corporate conflicts, including unlawful actions, when they conduct arrests and searches, launch criminal investigations and open criminal cases against lawful owners, and help raiders. If the police start determining which particular contract, action, or inaction of the company's management damages the company, then raiders can use this for the replacement of management and hostile takeovers.

As follows from media reports, the state apparatus is used for raiding large enterprises more and more actively. These enterprises would be able to defend themselves against ordinary raiders legally and physically, but it is hard for them to argue with the state organs.[31] The state apparatus appears to be quite an effective tool in this economically loaded activity. The Head of the NAK (National Anti-Corruption Committee), Kirill Kabanov, offered the following comments regarding the arrest of the co-owner and Director General of the retail chain "Arbat Prestige," Vladimir Nekrasov: "There are too many people who want to take over his profitable business. It seems like he will be freed in exchange for his business."[32] At the same time Khodorkovsky said that "No one offered me any deals after the arrest," while answering the question "Were there any deals

74 State and raider and state-raider

offered to you? What kind of deals?"[33] As follows from the response of the former Yukos's Head, the ruling political regime did not offer him any kind of "freedom in exchange for your business" swap, while taking away the oil company.

As far as the "Arbat Prestige" case is concerned, the situation developed under a somewhat different scenario. Indeed, the Arbitrage Court of Moscow ruled unlawful the decision of the tax authority which obligated the perfumes holding "Arbat Prestige" to pay 155.106 million rubles in taxes, interest, fees, fines, and penalties. Judge Igor' Korogodov fully satisfied the lawsuit demands of "Arbat & Co" and nullified the decision of the Interregional Inspection on the Federal tax services #48 in Moscow (MIFNS-48) of December 31, 2008 "On charging with the violation of the Tax Code." MIFNS-48 demanded the taxpayer company pay 66.151 million rubles as the profit tax, 47.097 million rubles as the value added tax (NDS), as well as appropriate fees, fines, and penalties. As of early 2008, "Arbat Prestige" was one of the largest retail chains of perfume stores in Russia. At the end of 2007, its revenue was $471.5 million. After the arrest of its owner, Vladimir Nekrasov, the company faced over 100 legal claims against it filed in Russian courts. By the fall of 2010, all of the company's stores had been closed and the premises occupied by other firms.[34] The prompt closure of this large company and its following sale in pieces reminds one of a well-organized raiding attack.

Nekrasov's lawyer said that his client received an offer to sell the business in exchange for freedom and ceasing the criminal investigation.[35] Eventually, the founder of "Arbat Prestige" turned out to be clean before the criminal investigation.[36] Moreover, the General Prosecutor's Office asked to release the co-founder of "Arbat Prestige" and partner of Nekrasov, Semen Mogilevich, from detention. Earlier this request was linked to the sale of "Arbat Prestige."[37] A few months earlier, in January of 2008, the Ministry of the Interior confirmed that Shnajder (one of last names used by Semen Mogilevich) would not be extradited to the US. Semen Mogilevich was on the list of the FBI's most wanted for years. He was accused of large-scale fraud and related crimes. Despite this, the Russian Ministry of the Interior responded that the information presented by the CIA could be evaluated in Russia, and there was no need for extradition.[38] US state agencies should also keep in mind that the extradition of Russian citizens from Russia is unconstitutional. Even though Semen Mogilevich may have multiple name-spellings and citizenships, he is still a Russian citizen while on the Russian soil. Requests for extradition have become very sensitive issues, for they touch on national sovereignty and extraterritoriality. The point advanced by the media is well-taken: one can avoid serious problems with law enforcement agencies and courts if one is to follow the requests of giving up a part of a business or its profits.

There are quite a few of such stories in post-Soviet Russia. For instance, former CEO of KrAZ, Anatoly Bykov, held under arrest in Lefortovo, was offered freedom in exchange for the control stock of KrAZ. His lawyer, Genrikh Padva, said at a press conference in Moscow that his client Bykov received such offers several times. Moreover, Padva said that such offers were made through him. Bykov was told to surrender his 28 percent of stock for only $25 million, while the market price on this package was at least $120–150 million. In exchange, he would be freed, but would have to leave the country immediately.[39] Such claims are impressive in their content and their frankness, but not in their impact. People who are deprived of their property through fabricated criminal cases and offered freedom-to-property swaps have no respect from the general public. Their ownership rights can be legal, but still illegitimate in the eyes of the people.

In this regard, one can recall the decision of the Strasburg Court regarding Vladimir Gusinsky.[40] A European appeals court ruled that Russia violated the human rights of Gusinsky, the media mogul who fled into exile and whose television and print operations were seized in a politically charged legal campaign. The European Court of Human Rights agreed with Gusinsky's assertions that a Russian criminal investigation against him in 2000 was politically motivated, finding that the state's actions "insistently suggest that the applicant's prosecution was used to intimidate him" into giving up his media empire (Baker & Glasser, 2005, p. 248). Some state officials wanted the Media-Most media holding to be acquired by the state oil and gas giant Gazprom for a much reduced price, so this may be considered a corporate raiding.

Western media comments on the merger of corrupt law enforcers and criminals in their attempt to conduct hostile takeovers of successful businesses. Matthews (*Newsweek*, August 14, 2010) states that,

> At the heart of the problem is an unholy alliance between Russian law enforcement and the criminal world – a combination that over the last decade has created "an alloy of almost unbreakable force," says lawyer Vladimir Pastukhov. Instead of enforcing the law, a large chunk of Russia's police, secret police, and government bureaucrats spend their energies on looking out for vulnerable businesses that can be targeted for a corporate raid, Russian style. Unlike the Wall Street version, a Russian hostile takeover almost invariably involves a violent raid by armed and masked police using a warrant issued on flimsy charges, followed by the confiscation of company documents, computers, and archives with a view to stealing the business and intimidating its lawful owners. The pattern was established in 2003 when the Kremlin dismembered Russia's biggest oil company, Yukos, and jailed its head, Mikhail Khodorkovsky, and a slew of executives and lawyers based on dubious evidence.[41]

In the 1990s, dismembering large Soviet enterprises was called restructuring, and now the proper term seems to be corporate raiding.

In late 2008, the State Duma adopted amendments to the laws "On police" and "On investigation and search operations." The MPs suggest that the proposed measures have anti-raiding and anti-corruption character. The amendments restrict the ability of the police officers to enter firms and take away financial documents. According to the amendments, the police will be able to conduct checks in firms only when "there is an immediate threat to lives and health of citizens, to the state, military, economic, or ecological safety and security." The amendments followed

76 State and raider and state-raider

Medvedev's demand to "stop causing nightmares for business."[42] Hostile take-overs often start from police visits to the targeted company and expropriating financial documentation. Sometimes illegal searches lead to extortions from the side of the police[43] or to interfering in the work of the targeted company, even if it is a cargo terminal of Moscow Sheremet'evo International Airport.[44] The searches in Sheremet'evo were done on suspicion of smuggling. Smuggling may be related to another type of raiding, commodity raiding.

The legislative project against commodity raiding was considered and adopted in the State Duma in January 2009. The amendment introduced in Article 82 of the Criminal Code allows the investigator to decide regarding the sale of material evidence during the investigation if its storage and preservation is either too difficult or too costly. Another amendment changes the federal law "On appraisals code in the RF." The amendment suggests introducing criminal responsibility for appraisers for abuse of their office regarding the seized property. Police officers can choose a target with high liquidity (i.e. easy to sell goods), take an already existing criminal case, and find some "evidence" that the targeted company has a stock of goods in its warehouse related to the case. They enter the warehouse and seize the goods, which are then sold by a mediator at a reduced price. For instance, in 2006, "Evroset" lost 160,000 cell phones. Cell phones were expropriated on the grounds of consumer safety concerns.[45] But this is nothing compared to the closure of Cherkizovsky rynok in Moscow, the largest wholesale and retail commodity market in the country.[46] Despite some significant and widely publicized cases of commodity raiding, this type of raiding is not as much on the media radar as other forms of raiding.

2.3 Concluding remarks

In conclusion, the attention can once again be placed on the relations between the state and raiding and the role of the state as raider. The process of privatization of socialist property was, in essence, raiding. Accordingly, there is an impression that the state became an object of raiding and a victim of aggression of external forces toward the state property, including all means of production. But, in fact, the object of raiding became the state property, while the state was an instrument used by raiders possessing state power to appropriate property. In this case, the state itself is seen as a raider. At the same time, state functions, state authority, and execution of state powers were taken over and "privatized." In scholarly literature this phenomenon is known as state capture.

The dualistic approach to the state's position in relation to privatization has a direct relevance to the question of nationalization and reprivatization. Dualism is the position of the modern post-Soviet Russian state in that it is both interested in the transfer of the means of production and other economic assets into private hands, and in maintaining economic control, monitoring, and exercising economic power. And this economic power is only possible while maintaining significant economic assets, because without them, the controls will be based only on noneconomic mechanisms, coercive power, and dictatorial coercion. Simply put, in order to have economic power, the state should have economic weight. Possible options include the presence of the state in the private sector and/or the presence of a significant public sector in the national economy.

Dualism of the position of the post-Soviet state is determined by the trajectory of the inverted development. The inversion in this case is due to the fact that the state, which owned everything, now refuses the part of a whole instead of gaining control over it. As a result, images are formed inevitably of the state that gives, the state that takes, and the state that preserves. The state continues facing the issue of optimizing its presence in the economy. The state has yet to decide how much of the national economy should be given into private hands, and how much is to be retained in state or public ownership. The state as a subject of economic activity or an acting economic agent tends to attract more funds into the budget, obtain more funds to maintain the political regime and implementation of national projects funded by the state. In this case it does not make sense at all for the state to give something away and into private hands, abandon any property, especially for free, with no compensation, on a pro bono basis. However, if one is to accept the suggestion that the private sector as a whole works better than the state or public sector as a basis, then the starting point will be the statement on the maximization of revenues flowing into the state budget by optimizing the structure of ownership on the means of production, and their distribution between the state and private companies. The state as a conveyor of the people's will, acting in their interests, aims to increase production, employment, economic growth, and economic efficiency, rather than simply filling the state budget as a goal in itself. In this case, it may be rational for the state to give up ownership of a significant part of its economic assets, including on a compensable basis, in order to optimize the structure of ownership of productive assets in the national economy.

In terms of relationships with private capital and business in general, modern Russian bureaucracy demonstrates the transition from the security and protection function to the redistribution function. Participation of the bureaucracy in the process of raiding marks this transition. In this regard, this study suggests a new term: economically active bureaucracy. The bureaucratic caste is traditionally considered as the community of civil servants working for a certain salary determined and paid by the state. Accordingly, bureaucrats as a rule have no special financial incentives to work more efficiently and effectively. In addition, bureaucrats collect bribes and other illicit benefits to the greatest extent possible while being cautious and weighing the possible risks of losing their "bread and butter" places and facing criminal prosecution.

Economically active bureaucracy means something more than being slow and ineffective. The post-Soviet bureaucracy in Russia is not satisfied with its salary received from the state budget and illicit benefits collected from businesses and other clients. Russian bureaucrats want to share in the profits, and this is known to be a function of the business owner, the one who owns at least a part of the production. And it is not that civil servants are forbidden to engage in private business – all those who have a business use well-known schemes to circumvent this prohibition set by the state. The fact is that not all bureaucrats have their

78   *State and raider and state-raider*

own business, including not only street-level bureaucrats, but also high-ranking bureaucrats with big "resolution" capacity. By resolution capacity, this study means the capability of highly ranking and well-positioned state bureaucrats to resolve problems based on their office authority delegated to them by the state. In Russia it is called *reshat' voprosy*; this phrase has a direct idiomatic translation "to solve the questions."

State bureaucrats are no longer satisfied with their function of protecting businesses against external aggressors and their raiding assaults on businesses, prescribed by the state. Bureaucrats offer services to facilitate redistribution of not only access to limited resources, public goods, spheres of influence, and market segments, but business assets as well. While helping raiders to capture someone else's business, state bureaucrats, in fact, participate in the redistribution of property, profit-generating assets and businesses, and expect a reward from this future profit, obtained by the raiders or the new owners. Therefore, bureaucrats reach the stage and the level of profit participation. This is no longer the use of functions delegated by the state for personal purposes or personal enrichment, but an explicit economic activity.

Notes

1 Composed by the author based on the data from Social and Economic Indicators of the Russian Federation: 1991–2014, Appendix to the "Statistical Yearbook of Russia. 2015," Section 11, Privatization. Moscow: Federal State Statistics Services. Retrieved March 1, 2017, from www.gks.ru/wps/wcm/connect/rosstat_main/rosstat/en/main/; Privatization. Russia in Figures. Moscow: Federal State Statistics Service Yearbook, 2016, p. 230. Retrieved March 1, 2017, from www.gks.ru/free_doc/doc_2016/rusfig/rus16e.pdf; http://cbsd.gks.ru/
2 Kommunisticheskaya partiya Rossijskoj Federatsii (KPRF).
3 Medvedeva poprosili natsionalizirovat' "Nornikel" [Medvedev was asked to nationalize "Nornikel"], *Newsru.com*, July 28, 2010. Retrieved July 28, 2010, from www.newsru.com/finance/28jul2010/iljukhin.html
4 Chaves s pomoshch'yu vojsk natsionaliziroval neftegazovye kompanii [Chavez nationalized oil and gas companies with the help of the army]. *Newsru.ua*, May 9, 2009. Retrieved May 9, 2009, from http://rus.newsru.ua/finance/09may2009/chavess.html
5 Russian Tsar Ivan the Terrible, also known as Ioann the IV, Grozny and Ioann Grozny, was known for his cruelty and purges conducted among the noblemen by his guards, called Oprichniki.
6 Rossiya, za kotoruyu menya posadili [Russia for which I was imprisoned]. *Kommersant*, 37(941), September 19, 2011. Retrieved September 19, 2011, from http://kommersant.ru/doc/1771803

   Khodorkovsky o "Rossii, za kotoruyu ego posadili": sovetuet Medvedevu, kak izmenit' stranu, ostavshis' prezidentom [Khodorkovsky about "Russia for which he was imprisoned": Giving advice to Medvedev on changing the country if remaining president]. *Newsru.com*, September 19, 2011. Retrieved September 19, 2011, from www.newsru.com/russia/19sep2011/newrussia.html
7 Russkie "Medvedi" prodolzhayut muchit' britanskih letchikov. No skoro bazu perehvatchikov mogut zakryt' [Russian "Bears" continue terrorizing British pilots: But soon the airbase of jetfighters may be closed]. *Newsru.com*, October 29, 2010. Retrieved October 29, 2010, from www.newsru.com/world/29oct2010/flyingbears.html
8 Vlast' davit na menya postoyanno. Tyur'moj. Interv'yu Reuters s Mikhailom Khodorkovskim (original'naya russkaya versiya) [State authorities put pressure on me all

time: By prison: Reuter's interview with Mikhail Khodorkovsky (the original Russian version)]. *Khodorkovsky.ru*, September 18, 2011. Retrieved September 18, 2011, from http://khodorkovsky.ru/mbk/articles_and_interview/2011/09/18/16606.html

Khodorkovsky v interv'yu Reuters predrek Rossii novy krizis i porassuzhdal o mesti [Khodorkovsky predicted a new crisis for Russia and talked about a revenge in an interview given to Reuters]. *Newsru.com*, September 18, 2011. Retrieved September 18, 2011, from www.newsru.com/russia/18sep2011/hodorkovsky.html

Forget reform if Putin stays in power – Khodorkovsky. *Reuters*, September 18, 2011. Retrieved September 18, 2011, from http://uk.reuters.com/article/2011/09/18/uk-russia-politics-khodorkovsky-idUKTRE78H0RD20110918

9 Completed by the author based on data from: Sakwa, Richard. (2009). *The Quality of Freedom: Khodorkovsky, Putin and the Yukos Affair.* Oxford: Oxford University Press, p. 182.

10 International Labour Organization (ILO) Resolutions Concerning Economically Active Population, Employment, Unemployment and Underemployment Adopted by the 13th International Conference of Labour Statisticians, October 1982, para. 5. Retrieved from www.ilo.org/public/english/bureau/stat/res/index.htm

See also: Glossary of the Organization for Economic Cooperation and Development (OECD), Statistics division. Retrieved from https://stats.oecd.org/glossary/detail.asp?ID=730

11 The World Bank interviewed a representative sample of the private sector composed of 4220 business establishments during August 2011 and June 2012 across the Russian Federation. The Enterprise Survey covers several topics of the business environment as well as performance measures for each firm. Enterprise Surveys. The World Bank. Washington, DC. Retrieved March 1, 2017, from www.enterprisesurveys.org/Graphing-Tool

12 V MVD nazvali srednij razmer vzyatki v Rossii – za god on vyros na 75% [Ministry of the Interior reports that the average bribe in Russia increased 75 percent over the last year]. *Newsru.com*, March 16, 2017. Retrieved March 16, 2017, from www.newsru.com/russia/16mar2017/mvd.html

13 For details on the case, see Leake, Christopher. (2007). Battle of the oligarchs … the amazing showdown between Roman Abramovich and his arch rival. *Daily Mail*, October 6, 2007. Retrieved October 6, 2007, from www.dailymail.co.uk/news/article-486164/Battle-oligarchs-amazing-showdown-Roman-Abramovich-arch-rival.html#ixzz1pWFzMGlq

14 VDV, vozdusno-desantnye vojska, i.e. paratroopers' brigades.

15 Kvasha, Maksim. (2007). "Partiju dlya nas olitsetvoriaet silovoj blok, kotory vozglavliaet Igor' Ivanovich Sechin" – glava Finansgrupp Oleg Shvartsman o novyh dobrovol'no-prinuditel'nyh sposobah konsolidatsii aktivov v rukah gosudarstva ["The party for us is represented by the power bloc, led by Igor Ivanovich Sechin" – the head of Finansgrupp, Oleg Shvartsman, told in an interview about new voluntary-forceful ways of consolidation of assets in the hands of the state]. *Kommersant*, 221(3797), November 30, 2007. Retrieved May 9, 2009, from www.kommersant.ru/doc.aspx?DocsID=831089

16 Reiderstvo kak sotsial'no-ekonomicheskij i politicheskij fenomen sovremennoj Rossii: otchet o kachestvennom sotsiologicheskom issledovanii. Issledovanie "Tsentra politicheskih tehnologij" pod rukovodstvom Bunina. Moskva, 2008. [Raiding as a socioeconomic and political phenomenon of the modern Russia: A report on the qualitative sociological investigation. An investigation conducted by the Center of Political Technologies led by Bunin]. Moscow, May 2008. Retrieved June 12, 2009, from www.politcom.ru/; www.compromat.ru/main/mix1/raiderycpt.htm

17 See video-materials: Court bailiffs expropriated an SUV. Retrieved from www.youtube.com/watch?v=5k8dD_Ac9sM&feature=related

18 Sudebnye pristavy otsenili dzhip Evgeniya Kiseleva v pyat' tysyach rublej [Bailiffs priced jeep of Yevgeny Kiselev at 5,000 rubles]. *Newsru.com*, February 4, 2002. Retrieved May 9, 2009, from http://palm.newsru.com/russia/04feb2002/kiselev_car.html

80 *State and raider and state-raider*

19 See video-materials of court bailiffs at work, using their new privileges. Retrieved May 9, 2009, from www.youtube.com/watch?v=ONKqDdg5ASA&NR=1; www.youtube.com/watch?v=k1rVX27sHaY&feature=related

20 Orfenov, Aleksandr. (2008). Chernye piarshchiki koshmaryat yekaterinbirgskie banki [Black PR companies are a nightmare for Yekaterinburg banks]. *Notheft.ru*, November 25, 2008. Retrieved November 25, 2008, from www.notheft.ru/chernye-piarshhiki-koshmarjat-ekaterinburgskie-banki

Orfenov, Aleksandr. (2009). Krizis i kollektorstvo [Crisis and collecting]. *Notheft.ru*, February 24, 2009. Retrieved February 24, 2009, from www.notheft.ru/krizis-i-kollektorstvo

Orfenov, Aleksandr. (2009). Krizis, dolgi, reiderstvo [Crisis, debts, raiding]. *Notheft.ru*, April 16, 2009. Retrieved April 16, 2009, from www.notheft.ru/krizis-dolgi-rejderstvo

21 Byvshij zampred Torgovo-promyshlennoj palaty RF poluchil 7 let za reiderstvo [Former vice chair of the Chamber of Trade and Commerce of the RF was sentenced to seven years for raiding]. *Newsru.com*, March 4, 2009. Retrieved May 9, 2009, from www.newsru.com/russia/04mar2009/birukov.html

22 Ibid.

23 Sovladelets Finansgrupp rasskazal ob iz'yatii chastnogo biznesa v interesah gosudarstva i Sechina [One of the owners of Finansgrupp told about the expropriation of private business in the interest of the state and Sechin]. *Newsru.com*, November 30, 2007. Retrieved May 9, 2009, from www.newsru.com/russia/30nov2007/finansgrupp.html

24 Kvasha, Maksim. (2007). "Partiju dlya nas olitsetvoriaet silovoj blok, kotory vozglavliaet Igor' Ivanovich Sechin" – glava Finansgrupp Oleg Shvartsman o novyh dobrovol'no-prinuditel'nyh sposobah konsolidatsii aktivov v rukah gosudarstva ["The party for us is represented by the power bloc, led by Igor Ivanovich Sechin" – the head of Finansgrupp, Oleg Shvartsman, told in an interview about new voluntary-forceful ways of consolidation of assets in the hands of the state]. *Kommersant*, 221(3797), November 30, 2007. Retrieved May 9, 2009, from www.kommersant.ru/doc.aspx?DocsID=831089

25 Zapret azartnyh igr lishil raboty polmilliona chelovek [The ban on gambling forced half a million people out of jobs]. *Newsru.com*, June 30, 2009. Retrieved June 30, 2009, from www.newsru.com/finance/30jun2009/zapret.html

26 Danilova, Ekaterina. (2009). Belyh net: igornyj biznes ne ischeznet posle zapreta. Kakim on stanet? [No whites: Gambling business will not disappear after the ban: How will it change?]. *Ogonek*, 4.

27 Prekrashcheno ugolovnoe delo v otnoshenii direktora muzeya "Mikhajlovskoe" [A criminal investigation of the director of "Mikhajlovskoe" is stopped]. *Newsru.com*, September 19, 2009. Retrieved September 19, 2009, from www.newsru.com/russia/19sep2009/mih.html

Skandal v pushkinskom muzee "Mikhajlovskoe": direktora obvinyayut v sluzhebnom podloge [A scandal in the Pushkin's museum "Mikhajlovskoe": The director is accused in fraud]. *Newsru.com*, May 15, 2009. Retrieved September 19, 2009, from www.newsru.com/russia/15may2009/vasilevi4.html

Prestupnaya gruppa v sostave grazhdan Pushkina, Onegina i nekoj Ariny Rodionovny [A criminal group of Pushkin, Onegin, and Arina Rodionovna]. *Novaya gazeta*, 46, May 6, 2009. Retrieved September 19, 2009, from www.novayagazeta.ru/data/2009/046/23.html

28 Minoborony proverit komanduyushchego VDV na svyazi s kriminal'nym mirom [The Ministry of Defense will check the head of VDV regarding his possible connections with the criminal underworld]. *Newsru.com*, September 22, 2009. Retrieved September 22, 2009, from www.newsru.com/russia/22sep2009/razb.html

Glavkom VDV Shamanov poradel za rodstvennuyu dushu – glavu OPG Glybu? [Did the head of VDV Shamanov tried to help a relative – leader of the organized criminal group Glyba?]. *Moskovskij komsomolets*, September 22, 2009. Retrieved September 22, 2009, from www.mk.ru/politics/publications/354122.html

State and raider and state-raider 81

29 Militsiyu vyzvali na korporativnyj konflikt [Police was called to a corporate conflict]. *Kommersant*, December 1, 2008. Retrieved July 22, 2009, from www.notheft.ru/miliciju-vyzvali-na-korporativnyj-konflikt
30 FSFR predlagaet sudit' top-menedzherov za neradivost' i nerazumnost' [FSFR suggests suing top managers for negligence]. *Newsru.com*, June 17, 2010. Retrieved June 17, 2010, from www.newsru.com/finance/17jun2010/fsfr.html
31 Na skryvayushegosya ot pravosudiya predprinimatelya iz Ekaterinburga zavedeno ocherednoe ugolovnoe delo [One more legal investigation is launched against an entrepreneur from Yekaterinburg, who is on the run]. *Notheft.ru*, June 15, 2009. Retrieved July 22, 2009, from www.notheft.ru/na-skryvajushhegosja-ot-pravosudija-predprinimatelja-iz-ekaterinburga-zavedeno-ocherednoe-ugolovnoe
    Byvshij nachal'nik kriminal'noj militsii Adilhan Muhamedzhanov osuzhden za reiderstvo [Former chief of the criminal police Adilhan Muhamedzhanov is sentenced for raiding]. *Notheft.ru*, November 26, 2008. Retrieved July 22, 2009, from www.notheft.ru/byvshij-nachalnik-kriminalnoj-milicii-adilhan-muhamedzhanov-osuzhden-za-rejderstvo
    Na koordinatsionnom sovete Omskogo oblastnogo soyuza predprinimatelej obsudili problemu reiderstva [Problem of raiding was discussed at the meeting of Omsk regional union of entrepreneurs]. *Notheft.ru*, November 26, 2008. Retrieved July 22, 2009, from www.notheft.ru/na-koordinacionnom-sovete-omskogo-oblastnogo-sojuza-predprinimatelej-obsudili-problemu-rejderstva
32 Chebatko, Mariya. (2009). Svoboda v obmen na biznes [Freedom in exchange for business]. *RBK Daily*, January 25, 2008. Retrieved July 25, 2009, from www.rbcdaily.ru/2008/01/25/focus/316283
    Advokat glavy "Arbat Prestizha": Nekrasovu predlozhili prodat' biznes v obmen na svobodu i prekrashchenie dela [Lawyer of the head of "Arbat Prestige": Nekrasov was offered to sell the business in exchange for cease of investigation]. *Newsru.com*, February 11, 2008. Retrieved July 25, 2009, from www.newsru.com/russia/11feb2008/shantaj.html
33 Vlast' davit na menya postoyanno. Tyur'moj. Interv'yu Reuters s Mikhailom Khodorkovskim (original'naya russkaya versiya) [State Authorities put pressure on me all the time: By prison: Reuter's interview with Mikhail Khodorkovsky (the original Russian version)]. *Khodorkovsky.ru*, September 18, 2011. Retrieved September 18, 2011, from http://khodorkovsky.ru/mbk/articles_and_interview/2011/09/18/16606.html
    Khodorkovsky v interv'yu Reuters predrek Rossii novy krizis i porassuzhdal o mesti [Khodorkovsky predicted a new crisis for Russia and talked about a revenge in an interview given to Reuters]. *Newsru.com*, September 18, 2011. Retrieved September 18, 2011, from www.newsru.com/russia/18sep2011/hodorkovsky.html
    Forget reform if Putin stays in power – Khodorkovsky. *Reuters*, September 18, 2011. Retrieved September 18, 2011, from http://uk.reuters.com/article/2011/09/18/uk-russia-politics-khodorkovsky-idUKTRE78H0RD20110918
34 Sud priznal nezakonnymi nalogovye pretenzii k "Arbat Prestizhu" [The court dismissed the claims of tax authorities to "Arbat Prestige"]. *Newsru.com*, October 8, 2010. Retrieved October 8, 2010, from http://newsru.com/finance/08oct2010/arbat.html
35 Advokat glavy "Arbat Prestizha": Nekrasovu predlozhili prodat' biznes v obmen na svobodu i prekrashchenie dela [Lawyer of the head of "Arbat Prestige": Nekrasov was offered to sell the business in exchange for cease of investigation]. *Newsru.com*, February 11, 2008. Retrieved July 25, 2009, from www.newsru.com/russia/11feb2008/shantaj.html
36 Osnovatel' "Arbat Prestizha" Nekrasov okazalsya chist pered sledstviem [Founder of "Arbat Prestige" turned out to be clean before the investigation]. *Newsru.com*, April 8, 2011. Retrieved April 8, 2011, from www.newsru.com/finance/08apr2011/arbatp.html

82 State and raider and state-raider

37 Genprokuratura prosit vypustit' Mogilevicha iz-pod aresta. Ranee eto uvyazyvali s prodazhej "Arbat Prestizha" [The general prosecutor's office is asking to release Mogilevich from detention: Earlier this request was linked to the sale of "Arbat Prestige"]. *Newsru.com*, April 2, 2008. Retrieved April 2, 2008, from http://newsru.com/russia/02apr2008/arbatt.html

38 Shnajdera SShA ne vydadut, podtverdili v MVD. Materialy CRU mozhno otsenit' i v Rossii [The Ministry of the Interior confirmed that Shnajder will not be extradited to the US. information presented by the CIA can be evaluated in Russia]. *Newsru.com*, January 30, 2008. Retrieved January 30, 2008, from http://newsru.com/russia/30jan2008/noshnaider.html

39 Bykovu predlozhili obmenyat' blokiruyushchij paket aktsij KrAZa na svobodu [Bykov was offered freedom in exchange for the blocking package of KrAZ stocks]. *Newsru.com*, January 31, 2001. Retrieved July 25, 2009, from www.newsru.com/russia/31jan2001/bikov.html

40 Pretsedent Gusinskogo. Evropa zasudila Rossiyu [Gusinsky precedent: Europe sued Russia]. *Newsru.com*, May 20, 2004. Retrieved July 25, 2009, from www.newsru.com/russia/20may2004/gusinsky.html#1

41 Matthews, Owen. (2010). Generation exile: Corruption is forcing Russia's best and brightest to flee the country. *Newsweek*, August 14, 2010. Retrieved August 14, 2010, from www.newsweek.com/2010/08/14/putin-s-russia-exile-businessmen.html

42 Popravki v zakony "o militsii" i "ob operativno-rozysknoj deyatel'nosti" ne dadut organam vlasti "koshmarit'" biznes [Amendments to laws "On militia" and "On search and investigation" will not allow the authorities to disturb business]. *Notheft.ru*, December 11, 2008. Retrieved July 22, 2009, from www.notheft.ru/popravki-v-zakony-%C2%ABo-milicii%C2%BB-i-%C2%ABob-operativno-rozysknoj-dejatelnosti%C2%BB-ne-dadut-organam-vlasti-%C2%ABkosh

43 Moskovskij sledovatel' vymogal u biznesmenov 25 mln rublej za ukradennye im zhe dokumenty [A police investigator in Moscow was trying to extort 25 million rubles from businessmen in exchange for the documents that he himself had stolen from them]. *Newsru.com*, February 24, 2010. Retrieved February 24, 2010, from www.newsru.com/russia/24feb2010/usach.html

44 Sledovateli obyskivayut ofis kompanii "Sheremet'evo-Kargo" – rabota krupnejshego gruzovogo kompleksa blokirovana [Investigators conduct searches in the offices of the "Sheremet'evo-Kargo" company: Work of a largest cargo terminal is blocked]. *Newsru.com*, November 12, 2009. Retrieved November 12, 2009, from www.newsru.com/finance/12nov2009/cargo.html

45 Zakonoproekt o protivodejstvii tovarnomu reiderstvu prinyali v Gosdume RF [A law on anti-raiding for commodities was approved in Russia's State Duma]. *Notheft.ru*, January 29, 2009. Retrieved July 22, 2009, from www.notheft.ru/zakonoproekt-o-protivodejstvii-tovarnomu-rejderstvu-prinjali-v-gosdume-rf

46 Rosimushchestvo unichtozhaet tovary s "Cherkizona," dlya etogo zakupili spetsial'nye katki iz Finlyandii [Rosimushchestvo destroys goods from "Cherkizovsky" market and for that reason it bought special machines from Finland]. *Newsru.com*, January 21, 2010. Retrieved January 21, 2010, from www.newsru.com/finance/21jan2010/cherkizon.html

References

Baev, Pavel. (2011). Crooked Hierarchy and Reshuffled Networks: Reforming Russia's Dysfunctional Military Machine. In Vadim Kononenko & Arkady Moshes (eds.). *Russia as a Network State: What Works in Russia When State Institutions Do Not?* (pp. 62–80). New York: Palgrave Macmillan.

Baker, Peter, & Glasser, Susan. (2005). *Kremlin Rising: Vladimir Putin's Russia and the End of Revolution*. New York: Simon & Schuster.

Dugin, Aleksandr. (2010). *Konets ekonomiki* [*The End of Economics*]. Sankt Petersburg: Amfora.

Karatuev, Aleksandr Grigorievich. (1998). Sotsial'no-ekonomicheskie osnovy gospodstva byurokratii v SSSR i v sovremennoj Rossii [Socio-Economic Foundations of Domination of Bureaucracy in the USSR and in Modern Russia]. DSc Economics dissertation, Volgograd, 08.00.01 Political Economy, p. 268. Retrieved from www.dissercat.com/content/sotsialno-ekonomicheskie-osnovy-gospodstva-byurokratii-v-sssr-i-v-sovremennoi-rossii

Kazun, Anton. (2014). Violent Corporate Raiding in Russia: Preconditions and Protective Factors. *Demokratizatsiya: The Journal of Post-Soviet Democratization*, 23(4), pp. 459–484.

Kononenko, Vadim & Moshes, Arkady (eds.). (2011). *Russia as a Network State: What Works in Russia When State Institutions Do Not?* New York: Palgrave Macmillan.

Markus, Stanislav. (2015). *Property, Predation, and Protection: Piranha Capitalism in Russia and Ukraine*. New York: Cambridge University Press.

Skidanova, Lilia. (2010). Raiding as a Socio-Economic Phenomenon. PhD dissertation. Moscow: Moscow State University.

Taylor, Brian D. (2011). *State Building in Putin's Russia: Policing and Coercion after Communism*. Cambridge: Cambridge University Press.

Volkov, Vadim. (2005). Po tu storonu sudebnoj sistemy, ili Pochemu zakony rabotayut ne tak, kak dolzhny [On the Other Side of the Justice System or Why Don't Laws Work as They Should]. *Neprikosnovennyj zapas*, 4(42). Retrieved from http://magazines.russ.ru/nz/2005/42/vv6.html

Weber, Max. (1990). *Selected Works*. Translated from German. Moscow: Progress.

Zon, Hans van. (2008). *Russia's Development Problem: The Cult of Power*. New York: Palgrave Macmillan.

3 Raiding in transition

3.1 Problem of raiding in the transition economy

Ways of hostile takeovers

Mergers, acquisitions, hostile takeovers, and other digestive processes of the modern market, where raiders serve as an accelerator of economic processes – or speaking in medical language, a gastric acid – are now commonplace in post-Soviet Russia. Moreover, on par with corruption, raiding becomes one of the most popular topics in the economic section of the mass media and national news. Not only large companies, but small enterprises also become targets of raiders. Raiders moved from hostile takeovers of large metallurgic plants and oil refineries to takeovers of stores and laundry and cleaning services.[1] Police are taking back state enterprises from raiders by court decisions. Company management teams are changed by the ministerial orders, but no one is going to leave profitable enterprises without a fight.

Russian media highlights the problem of raiding in numerous reports and commentaries. This study has identified well over 3,000 such reports filed from 2004 to 2016. All regions in Russia are now subject to raiding.[2] No doubt, the chronicles of major raiding attacks will eventually be entered in the annals of Russian national history. Russia is a big country – the largest in the world by territory – and the geographic spread of raiding is impressive too. All Russia's numerous regions suffer from raiding. News reports about raiding attacks come from all corners of the country. In Pskov, raiders were especially interested in a city bakery plant,[3] a new raiding attack on "AGRO-Trast" agricultural enterprise was registered in Omskaya oblast',[4] a raiding attack on a condominium building occurred in Kemerovo.[5] In Kazan, members of the organized criminal group of raiders stole over 91 million rubles,[6] and in Yaroslavskaya oblast' entrepreneurs suffered raiding attacks.[7] This list can be continued for a long time, especially since it becomes longer every year.

Those who claim that violent storming raids were left to history in the rough 1990s are inadvertently incorrect. Hostile takeovers with the use of violent clashes of competing parties and storming of enterprises continue. A good example of such a violent takeover is that of a major machine-building plant in Chelyabinskaya

Raiding in transition 85

oblast', Ural Federal District, in 2015. The storming of the plant involved a police blockade, dozens of armed storm troopers, shooting, fights that left a few with broken skulls and fractured ribs, and all other elements of a good Hollywood blockbuster.[8] Corporate raiding in Russia may have become more sophisticated and intellectually developed, but this does not eliminate the importance of the violence component of the raiding phenomenon.

Let us turn to the question of who are Russian raiders. As of today, there is no uniform portrait of a raider organization, a pattern under which one could try to fit different players of the market in order to classify them as raiders or otherwise. Raider organizations wear many guises and have many faces. Raiders may be individuals holding public office or positions in business and skillfully using these positions, connections, and capital in order to conduct appropriation and alienation of someone else's property with the use of nonmarket mechanisms and corruption schemes. This stratum of economic agents includes both hostile invaders of apartments that belong to old retirees and prominent leaders of entire notorious raiding companies whose names represent the raider business and are synonymous to raiding in the minds of local businessmen. Raiding engages teams of associates and complete specialized firms, which include lawyers, financiers, and accountants. Often these groups and firms acquire someone else's property on order, for their customers. They themselves are not new owners but rather operators on the property market. The range of their interests includes only assets ordered for takeover by their firms' customers. And if their clients are willing to cover the cost of appropriating any asset, including land, enterprises, public facilities, and real estate, raiding companies are here to help.

Large companies, holding companies, and financial-industrial groups can also engage in raiding. Although not their main type of business activity, raiding serves as one of the tools for expansion. Large companies use raiding techniques because of the need for further business development. This may include the elimination of competitors, monopolization of certain market segments, alienation of land for future construction, exploration and development of mineral deposits, and seizure of buildings, including the one that may be used as the company's headquarters. Large firms also capture entire enterprises, not for resale, as is the case with specialized raider companies, but for their own use. All these groups belong to outside raiders sometimes referred to as external raiders.

Enterprises can face internal raiders as well. These are insiders and include, first of all, business leaders who have a tendency to lay their hands on the company. Insider raiders raid their own firms by deceiving the company's employees and by committing fraud with the assistance of external agents. Their advantage is that they have access to all the charter documents, knowledge of management schemes, the structure of the company, and its financial status, and they also have the ability to manage enterprise assets. The intentional bankruptcy is a classic example of an internally planned and staged raid. In cases of internal or so-called insider raiding, the notion of information as a valuable asset is clearly distinguished. Raiders may be business partners and small shareholders. Here, open

86 *Raiding in transition*

access to information about the company, possessed by the insiders, also plays a significant role.

As seen from this brief excursion on images of raiders and raider organizations, the term "raider" or "raider organization" has several meanings: it can be an individual, a manager or director, a raider group, a specialized company, or industrial and financial conglomerate. Moreover, these economic agents can collude in order to conduct raids and as such, also be known as raiders. The mosaics of the transitional system with its rich palette explains the heterogeneity of the raider stratum: in post-Soviet Russia raiding companies are not exclusively investment funds involved in corporate raiding, but a whole range of different participants, including criminals.

The term "raiding" is a derivative of the word "raider." The usage of the word "raider" dates back to 1863. A raider is an active participant in a hostile takeover. Raid denotes an event, i.e. a hostile takeover committed by raiders. The usage of "raid" starts around 1865. Raiding characterizes a phenomenon. Raid, from English "raid" denotes a hostile or predatory incursion; a surprise attack by a small force. Raid also means a sudden invasion by officers of the law; a daring operation against a competitor; the act of mulcting public money; the recruiting of personnel (as faculty, executives, or athletes) from competing organizations. Raider has historical meanings as well: a raider is a fast lightly armed ship operating against merchant shipping; a soldier specially trained for close-range fighting; one that attempts a usually hostile takeover of a business corporation. In the world of finance, the term "raid" is used to denote an attempt by professional operators to depress stock prices by concerted selling.[9] The term "raider" refers to corporate raiders.

This work introduces the definition of raiding [reiderstvo] as a hostile takeover that manifests a fight for property or other assets that involves corruption and fraud. Raiding does not necessarily imply a raider storm or assault on the property in dispute. In some cases, raiding does not involve violence. A hostile takeover that involves corruption and fraud may occur without such extreme acts, as an armed assault. However, in many instances, such an assault is the culmination of legal disputes. In other cases, such an assault may be just the beginning of the hostile takeover and may be repeated by both parties a few times.

The distinction between a military occupation, military assault, criminal assault, simple robbery on one hand and raiding on the other hand lies in the realm of legally binding relations. Raiding occurs under the cover of existing laws but does not stay within its limits. Raiders enjoy the protection given to them by the law, when they are already in possession of the targeted property. The key point in raiding is in buying the necessary legal decision. All the other operations, including the (armed) assault on the disputed property are technicalities that can be organized with the help of private security firms. Raiders use legal loopholes and the corruptibility of courts and other state authorities in order to achieve the takeover. Tkachenko and Lobodenko (2007, p. 212) offer the following definition of raiders: "Raiders are companies whose activities are aimed at the change of structure of property on targeted companies to their own benefit or the benefit of their client companies ordering the raid."

Both the scholarly literature and the mass media normally mention four major ways of hostile takeovers. For instance, Varnalij and Mazur (2007, p. 131) identify stock capital, hired management, credit debt consolidation, and disputing results of privatization as areas where raiders can challenge present owners. The first is raiding through the stock capital, when raiders buy stock from minority shareholders. Normally this initial action is sufficient to call for a meeting of stockholders and vote for necessary decisions, such as changing the company's management. In some cases, there is no actual hostile takeover of the company. Instead, majority shareholders are literally forced to buy out shares acquired by the raiding company at a very high price. The second way is raiding through the hired management when the management team takes assets away from the company in the firms controlled by the raider or takes credits with unrealistically high interest rates using the company's property as collateral. The third way is raiding through credit debt consolidation when an enterprise has several small credit debts and a raider buys them and presents for pay at once. The fourth way is raiding through disputing results of privatization; the basis for this type of raiding is laid down at the time of privatization when some routine violations take place.

Reports also suggest that in modern Russia the first two ways of raiding are most commonly met. These two ways of hostile takeovers – through the stock capital and through the hired management – have clear criminal character. The third way of raiding – through credit debt consolidation – in principle does not contradict the law, but can be met only rarely. It can be used by raiders when a targeted enterprise borrows money without proper precautions. The fourth way of raiding – through disputing results of privatization – can be met not very frequently because the major wave of Russian privatization was that of the 1990s and the statute of limitation on most of the privatization deals has expired by now. A combination of different methods and tricks makes hostile takeovers most dangerous especially since such combinations require a set of different kinds of resources of raiding, including administrative and financial resources.[10] The more resources raiders have to employ for their attempts of hostile takeovers, the more it will cost them. As any other businessmen, raiders have to do their cost-benefit analysis while considering different options and possible ways of raiding a targeted firm.

In addition to raiding through stock capital, hired management, credit debt consolidation, and disputing results of privatization, extortion is also used as a way of hostile takeover.[11] A priori lost arbitration court cases are being compensated with the threats of releasing compromising materials. In such cases, both sides accuse each other of raiding.

The research conducted by the Center of Political Technologies exposed six major methods of hostile takeovers used by raiders in Russia. Fraud: This includes the production and use of fraudulent documents, including records of shareholders' meetings, bribes to registration or state officials. Greenmail or psychological attack: This method may be listed as a quasi-legal. Greenmail does not enter in the direct contradiction with the law, but has a psychological pressure on the owner of the targeted company. Violent storming: This is a clear-cut illegal method of

88   Raiding in transition

hostile takeover (slowly vanishing). Bankruptcy: The bankruptcy method is now used less frequently, because the bankruptcy legislation is now developed much better than it used to be in the past. Administrative methods: This is used by local or federal authorities. Buying shares: This means washing out of the stock value of minority holders with the help of additional emission of shares and without taking into consideration the interests of the minority holders. This method is quasi-legal.[12]

Restructuring plays a significant role in raiding, and is considered a powerful instrument in the hands of raiders. Tkachenko and Lobodenko (2007, p. 212) point out that

> oftentimes a raiding attack is aimed not only at taking the enterprise, but also includes this enterprise's bankruptcy with the exertion of the most valuable assets and sale of land. The latter especially concerns enterprises which are located close to central districts of a given city and occupy large territories.

Sometimes the plot of land on which the targeted enterprise stands is more expensive than the enterprise itself.

In Soviet Russia, such issues as breach of fiduciary duty and insider trading were simply unknown, which is of no surprise. The plan and directive economy based exclusively on state enterprises assumed no personal interest in insider information, especially since there was no trade in a sense commonly accepted in a market economy. By the way of infiltrating the company, outsiders become insiders. Neutze and Karatnicky (2007, p. 13) say that,

> Raiders infiltrate the company of interest with agents who collect information. A small share of stock is purchased. Then, a usually frivolous lawsuit is filed with a lower-level court in a remote town. Armed with an often anomalous court injunction, raiders resort to force, sending a pseudo "security firm" to take possession of the property (through forcible entry). Further, by bribing law enforcement agencies, they keep the object under their control – even in the face of a corrected court decision. Then, they try to re-sell property to themselves or to those who ordered the raid, to change the composition of charter capital (which requires changing the statute of the enterprise).

A hostile takeover may be a lengthy process and anticipates certain stages. Tkachenko and Lobodenko (2007, pp. 212–213) highlight the following stages of a hostile takeover: gathering information and intelligence about the targeted company, estimating the ability of the targeted company to defend itself against raiders and its possible reaction to a change in ownership, working out the scheme of capture of the target business, organizing the attack and other measures necessary to guarantee the success of the entire operation.

Methods of raiders include actions punishable as crimes. The most obvious methods of raiders include document fraud, falsification of protocols of shareholder meetings, production of signatures, bribery of the state registry officers and state bureaucrats, and production of false documents. One of the most popular methods of this kind is the production of a fraudulent court decision handed down in a distant region. With such a decision, delivered by a court let us say in Primor'e, raiders come to a court bailiff in Moscow. Based on this court decision, this court bailiff initiates the procedure of claims on the property of a Moscow-based firm, targeted by raiders.

A psychological attack on a targeted firm owner is a quasi-legal method of raiding. Such kind of pressure on a company's managers or owners stays within the limits of law, but is considered as unethical or not appropriate morally. Yet another method used by raiders is diminishing the value of shares held by minority shareholders without their prior consent by the way of issuing additional shares. Raiding includes not only buying a stock of shares, but involves a whole complex of activities. These activities may include doubling the charter capital of the targeted enterprise and buying the stock that comes with the additional emission of shares. The media also mentions violent takeovers of enterprises as illegal methods of raiding.[13] Violent hostile takeovers, no doubt, earn the lion's share of the media attention simply due to their high visibility and the sense of urgent action.

Raiding is now traditionally being divided into three types: "black," "grey," and "white." Such a gamut is necessary to reflect the degree of darkness of different elements of raiding, from most violent and illegal to most legal. An investigation conducted by the Center of Political Technologies entitled "Raiding as a Socio-Economic and Political Phenomenon of Modern Russia: A Report on the Qualitative Sociological Investigation" discovers these three types of raiding (Bunin, 2008). Such a typology or even gradation of raiding by its colors and shades based on methods used by raiders is generally accepted without much argumentation.

Black raiding is the most criminalized type of the raiding phenomenon. Methods used in connection with this type of raiding are always illegal and involve physical violence. These methods may include bribery, blackmail, a violent entry in the targeted enterprise, or production of a false register of shareholders. According to the reports of the majority of the respondents, this type of raiding is slowly vanishing. Grey raiding is a soft type of raiding, partially connected to bribery, such as for instance bribing a judge in order to speed up the process of producing a necessary and lawful court decision. Another case of grey raiding is when a third party buys out one of the partners and offers negotiations or a deal. One shareholder does not want to sell shares to another shareholder. This shareholder finds a third party, transfers his/her shares to the third party, which concludes the sale and closes the deal. This method looks legal, but it is wrong in its essence. It is wrong because according to the law a shareholder should first offer his/her shares to his/her partner and only then to a third party, explains one of the interviewed experts. White raiding is most frequently met in the Western world, while in Russia, in the experts' view, it is not cost efficient. "White" raiding includes, for instance, organizing worker strikes or unscheduled audits initiated by state controlling agencies. This type of raiding is normally employed by experienced lawyers, who quite skillfully use legal loopholes to the benefit of the raiders. This practice allegedly facilitates economic development and does not cause any damage.

90 *Raiding in transition*

It appears that while in the West raiders act within legal limits set by the state, in the post-Soviet space legal actions of raiders are oftentimes not considered as raiding at all. Respondents of the Center of Political Technologies arrived at a mutual agreement on this particular issue: what is done with the help of lawful methods cannot be considered raiding. In reality, it became very difficult to differentiate raiding from some other activities from the time the former Soviet republics entered the realm of the pseudo-market economy. It is hard to delineate between raiding and the honest way to receive property rights within the limits of the enacted legislation, say one of the legislators (Bunin, 2008). Apparently, the issue of definition and clear demarcation of raiding and nonraiding persists not only in scholarly discussions, but in political debates as well.

In addition to production facilities, real estate and land are major targets of raiding. Raiding goes far beyond hostile takeovers of private enterprises. Raids are organized against the state enterprises and state property as well. Documents show that industrial disposal fields; industrial waste; oil refineries; private banks; public utility companies; electricity and oil distribution centers, facilities, and pipelines; abandoned state and private plants; entertainment centers; sea ports; construction sites; agricultural land; resort areas; economic quotas on exploitation of natural resources; resort areas; tanks and ammunition; technologies and technical documentation; TV companies; radio frequencies, and even dolphins are all targets of raiders. Essentially, anything of value is potentially an object for a raiding attack. Apartments are also illegally occupied, often with the use of legislative loopholes, threats, and violence. This comes as no surprise, since these apartments are often priced higher than a working individual can earn in an honest way in thirty years. Raiders use any problems with the ownership titles and other related documents along with the outright bribery of state officials in order to gain valuable assets.

Scholars traditionally miss one very important and very vivid way of raiding met in Russia: the use of the confusing tax system. Having a confusing and contradictory tax system, entrepreneurial bureaucrats can pressure businesses and rightful owners to sell their assets at the prices well below the market rates. However, the Head of Finansgrup, Oleg Shvartsman, does not think that this may be interpreted as a mandate for forceful raiding. He suggests that,

> This is not raiding. We do not take away enterprises. We minimize their market value with the help of different instruments. Normally, these are voluntary-forceful instruments. There is a market value and there are mechanisms to block its growth, of course, with different administrative tools. But normally people understand where we come from.... All though these conflicts are smoking, as a rule, and are under the watch of existing financial and industrial groups. In such cases our bosses have to agree and arrive at some kind of consensus. Normally, this is a low benchmark of market value. But this is not like taking away Yukos; people receive decent money.... At this moment we are busy with acquiring an enterprise that produces chromium in Orenburgskaya oblast'. This is one of the best producers of Russian chromium, first in

Raiding in transition 91

EBITDA, second by volume of production in the world.... Chromium will go for $700–800 million while we buy it for only $300 million.

People who do this job come from different places, says Shvartsman: "First of all, the Moscow raiding market has shrunk, and there is nothing to do there. Some people came from 'Rosbilding,' some people came from other places."[14] Judging by the previous occupations held by the managers, one can think of the methods used by the company, where Shvartsman is the head.

The state is unlikely to stay outside of the process of raiding. The media points to a possible link between the Members of Parliament (MPs) and the raiding. Hostile takeovers, mergers and acquisitions sometimes happen with the help of MPs. It appears that the state plays a significant role in the phenomenon of raiding in Russia. Such a significant role can be explained by a few factors. First, all of the enterprises and organizations were state property. Second, the state retains a significant presence in the national economy. By now, slightly more than a half of all the production capacities in the former Soviet republics are privatized, but the public sector remains very large. Third, contradictory and mutually exclusive decisions that serve as a ground for raiding attacks are made by state institutions, such as courts, state ministries, and local authorities. Fourth, the state apparatus is often used to plan and stage a hostile takeover. Bribes are paid to state officials in order to break laws, avoid the responsibilities, and pervert the judgment. Similar reasons apply to the future prospects on raiding in the healthcare, education, and science sectors. Due to the historically very significant role of the state in these sectors of the national economy, the role of the state institutions in raiding in this sector may be even more significant than in other industries.

In Russia, it may be important to delineate the state and the ruling political regime in order to better understand the role of the state institutions in raiding. The state is represented by the state institutions, including the set laws, while the ruling political regime uses the state machine in order to advance its own interest, including self-sustainability and a transfer of property to the hands of those who support the regime financially, including its members. Members of the ruling regime exist in the perpetual search of popular support and are unlikely to advance any decision that explicitly threatens their popularity. This form of political behavior is known as populism.

Objects of raiding: risks and victims

The questions remain about risks and victims or raiding. Who are the targets of raiders in Russia? Based on what criteria do raiders choose their victims? Which companies are most attractive for raiders and why? What makes a company high risk in terms of its potential to become a target of a raiding attack? Apparently, raiders face a certain dilemma: on one hand, they are attracted by the most economically strong companies either due to future profits or valuable property and other assets; on the other hand, raiders are attracted to poorly protected companies, which can be taken over with no exhaustive effort. Raiders have to do cost-benefit

92 *Raiding in transition*

analysis. Economically strong companies are normally well protected, because these companies can afford a good defense. At the same time weak companies are not necessarily economically attractive for raiders.

Raiders in market economies are often compared to wolves. Wolves as forest cleaners attack weak animals, which are not capable of running away or defending themselves, and yet are quite attractive as a one-time prey. Raiders in Russia have to be much more inventive than forest wolves. Their tasks are not limited by the functions of identifying, locating, choosing, estimating, and attacking a "weak and attractive" enterprise. Their task extends much further and includes converting a targeted enterprise in such a "weak and attractive" firm. They have to search for different kinds of tricks and weak sides which in combination with semi-legal or illegal methods will allow them to take over the targeted company. Raiding in Russia has a predatory character not because raiders prey on the bankrupting businesses, but because they attack healthy and profitable enterprises, firms in temporary financial distress. Raiders use unclear ownership structures of economically attractive firms and buy necessary decisions from corrupt bureaucrats instead of waiting for another financial crisis (Osipian, 2012). In fact, raiders intentionally bankrupt profitable businesses with the help of state bureaucrats.

Risks of raiding, faced by large, small, and medium companies, depend on their management, governance structures, business activities, assets, and external links. Demekhin (2010) suggests dividing risks of raiding into five groups, including corporate governance, presence and condition of property, financial and economic situation, management, and external environment. But the division of raiding risks may be much broader, depending on the overarching or large component of the business structure in focus as well as the incentives to act and vulnerabilities present in different types of businesses. For instance, in limited liability companies, presence of partners who do not take part in the business or in profit sharing may incentivize them to collude with raiders and use their formal rights for the hostile takeover to proceed.

Another category of raiding risks may be brought to life by the company's purchase of an already established and registered company from an outside register. A large number of such ready-to-go companies are registered with legal deficiencies. The registration problems include shell companies being registered on passports of convicted criminals, individuals who already left the country through immigration procedures, or even deceased people. In yet another example, a manager, whose name is in the state register also serves as the manager of several dozen companies, including shell companies. In many such instances the manager has no idea about these numerous companies and their character of business. Many shell companies lie idle and accounting reporting on them is not submitted, and that is why such a company may be just a time bomb.

Not only the use of a shell company or companies, but also the use of a shell or nominal director or top manager places a company at risk. On the one hand, companies use services of nominal directors for some situational and even legal reasons, while on the other hand the use of any nominal service always means risk. A nominal director can always sell property or make credit and borrowing agreements without consent from the partners or top management. Moreover, there is often a need to sign documents by someone other than the nominal director in his/her absence, whose signature is sometimes faked, or even worse, whose real signature is kept on blank letterhead.

A company can be created on the basis of standard registration documents borrowed from a sample documents package of similar companies. Instead, registration documents should be drafted based on specific needs and guaranteeing specific corporate and property interests. Such aspects cannot be reflected in standardized documents. A charter, drafted for guaranteeing specific interests, tailored for a specific company, is the fundament for developing a corporate defense system.

Joint-stock companies face some more challenges in addition to those faced by limited liability companies. In typically large joint-stock companies, risks associated with raiding may be different. Absence of the blocking package or control package of shares in the hands of one shareholder and the presence of many minority shareholders creates a threat of a hostile takeover through a buyout of shares from minority shareholders by raiders. This type of raiding may occur in joint-stock companies and be related directly to a specific corporate governance structure. Unreasonably tough and restrictive policies regarding minority shareholders, including restriction of their rights and interests by the corporate board and major shareholders can also serve as an incentive for the former to betray the latter by colluding with raiders or potential raiders. The lack of transparency in the policy of assigning and distributing dividends may also cause the dissatisfaction of shareholders, especially minority shareholders, and make them prone to cooperation with potential raiding companies.

Rules governing large joint-stock companies may be complicated and confusing. Violations of corporate protocols and procedures, including first of all violations or rules of concluding large deals and deals with potential conflicts of interest, can lead to dissatisfaction of shareholders and/or management of the company. Contradictions in corporate documents can also make a company an easy target for raiders. Yet another challenge arises from internal corporate conflicts that emerge between stakeholders and management. Internal tensions and confrontations present risks for any otherwise stable business structure or organization. Raiders often become involved in such conflicts initially disguised as outside consultants in order to gain access to critical information.

Raiders hunt for material assets that may be easily assessed, priced, and resold on the market. The presence of large property, such as real estate, especially in good condition, can urge raiders to take over the company. Demekhin (2010) points out that raiders hunt for material assets. High tech companies, where human capital is the major asset, are of little to no interest to raiders. However, the presence of intellectual property assets may also prompt raiders to take action. According to Rumyantseva and Meshkov (2014), intellectual property constitutes anywhere from 10 to 15 percent of the assets of Russian companies (p. 86). Although these figures are just rough estimates, they point to the significant amount of economic assets based on intellectual property that constitutes a potential target for raiders.

94 *Raiding in transition*

It is considered extremely risky to have valuable assets and conduct business under one company's umbrella. Improper or incomplete legal registration of assets and privatization of objects with violations of current legislation weaken defense options of the company. Presence on the company's territory of some real estate object which does not belong to the company is yet another minus in the company's defense. Finally, absence of the official confirmation of lawfulness regarding deals completed in the process of privatization and asset restructuring creates potential problems that may be used by raiders. For instance, for a hostile takeover of one large company, created during the process of grand privatization in the 1990s, raiders used the difference in documents regarding just one small object of real estate, located on the newly formed company's territory. The rights on this particular object belonged to individuals no one could identify. The entire privatization deal was then contested by raiders with the help of a corrupt court.

The financial and economic situation of a given company is perhaps one of the most important indicators when it comes to a company's vulnerability before raiders. On the one hand, high profitability or high economic potential makes the company attractive to raiders. On the other hand, presence of an overdue debt on the balance sheet of an otherwise successful company can make it an easy target for raiders. Increasing the debt to a high level creates a threat of raiders buying out the debt from different creditors and presenting it for payment as a lump sum. This allows raiders to dictate their conditions to the targeted company under the threat of initiating a bankruptcy procedure. Presence of wage arrears may be used as a ground to initiate a criminal investigation against the top management of the targeted company in order to partially paralyze its business activity. This investigation can also be used by raiders to their benefit, including through obtaining sensitive information on the targeted company and/or weakening it for future planned hostile takeover.

Financial misconduct, such as keeping double accountancy, makes a company potentially vulnerable to raiding. At the same time, aggressive, not well-developed, and excessively risky business activities allow raiders to set a trap for a firm. For instance, raiders can try to make an a priori costly and inefficient deal with the company, which will take away a lot of the company's resources. A good example of a raiders' trap may be when a company's management buys an asset without paying much attention to proper paperwork in order to get a better deal below the market price. Absence of proper attention to detail of the company's operation on the side of the company's owner or top management, and excessive self-esteem can also play a negative role in the company's defense and provoke someone from inside the company or an outsider to attempt a hostile takeover. Making deals and signing contracts without restricting the rights of creditors to sell debt to third parties allow aggressors to buy debts of a targeted company without legal obstacles.

Internal conflicts that include discord among shareholders and lack of cohesion in the workers' collective and form a negative climate in the company in general can weaken its positions in struggling with raiders. While Russia does not have strong traditions or extensive experiences of company management, management becomes of key importance in safeguarding the company against raiding attacks. A key role in success of raiders in a hostile takeover campaign belongs to low loyalty of the company's management. Either hidden or open participation of the company's major figures such as managers, chief accountants, consultants, or one of co-owners on the side of raiders increases the chances of raiders on successful takeover. Absence of strong motivation among the managerial team members also strengthens raiders' positions.

The role of the company's management in securing the company against raiders' attempts of hostile takeovers extends beyond the issues and functions presented above. Managers underestimate that employees are potential sources of confidential information. Such an underestimation, combined with an unfair or conflicting firing or job termination could place the business at risk. Disgruntled former employees may be under no legal responsibility to keep the company's secrets secret. They may well share these secrets with raiders without even knowing that they serve as informants. Using temporary management by shareholders may also be a trap. Absence of clear restrictions of authority imposed on temporary management may help raiders get closer to the targeted company. Company management can take assets away from the enterprise and move them to the raider-controlled company. Unfaithful company management can also take loans by using the company's real estate as collateral, doing this in exchange for bribes received from raiders or because they are being blackmailed or coerced by raiders. Another variation of this scheme may be when a hired management team intentionally puts the company in a critical situation and then "suddenly" a buyer shows up at the door.

In addition to internal factors, such as corporate governance, business structure, the financial situation, management, and level of cohesion among shareholders and employees, external factors are also important. External environments favorable to raiders include absence of an independent register with a high level of reputation and trust, absence of a contract or agreement with the register supplying additional information, and opportunity of an unsanctioned access of a third party to the register. In addition to bureaucratic components of the external environment, there are also economic components. Absence of a proper systemic control over the activities with shares of the company being actively sought or bought by third parties can create additional threats to the company.

Another potential threat to the company can emerge from an unfavorable social climate or absence of ties with and support from the local community. Not taking part in state or municipal programs and ignoring the concept of social responsibility may deprive the company of public and state support in case of a raiding attack. Unsuccessful raiding attempts on the company in the past, the closeness of the company, and absence of the public relations protection also play into a company's vulnerability. A company can use mass media in order to create an image of a very important company, significant for the region and locale and labor collective, pointing out that a hostile takeover will come at a cost to the company's numerous constituents, including not only business partners and customers, but the local authorities and local population in general.

96 *Raiding in transition*

Not only owners of enterprises and entrepreneurs suffer from raiding attacks. Regular people, including those living in apartments, suffer from raiding as well. For instance, dwellers of one of Vladivostok's new buildings became victims of "serious debates" [*razborki*], when raiders claimed rights on their apartment building.[15] It is of no surprise that both entrepreneurs and ordinary people suffer from raiders. Entrepreneurial activities are aimed at receiving profit. However, raiders are often interested not in the profit that a firm receives from its business activities, but in extracting profit from a hostile takeover and sale of certain valuable economic assets, be it an enterprise, real estate, housing unit, or any other asset that has market value. Accordingly, entrepreneurs who do not own any material assets are unlikely to be targeted by raiders. At the same time, those private citizens who own certain assets, such as housing, are potential targets of raiding attacks.

3.2 Magnitude of raiding

Scale of raiding

The scale of raiding may be conditionally estimated based on the number of reports of raiding incidences in the mass media. When it comes to Russia, media reports on corporate, property, and land raiding are numerous. Raiding is associated with the way of doing business in Russia.[16] The media also reports on the successes of the authorities in combating raiding and blocking the attempts of hostile takeovers.[17] The Deputy Chief of the Department of Economic Security of the Moscow City Government, Vyacheslav Ivanov, reports that there were forty-nine cases of raiding registered in Moscow in the first quarter of 2006. Of these forty nine-cases, only in five cases did raiders use criminal methods. As a result, three criminal cases were opened against raiders. Ivanov says that "to a larger or a lesser degree raiders worked on each of Moscow's enterprises." He also admits that "there are objects in Moscow that are still under the control of raiders, but we hope to remove them from these enterprises." According to Ivanov, there were 177 cases of hostile takeovers in Moscow in 2004 and 117 cases in 2005. He says that this trend of the declining number of hostile takeovers in Moscow shows that the work of the authorities bore fruit.[18] Ivanov's reporting may be deemed as positive and optimistic.

There are less optimistic prognoses and they are also based on some data. The First Vice Mayor of Moscow, Yuri Roslyak, said that "taking into consideration the high rate of return of this kind of business one should not expect a decline in raiding in the near future." The number of raiding takeovers continues to grow. There were eleven raiding cases in 2003, forty-four cases in 2004, and fifty-three cases in 2006.[19] In 2008, one media source reported a number of raiding cases in Russia as standing above 1,000.[20] Obviously, different sources present different numbers. Such a mismatch in numbers is based on speculative estimates and the absence of clear legal and commonly accepted understanding of raiding and what constitutes raiding. It is remarkable that despite the dramatic decline in the number of privatized state enterprises, raiding does not indicate any decline.

Raiding in transition 97

Privatization was an initial base for raiding, but raiding continues to develop due to further redistribution of property. If, initially, raiding signified the takeover of state property, later raiding demonstrates the struggle for already privatized assets. The dynamics of the number of privatized state unitary enterprises in Russia during 1992–2015 is presented in Figure 3.1.[21]

In 2008, the Center of Political Technologies (CPT), conducted an investigation into the raiding phenomenon. The major findings of this investigation were presented in the report entitled "Raiding as a Socio-Economic and Political Phenomenon of the Modern Russia: A Report on the Qualitative Sociological Investigation." Bunin says that

> Giveaways of property is unfortunately a national Russian feature. But if the process of giving away property continues, the country will remain in the condition of permanent chaos. If we start another raiding war, this may end up in a revolution.

According to Bunin, "top-ranking bureaucrats and the mid-level businesses are involved in raiding now, because they were late to the initial distribution of the pie." According to the Center of Political Technologies, there are over 1,000 cases of raiding taking place in Russia annually, while there are no more than 100 guilty verdicts handed down in raiding-related criminal cases every year.[22] Western media estimates the total number of raiding attacks in Russia at the astronomical 70,000 cases per year.[23] Apparently, Western media does not encourage Western investors to come to Russia, because otherwise their assets will be at risk.

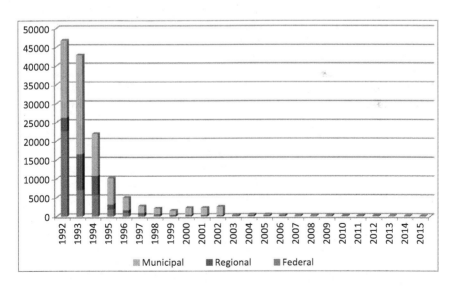

Figure 3.1 Number of privatized state unitary enterprises in Russia, 1992–2015

98   *Raiding in transition*

The Auditing Chamber of the Russian Federation [Schetnaya palata RF] reports the annual number of raiding attacks in Russia at 60,000 to 70,000. In Moscow alone, where the majority of professional raiding companies are located, there were over 1,200 enterprises attacked by raiders over the five-year period from 2003 to 2008. At the same time the Investigations Committee of the Prosecutor's General Office reports that there were only thirty-eight cases of raiding in the process of investigation from September 2007 to September 2008. These cases were concerned with the hostile takeover of property, proprietary and nonproprietary rights, and financial resources of enterprises. As the result of these investigations, twelve cases with charges were sent to the prosecutor, of which eleven reached the court, and only in one case was the court verdict handed down.[24] The Chair of the Ethics Committee of the State Duma, Gennady Rajkov, says that as of 2006, criminal hostile takeovers constitute anywhere from 5 to 8 percent of all the mergers and acquisitions in Russia.[25] However, the total number of M&A on the Russian market is not clear.

Control in the market sector of hostile takeovers is complicated due to existing numerous firms that last for a day or so, fictitious firms registered on outsiders or shell firms. A shell corporation or firm is a company which serves as a vehicle for business transactions without owning any significant assets or performing any business operations. These firms may be registered for a specific transaction and then disappear the next day. In Russia, they are called one-day firms, or *firmy-odnodnevki*. The Deputy Head of Moscow's police department, Lieutenant General Viktor Vasil'ev, said in 2005 that in Moscow, around 80 percent of all commercial firms are fictitious and registered on fake owners or outsiders. Moreover, of 960,000 legal entities registered in Moscow, 600,000 do not report economic and financial activities or report zero activities. Vasil'ev explained that these firms "are used not only in different tax evasion schemes, shady financial schemes, operations on unlawful return of the added value tax, fictitious export, and capital flight from Russia, but also in real estate dealings and other fraudulent schemes."[26] Normally so-called one-day firms are registered with fraudulent or stolen passports and other identity documents. Oftentimes citizens who lost their documents do not even have a slight suspicion that they in fact manage companies. Such firms are created in order to do particular financial operations, and then they are liquidated. It is virtually impossible to audit or check such a firm, because it is either not located at the legal address, or its manager cannot be found.

Head of the Investigations Committee of the Ministry of the Interior, Sergei Manahov, pointed out in 2006 that there are over one million one-day firms registered in Russia every year. They are used for illegal financial operations. In Moscow there are fifty such firms registered every day. Raiders use such firms in hostile takeovers of real enterprises. Manahov underlined that "normally, criminals are not interested in the production process. After the takeover they are busy stealing and selling out liquid assets of enterprises and first of all real estate."[27] One-day firms disappear as fast as they register and are used as a set of links in the chain of transactions, in order to make the process of tracing raided and resold assets especially difficult. Investigating crimes of raiding, which involve several one-day firms, especially if registered on fake passports of unrelated individuals, is very burdensome for the police; it takes time and effort and does not always result in catching the perpetrators.

The Deputy Head of the Prosecutor General, Alexander Buksman, reports that in 2007 the Investigations Committee of the Ministry of the Interior investigated over 500 criminal cases, linked to raiding of enterprises, and over 200 cases were sent to court. Nevertheless, some experts say that less than 10 percent of all the hostile takeovers done by raiders get in the official reports.[28] Raiders attack not only small enterprises, but also large companies, which are of a key importance to cities and towns. Raiding is directly associated with economic crimes. Economic crimes statistics in the Central Federal District of Russia for the period of 2000 to 2015 are presented in Table 3.1.

Central Federal District is Russia's largest federal district that accounts for 40 million people and includes Moscow. The data shows that the number of economic crimes fell fourfold, from 80,931 in 2000 to 20,148 in 2015. At the same time, the number of individuals who committed economic crimes fell even more dramatically, from 47,247 in 2000 to 5,578 in 2015. This significant fall may be linked to problems with registering economic crimes or replacing criminal responsibility for economic crimes with administrative responsibility. Another reason might be the order of the ruling regime to reduce the pressure on small businesses. The data on the number of individuals who committed economic crimes in 2003 is missing and it is exactly in this year that the number of individuals who committed economic crimes dropped from 40,917 to 15,738. Another interesting observation to be made is that in 2000, each perpetrator committed on average less than two economic crimes, while with the decline in total of both the

Table 3.1 Economic crimes statistics in the Central Federal District of Russia, 2000–2015

	Number of economic crimes	*Number of individuals who committed economic crimes*
2000	80931	47247
2001	78231	48245
2002	75915	40917
2003	72636	–
2004	65288	15738
2005	74675	17561
2006	78944	19089
2007	63996	17073
2008	65674	16269
2009	65376	14755
2010	48818	10108
2011	38472	6758
2012	35399	5560
2013	30654	5194
2015	20148	5578

Source: Composed by the author with the data obtained from the Central Statistical Database, the Ministry of Statistics, the Russian Federation. Retrieved March 9, 2017, from http://cbsd.gks.ru/

100 *Raiding in transition*

number of economic crimes and number of individuals who committed economic crimes over the years, in 2015 each perpetrator committed on average almost four economic crimes. This repetitive criminal behavior may point to further professionalization of economic crimes as a sphere of activity. The dynamics of economic crimes and number of individuals who committed economic crimes in the Central Federal District of Russia, for the period of 2000 to 2015 is presented in Figure 3.2.

In addition to the concentration of raiding in the large industrial centers, there is also a trend of spreading out of raiding to Russia's numerous regions. The Department of Economic Security of the Ministry of the Interior marks the trend of raiding companies moving to the regions. Large raiding companies are being replaced by small and mid-size raiding firms, which specialize on unlawful takeovers of property. The Head of the Department of Economic Security of the Ministry of the Interior, Yuri Shalakov, points out that "If earlier the majority of unlawful takeovers were taking place in Moscow and the Moscow region, today we see the trend of raiders moving to regions. Lately, raiders activated, for instance, in Rostovskaya oblast' and Yekaterinburg."[29] According to Shalakov, Moscow and

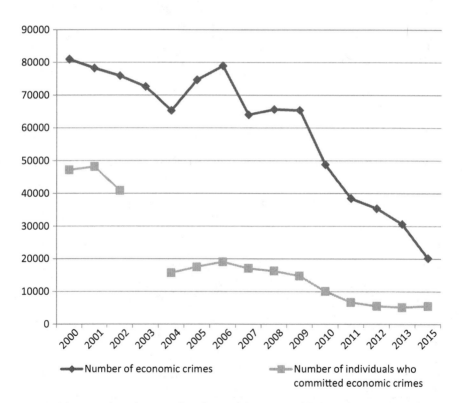

Figure 3.2 Dynamics of economic crimes and number of individuals who committed economic crimes in the Central Federal District of Russia, 2000–2015

the Moscow region are no longer sufficient bases for raiders; they need more space for their activities and more objects to apply their efforts to.

The large scale of raiding is a clear indication of the sorry state of property relations and the system of protection of property rights in particular in the Russian economy and even more so its prevailing destructive trends. Raiding points to the continuing dominant distributional processes in the economy that used to be known for slow but steady growth and accumulation of wealth in material production, primarily in heavy industry. Little new real value is created in the modern Russian economy, while the focus on virtual values facilitates the increase in such negative redistributional phenomenon as raiding. In addition to the function of redistribution, raiding is indicative of a high level and systemic corruption that eats away the Russian economy. Overall, raiding manifests the continuing process of the worker alienation from the means of production. This process of alienation takes place under the unstable structure of private property rights and is the fundamental process that underlies market transition.

Discussion and condemnation of raiding

The discussion of the raiding problem grows along with the growth in the raiding phenomenon. Law enforcement agencies take an active part in such discussions. For instance, a two-day seminar of the investigative bodies and operating forces of the Ministry of the Interior in the North-Western federal district took place in St. Petersburg. The major theme of the seminar was the process of investigating crimes linked to corporate raiding and committed in the process of hostile takeovers. The law enforcement agencies estimate the damage of raiding in 2008 at three-and-a-half billion rubles (over $100 million). This sum is insignificant for the Russian economy and even for the North-Western federal district. In 2007, there were many criminal cases related to raiding under police investigation. These cases were accumulated over the previous years. There were a total of 512 such cases, of which 130 cases were sent to court. In 2008, the number of such cases declined significantly to 352, of which only 52 were sent to court. By mid-2009, there were 152 criminal cases in process, linked to raiding in the North-Western federal district.[30] St. Petersburg, the second largest city in Russia, which was referred to as the criminal capital of Russia in the 1990s, is certainly not far behind Moscow in terms of hostile takeovers and raiding statistics.

The discussion of the raiding problem by law enforcement agencies, state and local authorities, and civil nongovernmental organizations takes place throughout Russia.[31] Since the cases of raiding were recorded in all of Russia's regions, the authorities, entrepreneurs, and civil activists react to this problem, including by discussing it in joint sessions, committees, and commissions. Local chambers of trade and commerce are especially active in organizing such events, meetings, and conferences. These chambers represent the interests of businessmen, and raiding threatens the normal functioning of businesses.[32] The problem of raiding is often linked with the problem of the recession of 2008 and 2009 in the Russian economy.[33] The whole process of discussing the raiding problem reminds one of

102   *Raiding in transition*

Soviet-type bureaucratic mechanisms invoked to react to unexpected problems. These meetings and discussions result in suggestions of preventive measures against raiding.[34] The effectiveness of such meetings and discussions remains unknown. The suggestions may be borrowed by different participants and travel from one meeting to the other.

Raiding and anti-raiding are actively discussed in police and prosecutors' offices.[35] The seriousness of the problem of raiding is being recognized at the highest levels of the state hierarchy, including the president. At the meeting of the Russian president with the leaders of the Federal Security Services (FSB) [Federal'naya sluzhba bezopasnosti, former KGB], Medvedev marked raiding in the banking sector and corruption as the two most serious problems that Russia faces.[36] The legislative organs also take the most active part in the discussion of raiding.[37] The Chair of the Council of the Federation, Sergei Mironov, addressed the Congress of Entrepreneurs entitled "Anti-Raiding 2008."[38] Similar to the reports presented in the media, the discussions link raiding to widespread corruption. There is an understanding that corruption is one of the necessary conditions or grounds for raiding to exist. Raiders are not considered as intellectual giants, evil geniuses of the stock market, but rather criminals acting in close cooperation with corrupt bureaucrats.

The essence of raiding is formulated in perhaps the most popular Russian magazine, "Ogonek":

> Raiders do not do anything intellectual. Simplistic schemes are realized by crooked entrepreneurs, real estate agents, and bureaucrats, well informed about the legal status of real estate or property and its owners. The unpunished successes of raiders are explained not by their diabolic sophistication, but by almost total widespread corruption among bureaucrats and law enforcement agencies.[39]

A typical scheme of raiding is based on the aggression and violence of private security agencies, the passive behavior of law enforcement agencies, and contradictory decisions of courts of different levels, regions, and jurisdictions. The examples of such schemes are numerous, including the raiding of small businesses, joint-stock companies, and state enterprises.[40]

President Putin personally takes part in anti-raiding campaigns and openly discusses the negative role that law enforcement agencies play in hostile takeovers. He acknowledges the fact that police agencies and particular officers pressure businesses and may in fact facilitate raiding of businesses, causing fear among businessmen and leaving their property unprotected by the state. In 2016, Putin suggested introducing criminal responsibility for law enforcement officers for violations of entrepreneurs' rights. In particular, President Putin stated that,

> It is necessary to reduce significantly the opportunities of unlawful criminal prosecution (of businessmen). Moreover, representatives of law enforcement agencies should carry personal responsibility for unjust actions that led to

destruction of a business. I think that this responsibility may include criminal responsibility.[41]

There is another side to this discussion, too. Businessmen, managers, owners of enterprises, and entrepreneurs discuss problems they face and the state comes in a negative light in these discussions. Moreover, many – if not most – of these problems and obstacles are created by the state apparatus. Out of fifteen areas of the business environment, the private sector in Russia cites tax rates as the biggest obstacle to its operations, followed by access to finance and corruption. Over one-third of firms in Russia, 36 percent, report tax rates as their biggest obstacle, compared to just about 10 percent of firms in other countries. For access to finance, 15 percent of the firms in the country rank it as the biggest obstacle. Over 8 percent of firms cite corruption is their biggest obstacle in the business environment. The areas of the business environment, estimated by the World Bank's Enterprise Survey include labor regulations, courts, crime, theft and disorder, electricity, tax administration, customs and trade regulations, access to land, transport, licensing and permits, poorly educated workers, informal competitors, political instability, corruption, access to finance, and tax rates.[42] The full ranking of the top business environment obstacles faced and reported by firms in Russia as compared to Europe and Central Asia regions in 2012 is presented in Figure 3.3.[43]

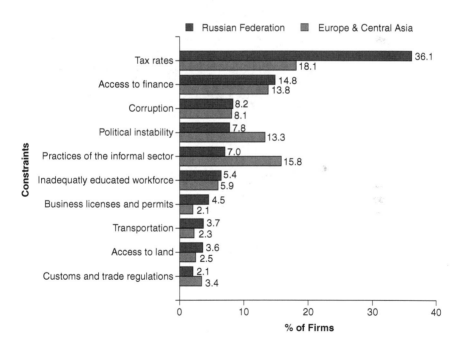

Figure 3.3 Ranking of the top business environment obstacles for firms in Russia and Europe and Central Asia regions, 2012

Source: Enterprise Surveys (www.enterprisesurveys.org), The World Bank

104 *Raiding in transition*

The full ranking of the top business environment obstacles for firms in Russia as compared to upper middle income group countries and the world in 2012 is presented in Figures 3.4 and 3.5, respectively.[44] As follows from results of surveys, worries about tax rates (36.1 percent) differentiate Russian businessmen as compared to their peers in Europe and Central Asia regions (18.1 percent), upper middle income group countries (13.4 percent), and the world (12.2 percent). At the same time, their worries about access to finance and corruption are about the same as those of their peers in the region, their income group, and the world average. It may sound confusing at first that in such an utterly corrupt country as Russia businessmen see corruption only as the third most significant obstacle for doing business, and not the first one. However, the corruption, coercion, and control model offered in this study serves as a perfect explanation for this seemingly confusing ranking of priorities.

High tax rates combined with confusing tax legislation and contradictory provisions make it very difficult – and sometimes virtually impossible – to comply with tax laws. The noncompliance, in its turn, leads to administrative and criminal responsibility of business owners and managers. This responsibility becomes a powerful tool in the hands of corrupt state bureaucrats. By using this leverage, top-ranking state officials exploit large corporations while street-level bureaucrats attack small enterprises. Business vulnerability based

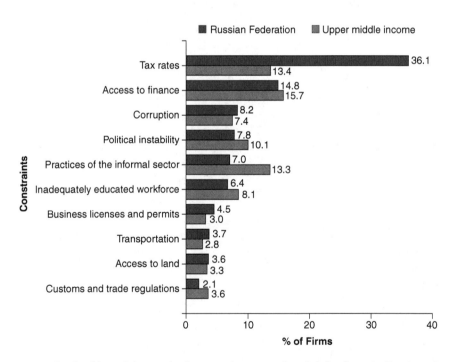

Figure 3.4 Ranking of the top business environment obstacles for firms in Russia and upper middle income group countries, 2012

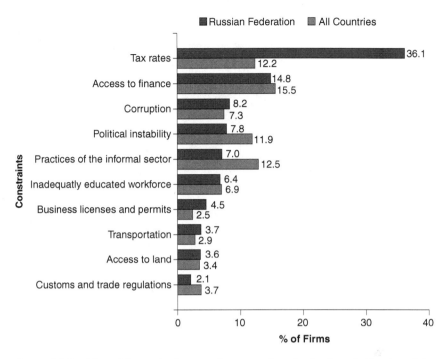

Figure 3.5 Ranking of the top business environment obstacles for firms in Russia and the world, 2012

on tax violations and selective justice forms the base for extortion and threats of hostile takeovers. In many instances, it is less costly for entrepreneurs to give bribes than to pay taxes.

The percentage of firms expected to give gifts during meetings with tax officials in Russia is incredibly small, only 7.3 percent, as compared to other countries in Europe and Central Asia regions. Comparisons with upper middle income group countries and the world averages bring similar results. This is of no surprise, since the corruption, coercion, and control scheme does not necessitate high pay to fiscal authorities. The percentage of firms expected to give gifts in meetings with tax officials in Russia and Europe and Central Asia regions in 2012 is presented in Figure 3.6.

It is also remarkable that political instability, so typical for the former Soviet bloc, is only the fourth most significant obstacle for doing business named by entrepreneurs in Russia. Only 7.8 percent of businessmen in Russia named political instability their primary concern when it comes to obstacles in doing business, as compared to 13.3 percent in Europe and Central Asia regions, 10.1 percent in upper middle income group countries, and 11.9 percent in the world. Russia's ruling authoritarian regime places significant effort in creating the illusion of stability, including political stability. Here, political stability is equated to sustainability

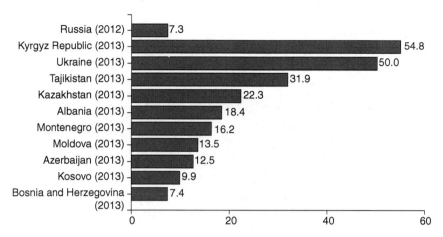

Figure 3.6 Percent of firms expected to give gifts in meetings with tax officials in Russia and Europe and Central Asia regions, 2012

of the ruling regime. Thus, businessmen are not much concerned with political instability, focusing instead on tax rates and corruption.

Access of entrepreneurs to financial resources is restricted not only by the undeveloped credit market, but by the need to give gifts in exchange for credits. The cost of regulation, measured by senior management's time spent dealing with government regulations, is higher in Russia compared to other countries. For an average firm, 15 percent of the senior management's time is consumed complying with regulations, considerably higher than the world average of 9 percent.[45] Obtaining key public services, such as licenses required to import products from abroad, construction permits, and connections to electricity grid and water supply networks is more difficult in Russia than in many other countries. An average firm in Russia waits for over four months to secure a construction permit, twice the figure for other countries and four times longer than in China. Gifts and informal payments are still indispensable to obtain key public services – water and electric connections. Over one quarter of firms in Russia report that informal gifts are needed to secure electricity connections, about nine times the figure reported as the average in the upper middle income countries' group, to which Russia belongs.

It is obvious that corrupt law enforcement agencies cannot fight themselves effectively in an attempt to eradicate unlawful corporate raiding, especially if they profit from it. The solution might be in developing institutions of civil society. Kazun (2014) suggests that the best way to improve the situation with property rights protection and reduce violent corporate raiding in Russia is to increase the risks for raiders by developing civil mechanisms for the protection of entrepreneurs. Such mechanisms will include, for example, business associations and other NGOs. This suggestion is similar to that of Duvanova (2013) and Markus (2015).

Unfortunately, Russia lacks civil society, its culture and principles. Moreover, the ruling authoritarian regime suppresses any serious attempts at constructing civil society in the country as it perceives civil society initiatives as threatening to the regime's sustainability.

3.3 Concluding remarks

Drawing the conclusion for the general characteristics of the raiding phenomenon in Russia, this study would like to highlight the following. As of today, there is still no uniform portrait of a raider organization, a pattern under which one could try to fit different players of the market in order to classify them as raiders or otherwise. Raider organizations wear many guises and have many faces. Raiders may be individuals holding public office or positions in business and skillfully using this position, connections, and capital in order to conduct appropriation and alienation of someone else's property with the use of nonmarket mechanisms and corruption schemes. This stratum of economic agents includes both hostile invaders of apartments that belong to old retirees and prominent leaders of entire notorious raiding companies whose names represent the raider business and are synonymous to raiding as perceived by local businessmen. Raiding engages teams of associates and complete specialized firms, which include lawyers, financiers, and accountants. Often these groups and firms acquire someone else's property on order for their customers. They themselves are not the new owners but rather operators on the property market, offering raiding services. The range of their interests includes only assets ordered for takeover by their firms' customers, including land, enterprises, public facilities, and real estate.

Large companies, holding companies, and financial-industrial groups can also engage in raiding, although not as the main type of their business activity, but rather because of the need for further expansion and business development. This may include elimination of competitors, monopolization of the market segment, alienation of land for future construction and exploration and development of mineral deposits, and the seizure of buildings for the company's headquarters. Large firms also capture entire enterprises, not for resale, as is the case with specialized raider companies, but for their own use. All these groups belong to the outside raiders or external raiders. Enterprises can face internal raiders as well. These are insiders and include first of all business leaders who have a tendency to lay their hands on the company. Insider raiders raid their own firms with the use of deception of the company's employees and fraud committed with the assistance of external agents. Their advantage is that they have access to all the charter documents, knowledge of management schemes, the structure of the company and its financial status, and also have the ability to manage enterprise assets. The intentional bankruptcy is a classic example of an internally planned and staged raid. In cases of internal or insider raiding the notion of information as a valuable asset is clearly distinguished. Raiders may be business partners and small shareholders. Here, open access to information about the company, possessed by the insiders, also plays a significant role.

108 *Raiding in transition*

Methods of raiders include actions punishable as crimes. The most obvious methods of raiders include document fraud, falsification of protocols of shareholder meetings, production of signatures, bribery of the state registry officers and state bureaucrats, and production of false documents. One of the popular methods of this kind is production of fraudulent court decisions, handed down in a distant region. Raiding is now traditionally being divided into three types: "black," "grey," and "white." Such a gamut apparently reflects the degree of darkness of different elements of raiding, from most violent and illegal to almost legal or even perfectly legal. It appears that while in the West raiders act within the acceptable legal limits, in the post-Soviet space legal actions of raiders are oftentimes not considered as raiding at all. Both entrepreneurs and ordinary people suffer from raiders. Entrepreneurial activities are aimed at receiving profit. However, raiders are often interested not in the profit that a firm receives from its business activities, but in extracting profit from a hostile takeover and sale of certain valuable economic assets, be it an enterprise, real estate, a housing unit, or any other asset that has market value. Accordingly, entrepreneurs who do not own any material assets are unlikely to be targeted by raiders. At the same time, those individuals who own certain assets, such as housing, are potential objects of raiding attacks.

Open public discussion of the raiding problem is increasing, along with the growth in the raiding phenomenon. Law enforcement agencies take an active part in such discussions. The discussion of the raiding problem by law enforcement agencies, state and local authorities, and civil nongovernmental organizations takes place throughout Russia. Since the cases of raiding were recorded in all of Russia's regions, the state authorities, entrepreneurs, and civil activists react to this problem, including by discussing it in joint sessions, committees, and commissions. Local chambers of trade and commerce are especially active in organizing such events, meetings, and conferences. These chambers represent the interests of businessmen, and since raiding threatens the normal functioning of businesses, it is of their concern. The problem of raiding is often linked to the recession of 2008 and 2009 in the Russian economy. The whole process of discussing the raiding problem reminds one of Soviet-type bureaucratic mechanisms invoked to react to unexpected problems. These meetings and discussions result in suggestions of preventive measures against raiding. At the same time, the effectiveness of such meetings and discussions remains largely unknown.

Concerns about high tax rates differentiate Russian businessmen from their peers in Europe and Central Asia regions, upper middle income group countries, and the world. At the same time, their worries about access to finance and corruption are about the same as those of their peers in the region, their income group, and the world. It may sound confusing at first that in such a highly corrupt country as Russia, businessmen see corruption only as the third most significant obstacle for doing business. The corruption, coercion, and control model serves as a perfect explanation for this seemingly confusing ranking of priorities. High tax rates combined with confusing tax legislation and contradictory provisions make it very difficult or even impossible to comply with tax laws. The noncompliance, in its turn, leads to administrative and criminal responsibility of business owners and managers. This responsibility becomes a powerful tool in hands of corrupt state bureaucrats. By using this leverage, top-ranking state officials exploit large corporations while street-level bureaucrats attack small enterprises. Business vulnerability based on tax violations and selective justice forms the base for extortion and threats of hostile takeovers. In many instances, it is less costly for entrepreneurs to give bribes to state officials than to pay taxes to the state budget.

Given the high level of corruption in law enforcement agencies, it should not be expected that these agencies will literally fight themselves – and do so effectively – in an attempt to eradicate unlawful corporate raiding, especially if officers of law enforcement agencies benefit from it directly. The solution might be in developing institutions of civil society, including those aimed at protecting private property rights of entrepreneurs. At present, however, this solution appears to be unrealistic; Russia lacks civil society, its culture and principles. It is remarkable that political instability, so typical for the former Soviet bloc, is only the fourth most significant obstacle for doing business named by entrepreneurs in Russia. Russia's ruling authoritarian regime places significant effort in creating the illusion of stability, including political stability. Here, political stability is equated to sustainability of the ruling regime. Thus, businessmen are not much concerned with political instability, focusing instead on tax rates and corruption. Furthermore, the ruling authoritarian regime suppresses any attempts at constructing civil society in the country as it perceives civil society initiatives as being threatening to the regime's sustainability.

Notes

1 See, for instance: Malyj biznes v opasnosti: reidery zahvatyvayut magaziny i himchistki [Small business is in danger: Raiders take over stores and laundries]. *Vedomosti*, 2(26), July 12, 2007. Retrieved May 14, 2009, from www.vedomostivuz.ru/article.shtml?2007/07/12/4101

   Kak ukrast' osobnyak [How to steal a mansion]. *Vek*, June 4, 2009. Retrieved July 22, 2009, from www.notheft.ru/kak-ukrast-osobnjak

2 Sukhorukova, Natal'ya. (2008). Reiderskij ohvat [Raiding reach]. *Vremya i Den'gi*, 147(2848), August 7, 2008. Retrieved August 7, 2008, from www.e-vid.ru/index-m-192-p-63-article-24438.htm

3 V Pskove reidery proyavlyayut povyshennyj interes k OAO "Pskovskij hlebokombinat" [In Pskov, raiders are especially interested in a city bakery plant "Pskovskij hlebokombinat"]. *Notheft.ru*, March 27, 2009. Retrieved July 22, 2009, from www.notheft.ru/v-pskove-rejdery-projavljajut-povyshennyj-interes-k-oao-%C2%ABpskovskij-hlebokombinat%C2%BB

4 Novaya ataka reiderov zahlestnula "AGRO-Trast" v Omskoj oblasti [A new raiding attack on "AGRO-Trast" in Omskaya oblast']. *Notheft.ru*, March 4, 2009. Retrieved July 22, 2009, from www.notheft.ru/novaja-ataka-rejderov-zahlestnula-%C2%ABagro-trast%C2%BB-v-omskoj-oblasti

5 V Kemerovo idet ataka reiderov na zdanie TSZh [There is a raiding attack on the TSZh building going on in Kemerovo]. *Notheft.ru*, March 2, 2009. Retrieved July 22, 2009, from www.notheft.ru/v-kemerovo-idet-ataka-rejderov-na-zdanie-tszh

6 V Kazani uchastniki organizovanoj prestupnoj gruppy reiderov pohitili bole 91 milliona rublej [In Kazan, members of the organized criminal group stole over 91 million rubles]. *Notheft.ru*, December 18, 2008. Retrieved July 22, 2009, from www.notheft.

110 *Raiding in transition*

ru/v-kazani-uchastniki-organizovannoj-prestupnoj-gruppy-rejderov-pohitili-bolee-91-milliona-rublej

7 V Yaroslavskoj oblasti predprinimateli stradayut ot reiderskih atak [In Yaroslavskaya oblast' entrepreneurs suffer of raiding attacks]. *Notheft.ru*, December 9, 2008. Retrieved July 22, 2009, from www.notheft.ru/v-yaroslavskoj-oblasti-predprinimateli-stradajut-ot-rejderskih-atak

8 Stenka na stenku, kak v 90-e: v Chelyabinskoj oblasti proizoshel rejderskij zakhvat gradoobrazuyushchego zavoda [Gang on gang, as in the 1990s: In Chelyabinskaya oblast', a hostile takeover of a major plant took place]. *Newsru.com*, February 24, 2015. Retrieved February 24, 2015, from www.newsru.com/russia/24feb2015/zavod.html

9 *Merriam-Webster's New Explorer Encyclopedic Dictionary.* (2006). Springfield, MA: Federal Street Press; Merriam-Webster On-Line Dictionary. Raider. Retrieved from www.merriam-webster.com/dictionary/raider

10 Krajnov, Yaroslav. (2008). Istoriya reiderstva: osobennosti natsional'nogo peredela [History of raiding: Specifics of national raiding]. *Notheft.ru*, July 17, 2008. Retrieved July 26, 2009, from www.notheft.ru/istorija-rejderstva-osobennosti-nacionalnogo-peredela

11 Sledstvie: zamdirektora oboronnogo predpriyatiya izobrel novuyu shemu vymogatel'stva – "pravozashchitnuyu" [The investigation: The deputy-director of a defense industry plant invented a new scheme of extortion – "right watch"]. *Newsru.com*, July 5, 2010. Retrieved July 5, 2010, from www.newsru.com/russia/05jul2010/baranovsky.html

12 Reiderstvo kak sotsial'no-ekonomicheskij i politicheskij fenomen sovremennoj Rossii: otchet o kachestvennom sotsiologicheskom issledovanii. Issledovanie "Tsentra politicheskih tehnologij" pod rukovodstvom Bunina. Moskva, 2008. [Raiding as a socioeconomic and political phenomenon of the modern Russia: A report on the qualitative sociological investigation: An investigation conducted by the Center of Political Technologies led by Bunin]. Moscow, May 2008. Retrieved June 12, 2009, from www.politcom.ru/; www.compromat.ru/main/mix1/raiderycpt.htm

13 Reiderstvo vstanet v odin ryad s korruptsiej [Raiding will stand in one line with corruption]. *Nezavisimaya gazeta*, May 23, 2008. Retrieved July 26, 2009, from www.notheft.ru/rejderstvo-vstanet-v-odin-rjad-s-korupciej

14 Kvasha, Maksim. (2007). "Partiju dlya nas olitsetvoriaet silovoj blok, kotory vozglavliaet Igor' Ivanovich Sechin" – glava Finansgrupp Oleg Shvartsman o novykh dobrovol'no-prinuditel'nykh sposobakh konsolidatsii aktivov v rukakh gosudarstva ["The party for us is represented by the power bloc, led by Igor Ivanovich Sechin" – the head of Finansgrupp, Oleg Shvartsman, told in an interview about new voluntary-forceful ways of consolidation of assets in the hands of the state]. *Kommersant*, 221(3797), November 30, 2007. Retrieved May 9, 2009, from www.kommersant.ru/doc.aspx?DocsID=831089

15 Zhiteli odnoj iz vladivostokskih novostroek stali zhertvami "ser'eznyh razborok" [Dwellers of one of Vladivostok's new buildings became victims of "serious debates"]. *Notheft.ru*, December 17, 2008. Retrieved July 22, 2009, from http://roscrime.ru/zhiteli-odnoj-iz-vladivostokskih-novostroek-stali-zhertvami-sereznyh-razborok

16 Poltavsky, Dmitriy. (2008). Reiderstvo ili stil' vedeniya biznesa v Rossii? [Raiding or a style of making business in Russia?]. *BBC*, June 24, 2008. Retrieved June 24, 2008, from http://news.bbc.co.uk/hi/russian/uk/newsid_7470000/7470519.stm

17 V Ul'yanovskoj oblasti predotvrashchen reiderskij zahvat predpriyatiya [An attempt of a hostile takeover was averted in Ul'yanovskaya oblast']. *IA REGNUM*, June 24, 2008. Retrieved July 26, 2009, from www.regnum.ru/news/1018297.html

GUVD: reidery trizhdy pytalis' zahvatit' nizhegorodskie predpriyatiya [GUVD: Raiders made three attempts to take over enterprises in Nizhny Novgorod]. *Rosbalt*, July 25, 2008. Retrieved July 22, 2009, from www.rosbalt.ru/2008/07/25/507496.html

18 S nachala goda v stolitse zafiksirovano 49 sluchaev reiderstva [49 cases of raiding have been registered in the capitol since the beginning of the year]. *Newsru.com*, July 20, 2006. Retrieved May 9, 2009, from www.newsru.com/finance/20jul2006/raider.html

Raiding in transition 111

19 FNS vvela v internete servis dlia zashchity kompanij ot reiderov [The Federal Tax Services office (FNS) introduced an internet service intended to protect companies from raiders]. *Newsru.com*, March 26, 2007. Retrieved May 9, 2009, from www.newsru.com/finance/26mar2007/fns_raiders.html

20 Kazhdy god v Rossii proishodit bolee tysiachi reiderskih zahvatov [Every year in Russia, there are over a thousand raiding takeovers taking place]. *Newsru.com*, May 21, 2008. Retrieved May 9, 2009, from http://realty.newsru.com/article/21May2008/raid

21 Composed by the author based on the data from Social and Economic Indicators of the Russian Federation: 1991–2014, Appendix to the "Statistical Yearbook of Russia. 2015," Section 11, Privatization. Moscow: Federal State Statistics Services. Retrieved March 1, 2017, from www.gks.ru/wps/wcm/connect/rosstat_main/rosstat/en/main/; Privatization. Russia in Figures. Moscow: Federal State Statistics Service Yearbook, 2016, p. 230. Retrieved March 1, 2017, from www.gks.ru/free_doc/doc_2016/rusfig/rus16e.pdf; http://cbsd.gks.ru/

22 V Rossii kazhdyj god proishodit tysyacha reiderskih zahvatov [Every year in Russia, there are a thousand raiding takeovers taking place]. *Novye Izvestiya*, May 21, 2008. Retrieved May 9, 2009, from www.newizv.ru/news/2008-05-21/90363/

23 Harding, Luke. (2008). Raiders of the Russian Billions. *The Guardian*, June 24, 2008. Retrieved May 9, 2009, from www.guardian.co.uk/world/2008/jun/24/russia.internationalcrime

24 Deputaty Gosdumy predlagajut propisat' v UK RF poniatie "reiderstva" [Members of the State Duma suggest to include the term "raiding" in the Criminal Code of the RF]. *Newsru.com*, November 13, 2008. Retrieved May 9, 2009, from www.newsru.com/finance/13nov2008/reiderstvo.html

25 Deputaty Gosdumy i predstaviteli TPP RF obsudili popravki v zakon, regulirujushchij rynok sliyanij i pogloshchenij [The members of the State Duma and representatives of the Trade and Commerce Chamber of the Russian Federation discussed amendments to the law that regulates the market of mergers and acquisitions]. *Newsru.com*, October 17, 2006. Retrieved May 9, 2009, from www.newsru.com/finance/17oct2006/nedrug.html

26 V Moskve okolo 80% kommercheskih firm zaregistrirovany na podstavnyh lits [In Moscow, around 80 percent of all firms are registered on fake owners]. *Newsru.com*, April 6, 2005. Retrieved May 9, 2009, from www.newsru.com/crime/06apr2005/podstava.html

27 MVD rasskazalo o zahvatah predpriyatij v Rossii [MVD told about hostile takeovers of firms in Russia]. *Newsru.com*, February 9, 2006. Retrieved May 9, 2009, from www.newsru.com/finance/09feb2006/mvd.html

28 Reiderstvo vstanet v odin ryad s korruptsiej [Raiding will stand in one line with corruption]. *Nezavisimaya gazeta*, May 23, 2008. Retrieved July 26, 2009, from www.notheft.ru/rejderstvo-vstanet-v-odin-rjad-s-korupciej

29 Departament ekonomicheskoj bezopasnosti MVD Rossii otmechaet tendentsiyu "uhoda" reiderskih struktur v region [Department of Economic Security of MVD Russia notes the trend of raiders "moving" to regions]. *Prime-TASS*, March 17, 2008. Retrieved May 9, 2009, from www.prime-tass.ru/news/show.asp?id=766590&ct=news

30 Ushcherb ot reiderskih atak v proshlom godu sostavil 3.5 mlrd rubley [The damage from raiding attacks during the last year is estimated at 3.5 billion rubles]. *Notheft.ru*, June 25, 2009. Retrieved July 22, 2009, from www.notheft.ru/ushherb-ot-rejderskih-atak-v-proshlom-godu-sostavil-35-mlrd-rublej

31 V Sverdlovskoj oblasti sostoyalos' zasedanie komiteta po promyshlennoj i agrarnoj politike, na kotorom obsudili reiderstvo [A meeting of the Industrial and Agrarian Policies Committee was held in Sverdlovskaya oblast' to discuss raiding]. *Notheft.ru*, March 15, 2009. Retrieved July 22, 2009, from www.notheft.ru/v-sverdlovskoj-oblasti-sostojalos-zasedanie-komiteta-po-promyshlennoj-i-agrarnoj-politike-na-kotorom

32 V Saratovskoj oblasti sostoyalos' zasedanie Komiteta po bezopasnosti v TPP, na kotorom obsudili problemu reiderstva [A meeting of the Security in TPP committee

112　*Raiding in transition*

was held in Saratov oblast' to discuss the problem of raiding]. *Notheft.ru*, March 4, 2009. Retrieved July 22, 2009, from www.notheft.ru/v-saratovskoj-oblasti-sostojalos-zasedanie-komiteta-po-bezopasnosti-v-tpp-na-kotorom-obsudili-proble

33 V Barnaule obsudyat problem krizisa i reiderstva [Problems of crisis and raiding will be discussed in Barnaul]. *Notheft.ru*, November 12, 2008. Retrieved July 22, 2009, from www.notheft.ru/v-barnaule-obsudjat-problemy-krizisa-i-rejderstva

34 Predlozheniya po povysheniyu effektivnosti bor'by s reiderstvom (nezakonnym zahvatom sobstvennosti) [Suggestions for anti-raiding campaign (illegal hostile takeovers of property)]. *Notheft.ru*, September 17, 2008. Retrieved July 22, 2009, from www.notheft.ru/predlozhenija-po-povysheniju-jeffektivnosti-borby-s-rejderstvom-nezakonnym-zahvatom-sobstvennosti

35 UVD po Murmanskoy oblasti i Obshchestvennyj sovet pri UVD proveli kruglyj stol po problemam bor'by s reiderstvom [UVD in Murmanskaya oblasti and Obshchestvenny sovet of UVD organized a roundtable discussion of raiding problems and anti-raiding strategies]. *Notheft.ru*, January 14, 2009. Retrieved July 22, 2009, from www.notheft. ru/uvd-po-murmanskoj-oblasti-i-obshhestvennyj-sovet-pri-uvd-proveli-kruglyj-stol-po-problemam-borby-s-r

36 Na rasshirennom zasedanii kollegii FSB Dmitry Medvedev oboznachil glavnye problemy strany: reiderstvo bankov i korruptsiyu [Dmitry Medvedev pointed to two major problems in the country: Bank raiding and corruption, during the meeting in the FSB]. *Notheft.ru*, January 31, 2009. Retrieved July 22, 2009, from www.notheft.ru/na-rasshirennom-zasedanii-kollegii-fsb-dmitrij-medvedev-oboznachil-glavnye-problemy-strany-rejderstv

37 V Gosdume pogovorili o probleme reiderstva i reshili, chto antireiderskie zakony budut prinyaty v kontse 2008 goda [The problem of raiding was discussed in the State Duma: It was decided that the anti-raiding laws will be adopted at the end of 2008]. *Notheft.ru*, November 14, 2008. Retrieved July 22, 2009, from www.notheft.ru/v-gosdume-pogov orili-o-probleme-rejderstva-i-reshili-chto-antirejderskie-zakony-budut-prinjaty-v-kon

38 Predsedatel' Soveta Federatsii Sergej Mironov vystupil na kongresse predprinimatelej "Antireiderstvo-2008" [Chair of the council of federation, Sergej Mironov, gave a talk to the congress of entrepreneurs "anti-raiding 2008"]. *Notheft.ru*, November 24, 2008. Retrieved July 22, 2009, from www.notheft.ru/predsedatel-soveta-federacii-sergej-mironov-vystupil-na-kongresse-predprinimatelej-%C2%ABantirejderstvo-2

39 Moskvin, Oleg. (2009). Otnyat' i podelit': tri syuzheta iz istorii piterskogo rejderstva [To take away and split: Three stories about St. Petersburg raiding]. *Ogonek*, 16(5094), August 31, 2009, pp. 20–24.

40 Reidery dokazyvayut svoyu pravotu rukoprikladstvom [Raiders prove their rights with fists]. *Notheft.ru*, December 29, 2008. Retrieved July 22, 2009, from www.notheft.ru/ rejdery-dokazyvajut-svoju-pravotu-rukoprikladstvom

41 Putin predlozhil vvesti ugolovnuyu otvetstvennost' dlya silovikov za narushenie prav predprinimatelej [Putin suggested introducing criminal responsibility for law enforcement officers for violations of entrepreneurs' rights]. *Newsru.com*, June 17, 2016. Retrieved June 17, 2016, from www.newsru.com/russia/17jun2016/siloviki.html

42 The World Bank interviewed a representative sample of the private sector composed of 4,220 business establishments during August 2011 and June 2012 across the Russian Federation: The Enterprise Survey covers several topics of the business environment as well as performance measures for each firm. Enterprise Surveys. The World Bank. Washington, DC. Retrieved March 1, 2017, from www.enterprisesurveys.org/~/media/ GIAWB/EnterpriseSurveys/Documents/CountryHighlights/Russia-2012.pdf

43 Enterprise Surveys. The World Bank. Washington, DC. Retrieved March 1, 2017, from www.enterprisesurveys.org/Graphing-Tool

44 Ibid.

45 Enterprise Surveys. The World Bank. Washington, DC. Retrieved March 1, 2017, from www.enterprisesurveys.org/~/media/GIAWB/EnterpriseSurveys/Documents/ CountryHighlights/Russia-2012.pdf

References

Bunin, Igor. (2008). Reiderstvo kak sotsial'no-ekonomicheskij i politicheskij fenomen sovremennoj Rossii: otchet o kachestvennom sotsiologicheskom issledovanii. Issledovanie "Tsentra politicheskih tehnologij" pod rukovodstvom Bunina. Moskva, 2008. [Raiding as a Socio-Economic and Political Phenomenon of the Modern Russia: A Report on the Qualitative Sociological Investigation: An Investigation Conducted by the Center of Political Technologies Led by Bunin]. Moscow, May 2008. Retrieved June 12, 2009, from www.politcom.ru/; www.compromat.ru/main/mix1/raiderycpt.htm

Demekhin, Aleksey. (2010). Tehnologii reiderstva v usloviyah ekonomicheskogo krizisa [Raiding during the Economic Crisis]. *Yurist*, February 2, 2010. Retrieved February 2, 2010, from www.gazeta-yurist.ru/article.php?i=982

Duvanova, Dinissa. (2013). *Building Business in Post-Communist Russia, Eastern Europe and Eurasia: Collective Goods, Selective Incentives, and Predatory States.* New York: Cambridge University Press.

Kazun, Anton. (2014). Violent Corporate Raiding in Russia: Preconditions and Protective Factors. *Demokratizatsiya: The Journal of Post-Soviet Democratization*, 23(4), pp. 459–484.

Markus, Stanislav. (2015). *Property, Predation, and Protection: Piranha Capitalism in Russia and Ukraine.* New York: Cambridge University Press.

Neutze, Jan. & Karatnicky, Adrian. (2007). Corruption, Democracy, and Investment in Ukraine. The Atlantic Council of the US, Policy Paper, October 2007.

Osipian, Ararat. (2012). Predatory Raiding in Russia: Institutions and Property Rights after the Crisis. *Journal of Economic Issues*, 46(2), pp. 469–479.

Rumyantseva, Anastasiya & Meshkov, Sergei. (2014). Dekompozitsiya reiderstva v sfere intellektual'noj sobstvennosti [Specifics of Raiding in the Sphere of Intellectual Property]. *Sotsial'no-ekonomicheskie yavleniya i protsessy*, 59(1), pp. 86–91.

Tkachenko, N.I. & Lobodenko, M.U. (2007). Mekhanizm provedennya rejders'kyh atak ta shemy zahoplennya biznesu yak chinnyk ekonomichnoji nebezpeky diyal'nosti sub'yektiv gospodaryuvannya [Mechanism of Conducting Raiding Attacks and Schemes of Taking over Business as a Factor of Economic Insecurity for Economic Agents and Firms]. *Nauchnye trudy DonNTU. Ekonomicheskie nauki*, 31(3), pp. 211–215.

Varnalij, Zakharij & Mazur, Irina. (2007). Reiderstvo v Ukraini: peredumovy ta shlyahi podolannya. *Strategichni Pryoritety*, 2(3), pp. 129–136. Retrieved April 2, 2009, from www.niss.gov.ua/book/StrPryor/3/17.pdf

4 Corruption and raiding

4.1 Links between corruption and raiding

Ties between corruption and raiding

Corporate and property raiding in Russia would be impossible without widespread corruption at all levels of state bureaucracy. Raiding is the art of taking over someone else's asset in such a way that the whole operation would create an impression of legitimacy and legality. State decisions that legitimize actions of raiders are rendered by state bureaucrats in corrupt ways. In some cases, these are personal business interests and stakes that state bureaucrats have in such endeavors, while in other instances these are mere bribes given by raiders. Russian mass media openly and explicitly points to the fact that raiding "simply cannot exist without a no less negative phenomenon, that of corruption. In order to take over someone else's enterprise, one would need either a favorable court decision or a 'friendly' position of the authorities, or both."[1] The mass media says that modern Russian raiding is characterized by its wide and active use of the so-called "administrative resource," i.e. abilities of state bureaucrats and corrupt law enforcement agencies to influence the situation. Raiding in Russia is to a large extent connected to the autocratic actions of state bureaucrats performed under the cover of their official duties.[2] Raiders use discretionary powers of state bureaucrats in order to obtain certain documents and decisions that would help them to conduct hostile takeovers. Needless to say, such unlawful decisions, or in some instances simply inaction, are bought, i.e. obtained in exchange for bribes.

In developed nations, institutionally organized civil activists, known as the nongovernmental sector, facilitate and maintain an informal system of oversight of governmental actions. This system helps confront corruption with transparency and accountability. Russia's nongovernmental sector is extremely weak and undeveloped. Nevertheless, civil activists and nongovernmental organizations become involved and try to attract attention to the problem of insecure property and corporate raiding. The National Anti-Corruption Committee (NAK) [Natsional'ny antikorruptsionny komitet], a civil nongovernmental organization

Based in Russia, together with the "Feniks" company presented a report entitled "Suggestions for a More Effective Fight against Raiding." The major conclusion of this report is that the key role in hostile takeovers belongs to corrupt state officials and civil servants. Corrupt bureaucrats provide raiders with the necessary information, legalize their operations, organize pressure on the lawful owner and block his or her work. A co-author of the report, the director of the Russian Office of Transparency International, Elena Panfilova, says this document was written because the Russian authorities declared the fight against corruption separate from the fight against raiding. Panfilova says that "our goal was to prove that in essence it is all the same, that corruption is the essential part of raiding."[3] Criminal raiding would be almost impossible to commit without the assistance of corrupt bureaucrats exercising their authority in wrongful ways.

According to the study, conducted in 2008 by the Center of Political Technologies (Moscow), corruption is named by the respondents and experts as one of the most significant, or even the most significant cause of raiding in Russia (Bunin, 2008). Respondents identified several important causes of widespread raiding, among which is widespread corruption. A large-scale corruption, weak law enforcement and justice system, including corrupt courts, have been named as one of the major causes of raiding. Another cause of raiding is a weak legislative base. Clearly, Russia's legal system needs more work.

In addition to legal problems, economic issues are also at the base of the raiding phenomenon. An increase in wealth and asset valuation, including production facilities, real estate, and land, attract raiders and cause raiding to grow in scale and scope. Ineffective use of property, caused by the fact that property in Russia remains vulnerable, brings economic inefficiencies. Property is something that may be taken away by raiders, especially if it is not real estate or land. A low level of entrepreneurial culture may also be one of the indirect underlying causes of raiding. Business owners think a lot about developing their business and building relations with state officials, but much less about a potential risk of a hostile takeover. Tied to legislative developments, weakness of market institutions remains one of the important characteristics of the Russian business environment. The existing market institutions, in experts' view, are not the real regulators in the pseudo-market environment of modern Russia. Respondents also name apathy, indifference, passive social position, ignorance, and sometimes even aggressive behavior and low tolerance on the side of the public regarding successful businessmen and private property in principle.

An extremely high level of corruption combined with weak legislative initiatives of the state and a low level of trust among businessmen and the public constitute the base of raiding. Varnalij and Mazur (2007) highlight the following causes of raiding: weakness of the law enforcement system and the justice system; high level of corruption in the organs of state authority; absence of state institutions that would protect property rights; a low level of legal culture; legal nihilism that can be found among both entrepreneurs and representatives of the state authority; and a dubious history of privatization. It was already in the 1990s that

116   *Corruption and raiding*

privatization was recognized as unfair, unjust, ineffective, and wasteful. Glaz'ev (1997) points out in this regard that,

> As a result of strong criminalization of the mass privatization of state property and orientation of the participants of the privatization process on speculative and high profits, another important mechanism of economic growth was blocked. This mechanism includes economic motivation of the owner of the means of production. Organizers of the privatization campaign and their business partners oriented themselves to speculative and high revenues obtained from re-sale of shares of significantly undervalued enterprises. The majority of privatized enterprises still do not have owners interested in their development. At the same time the state budget lost hundreds of trillions of rubles in potential revenues from privatization.
>
> (p. 116)

The institution of private property, established in 1991 as one of the components of the market reform, is being undermined by bureaucratic corruption.

The presence of a large-scale raiding lowers the qualitative characteristics of the external business environment by increasing risks to businessmen. This risky and hostile environment in turn impacts businesses' competitiveness and investment attractiveness. It also hurts stability and persistency of economic growth in the Russian economy experienced on all levels of interaction of economic actors. The pace of development of the institutionalized raiding is determined by the specifics of the national model of regulating the institution of private property, the process and results of privatization, the degree of development of the market for corporate control, information transparency of management, and levels of conflicts that emerge in conducting business.

In view of the respondents of the Center for Political Technologies, the degree of danger of raiding is determined by several factors, including levels of violence, corruption, criminalization of the national economy, risks for investors, and economic damages.[4] Violent and corrupt property redistribution is linked to the corrupt law enforcement agencies and courts. Raiding serves as a source of legalization of criminal segments of the national economy. At the same time, raiding does not deal with developing the real sector of the economy and is not aimed at solving real economic problems in the country. To the contrary, raiding diverts economic and organizational efforts of many individuals and thus can exhaust the economy.

Case studies of corruption and economic development presented in Rose-Ackerman and Søreide (2011) focus on different countries that represent diverse cultures. Such heavy-weights as Brazil, India, Nigeria, and the USA are beneficially supplemented with smaller and more exotic nations such as Sao Tome and Principe. The strong focus on variety only underscores the importance of corruption and the context in which it occurs. The authors state that, "[O]ne must study corruption in context. Understanding the consequences of corrupt transactions requires one to know what is being bought with a bribe and how the behavior of public and private actors has been affected" (Rose-Ackerman and Søreide, 2011,

p. xiv). Russia's context is such that widespread corruption exists on the background of bleak economic growth frequently interrupted with financial downfalls.

Compared with developed nations, in developing and transition economies economic growth does not preclude increase in corruption. Wedeman (2012) attempts to resolve the contradiction between the worsening corruption and continuing rapid economic growth that has been taking place in China for almost three decades now. To start the analysis, he accepts the definition of corruption as "the improper use of public authority for private gain or advantage" (Wedeman, 2012, p. 1). The author points out that corruption, while not unknown during the Maoist period, flourished after the introduction of market reforms and even more so after these reforms gained momentum. Wedeman (2012) then formulates his "double paradox": "the core issue was not whether one could have corruption and growth ... but how it was possible to sustain rapid growth given high levels of predatory corruption in which officials seem to be engaged in looting the economy" (p. xi). Indeed, the case of China overturns a standard and empirically tested economists' supposition that there is a consistent negative correlation between corruption and growth. Similar to Russia, China also experiences high and steady levels of corruption, corporate raiding, and numerous property rights violations. However, in distinction from Russia, in China these negative phenomena are only secondary to steady and significant economic growth.

In Russia, with its authoritarian ruling regime, economic dynamics may appear secondary to the overwhelming task of sustaining the regime through corruption and volatility of property rights. Given the conflicting law environment and informational asymmetries, building institutional capacity remains one of the primary tasks. Pistor and Xu (2004) point out that in transition economies, including Russia and China, "[t]he incompleteness of law problem and the information problem are both more severe than in developed market economies" (p. 172). Yadav (2011) focuses on case studies of the two largest emerging democracies, Brazil and India, and supplements these cases with a sample of other developing nations, some of which are rapidly growing, while others are stagnating. She uses the data that span a two-decade period from 1984 to 2004 in analysis supported by interviews and surveys in order to discover differences in corrupt systems in developing nations.

Power and Taylor (2011) address corruption and democracy in Brazil, focusing on presidentialism, coalitions, accountability, corruption and political voting, campaign finance, reelection, the role of the media in political accountability, auditing and auditing institutions, federal judiciary and electoral courts, federal police, federalism, state criminal justice systems, and the web of accountability institutions, calling corruption "a troubling constant in the Brazilian political system" (p. 1). Courts in Russia are not independent, suggests Ledeneva (2004a, 2004b). And without independent courts, it is hard to fight corruption and raiding, especially state-initiated raiding. At the same time, and surprisingly, international assessments recognize that Russian legislation is compliant with the Model Law on International Commercial Arbitration (Chapaev, 2007, p. 13). Such a mismatch is hard to explain, unless one is to take into consideration a much more significant mismatch with what is written on paper in Russia and the way things are really done.

118   *Corruption and raiding*

Raiding decreases Russia's attractiveness for foreign investors, because raiding is an additional risk for investments. As such, raiding undermines the prestige of Russia on the world scene. In fact, the damage to the country's image is so significant that it creates obstacles for the innovation policies of the state. Despite the clearly negative impact of raiding on Russia's economy, precise economic damages caused by raiding are hard to estimate. This is due to the fact that raiding oftentimes carries latent, hidden forms. Raiding has some negative societal consequences as well: it increases the level of corruption in the state apparatus and thus undermines social cohesion. Also, some employees of raided enterprises lose their jobs due to economically unjustified interruptions and lockouts. Foreign direct investment flows in Russia during 2015 constituted the total of $6.7 billion, a decline of 92 percent from 2013, according to the data from the UN Conference on Trade and Development.[5] This decline in foreign direct investment reflects the increased risks that foreign investors face when doing business in Russia. As long as corruption in Russia persists, foreign investors are unlikely to come to the country in large numbers. Values of Corruption Perceptions Index for Russia, USA, China, and Nigeria for the period of 1995–2016 are presented in Table 4.1.

Based on expert opinion obtained with the help of large-scale surveys conducted around the world by Transparency International, the Corruption Perceptions Index

Table 4.1 Values of Corruption Perceptions Index for Russia, the USA, China, and Nigeria, 1995–2016

	Russia	*USA*	*China*	*Nigeria*	*Countries ranked*
1995	–	15	40	–	41
1996	47	15	50	54	54
1997	49	16	41	52	52
1998	76	17	52	81	85
1999	82	18	58	98	99
2000	82	14	63	90	90
2001	79	16	57	90	91
2002	71	16	59	101	102
2003	86	18	66	132	133
2004	90	17	71	144	146
2005	126	17	78	152	159
2006	121	20	70	142	163
2007	143	20	72	147	180
2008	147	18	72	121	180
2009	146	19	79	130	180
2010	154	22	78	134	178
2011	143	24	75	143	183
2012	133	19	80	139	176
2013	127	19	80	144	177
2014	136	17	100	136	175
2015	119	16	83	136	168
2016	131	18	79	136	176

Source: Completed by the author with the data obtained from Corruption Perceptions Index. Transparency International. Berlin. Retrieved January 31, 2017, from www.transparency.org/news/feature/corruption_perceptions_index_2016

Corruption and raiding 119

(CPI) measures the perceived levels of public sector corruption worldwide. A vast majority of countries are surveyed annually. In 2016, 176 countries took part in this project. The results show that not a single country comes close to top marks and is not free of corruption, while over 120 countries score below 50 on the scale of 0 (highly corrupt) to 100 (very clean). The higher the numerical value of the CPI assigned to a given country, the more corrupt this country is.

As follows from the trends on corruption estimates, depicted on Figure 4.1, Russia is bundled with Nigeria, very distant from the US and even China. This close coupling is reminiscent of a saying that Russia is nothing more than a snowy Nigeria. Apparently this saying makes sense, at least when it comes to corruption. This is of no surprise, since China indicates strong economic growth over last three decades, while Nigeria exports oil and raw materials and lacks development.

It is true that corruption, along with other factors, lies at the base of Russian raiding, but corruption is not analogous to raiding. There are significant differences between corruption and raiding, and these differences exist not only on the fundamental level, but on the functional level as well. Corruption is invisible; everything is done in the darkness. Shady dealings do not like the light and avoid

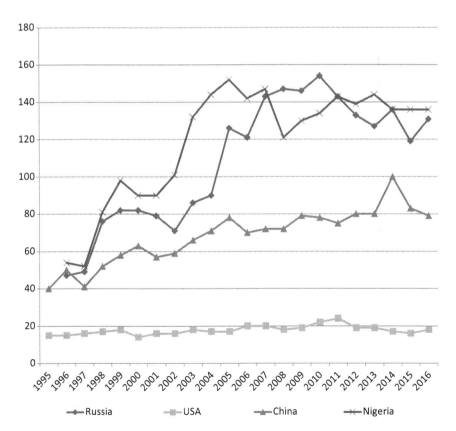

Figure 4.1 Dynamics of Corruption Perceptions Index for Russia, the USA, China, and Nigeria, 1995–2016

120 *Corruption and raiding*

attracting attention. One can judge about corruption only based on the results that surface every once in a while or otherwise are easily viewed and may be observed by the public or those especially interested. Such visible manifestations of corruption include an unaffordably high level of consumption and a luxury lifestyle. Another way of discovering corruption is catching the bribe-taker red-handed. However, it is insufficient simply to see or identify corruption; it has to be proven. Even when state bureaucrats get caught by the hand while accepting a cash bribe, they deny everything and often say that they asked for a loan or decided to borrow some cash for the short term.

Compared with corruption, raiding is visible. It is visible because raiders target material assets. The change of owner takes place. However, as is the case of corruption, the fact of raiding has to be proven. Raiding has become more civilized and less violent as an expression of raiding becoming more latent and better hidden or disguised. In such cases, raiding is being done through shares, management, real governance, and other civilized ways. It becomes even more difficult to understand who is right and who is wrong, who is the lawful owner and who is the raider? Accordingly, as raiding becomes more civilized, the fight against raiding will become even more complicated.

It is hard to prove the guilt of a bribe-taker because the bribe is the result of a consensus, and even in cases of extortion the bribe is still the result of a consensus reached between bribe-taker and bribe-giver. Raiding is different, because there is a struggle, in which one side is the winner and another is the loser, ready to complain to the state. The question is whether the state is ready to react to such a complaint properly and in a just manner?

Nepotism and inheritance as a basis of raiding

Nepotism and inheritance rights have long been considered as both the basis and the reason of sustainability of corrupt regimes. Those in power want to pass their accumulated fortunes to their offspring. This is natural. What is not so natural is that these fortunes were accumulated at the expense of the public and the business, both of which constitute the base for extortion and embezzlement, committed by the ruling regime and particular state bureaucrats. Kryshtanovskaya and White (2011) refer to Leon Trotsky's passage on the Soviet bureaucracy's possibility of appropriating not only the office of authority, but also property: "Privileges," as Trotsky had already pointed out in 1936, "have only half their value if they cannot be transmitted to one's children," and for this reason the bureaucracy would "inevitably" seek to consolidate their position through property relations" (p. 22). One is left to wonder why Russian politicians and scholars did not recall this prophetic statement in the late 1980s and the early 1990s, when ideas of market reforms and privatization were sold to the public and gained strength.

The key issue comes down to inheriting not the stream of income, illicit revenues, proceeds of corruption, access to graft, right to collect bribes, but the fundamental source of profit, that is, the enterprise, the company, the economic asset, the property itself. Inheriting a state office may be hard, but inheriting a state

Corruption and raiding 121

enterprise is simply impossible, especially in a formal, legal way. At the same time, while inheriting the state office is illegal, it is perfectly legal to inherit a private enterprise, company, or any piece of private property, including land. This seemingly axiomatic situation creates incentives for corrupt state bureaucrats to appropriate economic assets that they manage and formalize their property rights over these assets. And the best and most effective tool in securing not only the stream of bribes, but full-scale guaranteed profit participation is precisely raiding.

This view of sustainability of corrupt regimes plays well with the sense of stability developed and indeed imposed by the state during the Brezhnev era, also known as the slow down or *zastoj*. Russia's modern ruling regime wants to maintain this imagery of pseudo-stability in order to guarantee the sustainability of inheritance rights. In the late Stalinist system of state bureaucracy that existed under the Brezhnev regime, members of the state nomenklatura developed the practice of passing their positions to their children. This was done informally and even secretly, with family names being changed for conspiracy, but the state security services were very well aware of such instances.

Referring to the works of Whitefield (1993), Voslensky (1984), Vaksberg (1991), Simis (1982); and Barnes (2006, p. 41) points out that,

> With Brezhnev's emphasis on stability in the system and trust in the people who ran it, the Party lost control over the nomenklatura system. In its place developed informal norms that hid quality managers and administrators in low-level positions, promoted inferior ones instead of firing them, and even allowed members of the nomenklatura to pass their positions on to their children (Whitefield, 1993, pp. 83–86; Voslensky, 1984, pp. 101–102). In that environment, administrative officials and enterprise managers increasingly used state resources for individual profit – taking bribes, embezzling funds, selling goods on the black market, even using parts of state factories as their own private workshops – further clouding the lines of ownership and control in the system (Vaksberg, 1991; Simis, 1982, pp. 144–179).

Indeed, in the atmosphere of loss of control, party bosses, local administrators, and managers of Soviet enterprises drew extra benefits out of the socialist system. These benefits went to themselves and their family members. Modern Russia exists as a network state based on personal connections (see, for instance, Hanson, 2011; Kryshtanovskaya and White, 2011; Ledeneva, 2011; Ortmann, 2011; Petrov, 2011). Personal, business, and political networks are strengthened with family ties, and cronyism is perceived as a norm.

Contrary to the commonly shared view that the root of corruption originates from the state and public sector, which took over a part of the national economy, the reality oftentimes points to the opposite. Development of market reforms is accompanied by growing corruption. This is true for the former USSR, China, and perhaps all the other former socialist countries on their way to capitalism, without exception. The growing size of the economy enlarges the base for corruption, including primarily extortion, embezzlement from the state budget, and

122   *Corruption and raiding*

tax evasion. In Russia, however, the problem of corruption is more severe than in many other communist and post-communist regimes.

The problem of corruption has become so serious that former President Medvedev even mentioned the death penalty, while talking about growing corruption in state contracts. At the same time, the combination of state office and business is even welcomed (Ivanova, 2009, p. 19). And there is an indefinite moratorium on the death penalty in Russia. The President reported that bureaucrats embezzle from the state over one trillion rubles per year, and this is by quite modest estimates.[6] State contracts are numerous, with over ten million contracts signed every year. In this situation, embezzlement from the state budget and kickbacks become favorite tools of state bureaucrats for profiteering.

On February 16, 2011, President Medvedev sent to the State Duma a package of amendments to the Criminal Code and the Code on Administrative Violations, which anticipate increased terms in prison and larger fines for those involved in commercial bribery, bribe-taking, and bribe-giving. The maximum fine for those convicted of bribery will be one hundred times the size of the paid or received bribe, up to half a billion rubles, i.e. around $17 million. The lowest limit for a fine is set at 25,000 rubles, i.e. slightly less than $1,000. Bribe-givers will receive lesser punishments than bribe-takers. Moreover, those bribe-givers who actively cooperated with the investigation, informed law enforcement agencies about the fact of the bribery, or fell victim to extortion will be relieved of any punishment.[7]

The set of anti-corruption amendments was approved by the State Duma on April 20, 2011, and by the Council of Federation on April 27, 2011. On May 4, 2011, Medvedev signed these amendments into law. The media headline highlighting this event reads as follows: "President Introduced Multiplied Punishment for Bribes: The Greediest Bureaucrats Will Pay Half-a-Billion." Medvedev describes this change to be "an absolutely new punishment measure." In his view,

> this is quite an interesting measure, which may be applied without the actual deprivation of freedom, but creates serious conditions so those who committed a crime will understand that the sword of state responsibility will be aimed not only at him personally, but at his property as well; he will suffer materially.[8]

It may be good to have the president, who is a qualified lawyer, when it comes to legislative ideas regarding the anti-corruption effort. At the same time, there are price lists on services offered by members of the State Duma that go in contradiction with anti-corruption slogans and efforts. Price lists for the services of Russian MPs as well as size of kickbacks on state-funded projects occur in writing after writing. Ledeneva (2011) reports the prices of various services offered by politicians, state officials, and state bodies in Russia (p. 47). The credibility of such price lists is not beyond doubt and their trustworthiness rests with the readers.

The suggested amendments are based on the assumption, at least in part, that it is more painful for a bribe-taker to pay a huge fine than to serve time in prison. When bribe-takers will have to pay fines a hundred times the size of the accepted bribe, it will work as a deterrent. A fine or partial confiscation of property as an alternative to the real term in prison is perceived by many as a way for corrupt bureaucrats to buy their way out of prison before they even get there. Voloshin (2011) entitles his report in *Komsomol'skaya Pravda* as "Corrupt Bureaucrats Will Give the State a Hundred Times Enlarged 'Bribe.'"[9] If one is to simulate or predict an outcome of this new law, one may well conclude that bureaucrats will collect bribes from their clientele and when caught, pay part of the proceeds to the state budget. This sounds more like kickbacks paid by the bribe-takers to the state in return for their appointment to the office of authority. The state will de facto share in the illicit benefits obtained from corruption.

To the contrary, Medvedev says that for some this measure may turn out to be more significant than imprisonment or deprivation of freedom. In November of 2010, President Medvedev said that "The experiences indicate that even a threat of imprisonment for twelve years does not deter bribe-takers. It appears that in some instances economic measures such as fines may be more effective."[10] Moreover, Medvedev does not like confiscation of property as an ideal measure against corrupt bureaucrats. He says that it is easier for the state to receive a fine in cash instead of seizing the property and then placing it for sale in order to receive the proceeds in cash and send them to the state budget. One should not expect large revenues for the state, however. The Chair of the Supreme Court of the RF, Vyatcheslav Lebedev, says that during 2010, there were only thirty-five individuals sentenced for a bribe of over one million rubles, i.e. around \$35,000. The vast majority of prosecuted and sentenced bribe-takers are doctors and policemen, none of whom was occupying high-ranking offices.[11] Adaptation may be a most likely response to such anti-corruption governmental initiatives.

It appears that in order to avoid paying large sums in fines, if caught, bribe-takers will resort to the tactics of accepting one bribe in several parts or portions. They will do it piece-meal instead of as a lump-sum deal. As long as there are fundamental objective grounds for corruption, bribe-takers will adapt their strategies as long as there are grounds for corruption. The media reports on one such solution:

> What is a bribe according to the Criminal Code? A bribe includes receiving money, stocks and bonds, other property or services of material value, or delegating certain property rights. However, the ways of paying a bribe considered in the Criminal Code do not include, for instance, such a widely practiced form of corruption as appointing children, wives, sisters, brothers, fathers and mothers of a corrupt bureaucrat to the governing boards or management of companies.[12]

Similar to nepotism, this practice has been in place in Russia for decades.

The issue of nepotism in merging business and the state has been discussed by the Russian media since the mid-2000s.[13] This issue is being highlighted in the foreign media as well. In March of 2005, *Forbes* magazine reported that the 24-year-old son of Russia's Minister of Defense, Sergei Ivanov, became a vice

124   *Corruption and raiding*

president of Gazprombank, the third largest bank in Russia, affiliated with Gazprom, one of the largest state-owned oil and gas companies in the world.[14] Sometimes this kind of kinship-based appointment goes so far that the ruling regime itself has to react and publically denounce and disapprove such practices in general and in particular. For instance, in May of 2011 Russian mass media reported that the Kremlin prohibited the son of Sergei Ivanov from taking a bread-winning office in Rossel'khozbank, saying that "this is too much." When the idea came to remove state bureaucrats from some of the corporate governing boards of directors, the mass media reported "Western Media on 'Games in the Struggle for Power' in Russia: Friends of Putin in State Companies Will Be Replaced by Their Sons."[15] It is of no surprise that the newly formed elites delegate some of the authority over the state functions and property management to their heirs.

Oftentimes Russian mass media reports on the problem of nepotism only after it has been reported in the Western media. For instance, in July of 2011, French newspaper *La Tribune* reported how children of Russian statesmen receive breadwinning places in big businesses.[16] The day after, Russian media offered a report on this problem entitled "Children of Spies and Bankers Join Putin's Clan."[17] Despite all the critics and negative connotations, the tradition of nepotism and family-clan relations continues. Just recently, in March of 2017, Sergei Ivanov, son of Sergei Ivanov, was appointed the head of Alrosa. The state owns a 58 percent stake in the company, and that is why the news on the appointment came from Prime Minister Medvedev. Alrosa is the largest diamond company in the world, exploring and extracting diamonds not only in Russia's Sakha Yakutiya and Arkhangel'sk regions, but in Africa as well. Prior to this appointment, son of Sergei Ivanov served as the vice-president of Sberbank, the largest and state-owned bank in Russia. The media even reports it this way: "Sergei Ivanov Is Appointed the Head of Alrosa"[18] and "Sergei Ivanov's Son Is Appointed as the Head of Alrosa."[19]

In order to avoid confusion, father and son are identified as Sergei Ivanov Junior and Sergei Ivanov Senior. Sergei Ivanov Senior, a KGB operative, now serves as the Special Representative of the President in issues of nature, environment, and transportation and as the Permanent Member of the Security Council. This explains the fact that from now on, his son, Sergei Ivanov Junior, will lead the world's largest diamonds exploration in Eurasia and Africa. What more one can wish for in order to strengthen sustainability of the ruling political regime through nepotism? A similar case is with Aleksei Rogozin, son of Russia's Vice Premier Dmitry Rogozin. Dmitry Rogozin oversees Russia's huge military-industrial complex, and his son was appointed the vice president of United Aircraft Corporation.[20] Prior to this appointment, Aleksei Rogozin served as the deputy head of the department of property relations in the Ministry of Defense.

The fact that kinship in power is historically detrimental to economic development is of little concern to the ruling regime. Arguments in favor of the sustainability of the ruling authoritarian regime are placed above any other concerns, including economic reasoning. As a result, Russia finds itself in a stalemate, or a low steady state equilibrium, where overwhelming well-being of the elites does

Corruption and raiding   125

not facilitate and in fact prevents an increase in socioeconomic well-being of the masses.

Large state-owned banks and other companies eagerly accept children of top Russian bureaucrats and politicians for top managerial positions. In fact, they are not given much choice. Jointly owned companies and the private ones follow this practice as well. In this way, chief bureaucrats "outsource" their function of receiving illicit revenues, such as bribes, to their offspring and other close relatives, while companies establish close ties with the ruling political regime. As a result of such a reciprocal arrangement, state bureaucrats amass their wealth while securing themselves from formal state prosecution, while companies rely on their governmental connections in order to secure themselves from possible raiding attacks, including those led by the state.

4.2 Bureaucracy, corruption, raiding, and struggle against it

Russian bureaucracy and corruption

Perestroika and the market reforms that followed did not lead to a cut in the number of bureaucrats or a decrease in bureaucratic procedures. Soviet leader Mikhail Gorbachev was a vocal opponent of the Soviet bureaucracy, to which he himself belonged. Nevertheless, Gorbachev did not succeed in his epic struggle against bureaucracy. The state leaders that followed also shared his fate. Yeltsin, Putin, Medvedev, and Putin 2.0 failed to reduce the bureaucratic apparatus in Russia. Bureaucracy in Russia continues to grow. According to the data presented by the Russian Ministry of Statistics, the number of workers in state and municipal government in Russia constantly increases. It grew from 1,061,800 bureaucrats in 1995 to 1,623,900 in 2007 (Russian Statistical Yearbook, 2008). Such an increase in the number of civil servants manifests the growth of bureaucracy rather than its decline. Bureaucracy brings corruption, and more bureaucracy means more corruption. The data on the number of state employees is presented in Table 4.2.

Table 4.2 Number of employees in the state and municipal government in Russia, 1995–2007, in thousands

	Legislative branch	Executive branch	Courts, prosecutors	Other authorities	Total
1995	8.8	945.1	107.3	0.6	1061.8
2000	15.5	1029.5	115.2	3.1	1163.3
2001	19.2	983.7	134.3	3.5	1140.6
2002	20.4	1072.5	153.9	5.5	1252.3
2003	21.7	1102.9	168.5	7.4	1300.5
2004	22.9	1103.3	184.5	7.9	1318.6
2005	24.4	1236.6	192.8	8.3	1462.0
2006	26.1	1344.8	197.1	9.3	1577.2
2007	27.9	1387.6	197.6	10.8	1623.9

Source: Russian Statistical Yearbook (2008, p. 46).

126 *Corruption and raiding*

The officially released data points to a significant increase in corruption among Russian bureaucrats. The number of registered cases of bribery in Russia in 1990 was equal to 2,700, increasing to 4,700 in 1995, 7,000 in 2000, and 7,900 in 2001. Then the number of cases of bribery stabilized at the level of 7,300 cases per year in 2002 and 2003, followed by a period of consistent growth to 8,900 cases of bribery in 2004, 9,800 in 2005, 11,100 in 2006, and 11,600 in 2007. Thus, in less than twenty years the number of registered cases of bribery in Russia more than quadrupled (Russian Statistical Yearbook, 2008, p. 299). A steady growth of corrupt activities during Putin's reign as the president did not stop under Medvedev. In February of 2012, on the eve of the presidential elections, Russia's Prosecutor General, Yuri Chajka, admitted that the war on corruption in Russia has failed.[21] Clearly, Medvedev did not overplay his predecessor in the presidential office in regard to the anti-corruption campaign. Nor did Putin's return to the presidency change the situation with corruption for better, leaving the major challenge in place.

In 2017, the Chair of the Investigations Committee (SK) [Sledstvennyj komitet] of the Ministry of the Interior (MVD) [Ministerstvo vnutrennikh del], Aleksandr Bastrykin, reported that in 2016, the total value of property of corrupt bureaucrats, arrested on court order, almost doubled as compared with the previous year, and reached 38 billion rubles. Moreover, in 2016, his agency responded to 35,000 reports on corrupt activities. There were 25,000 criminal investigations opened and 12,500 criminal investigations completed. Of those criminal investigations of corrupt activities, 56 cases were of crimes committed by organized criminal groups and another six by entirely corrupt syndicates.[22]

Leader of the political party Spravedlivaya Rossiya [Just Russia] and former Speaker of the Council of Federation, Sergei Mironov, does not agree with Medvedev's approach to punishing corrupt state bureaucrats. He says that corruption should be considered equal to state treason and be punished by at least twenty-five years to life in prison.[23] Mironov is a strong believer in the carrot and stick approach when it comes to bureaucratic corruption. He suggests high salaries, benefits, and retirement packages for state bureaucrats and severe punishment for those of them who resort to corruption. Not only state bureaucrats are in focus in Mironov's rhetoric. He does not support Khodorkovsky, saying that the imprisoned oligarch "is guilty of economic crimes. We have plenty of guilty oligarchs. The fact that we only punished one is an absolute mistake, but this is a separate issue."[24] Apparently, Mironov points to the practice of selective justice and its deficiency. Three weeks later, in July of 2011, aids of MPs from Spravedlivaya Rossiya were detained for trading mandates to the future Duma. The Criminal Code article "Attempted fraud" was applied to two volunteers who demanded from an unidentified individual 7.5 million Euro in exchange for placing his name on the Party list of candidates for the 6th Duma elections scheduled to be held in December 2011. The MP himself denies that these aids ever worked for him and the Party considers the whole incident as a senseless provocation on the eve of the elections.[25] Places in the State Duma are considered as a valuable economic asset.

While politicians argue about the proper form of punishment for corrupt bureaucrats, a Moscow top government bureaucrat who allegedly deprived the

Corruption and raiding 127

city of over 252,000,000 rubles ($10,000,000) from 2004 to 2007, avoided punishment; it was a long time ago and the statute of limitation had expired due to the lengthy investigation.[26] Ministerial bureaucracies led by Kudrin, Levitin, and Golikova, who headed the Ministries of Finance, Transportation, and Healthcare and Social Development, respectively, became leaders in terms of media attention on corruption.[27] The volume of the media attention, however, is a far-from-perfect indicator of the level of corruptness of certain bureaucratic organizations.

While state bureaucrats fill their pockets with illicit benefits, some politicians clash in the presumptions versus perceptions argument. Presumptions of innocence versus perceptions of corruption become a hot topic when it comes to discussing anti-corruption measures. Some politicians think that the required annual declaration of incomes by state bureaucrats is insufficient as a measure of control over their illicit revenues and lavish spending. Mironov suggests that not only state bureaucrats, but their close relatives, including parents, children, brothers, and sisters, should present their income declarations and their spending or life expenditures:

> If a bureaucrat has an expensive car, house in Rublevka, helicopter, this bureaucrat should say where the money come from. If he fails to prove the honest origin of the money, then all of these assets should be expropriated to the benefit of the state treasury.[28]

It turns out that even though corruption is a crime, the target of the state would not be the corrupted bureaucrat, but his property.

The issue of declaring expenses in addition to income, property, and assets will continue to stay in the air for quite some time. In January of 2012, The Supreme Court of the Russian Federation rejected the claim of a doctoral student who wanted presidential candidates to declare their expenditures.[29] Andrei Kapliev, a doctoral student in the Institute of the State and Law at the Russian Academy of Sciences (RAN) [Rossijskaya akademiya nauk] filed a petition with the Supreme Court stating that Russia violates Article 20, "Unlawful enrichment," of the UN Convention against Corruption (see Article 40: "Convention against Corruption UN." New York, 2004), ratified by Russia in 2006. However, Russia did not ratify Article 20.[30] Presidential candidates have to declare their income, property, assets, and cars, and those of their spouses. However, they do not have to declare or justify their personal and family expenditures that often cover their lavish lifestyle.

In December of 2010, the State Duma received an anti-corruption law draft regarding the presumption of guilt for bureaucrats.[31] The concept of innocent until proven guilty, guaranteed by the Russian Constitution, should not apply to top bureaucrats, say the authors of the proposed legislative amendment. Mironov met with Putin and suggested abolishing presumption of innocence for corrupt bureaucrats. The Kremlin criticized Mironov for making this suggestion. Mironov says that

> the conversation is about the confiscation of property from bureaucrats and their family members. If a bureaucrat gets caught on such violations as

128   *Corruption and raiding*

bribe-taking, his property should be confiscated in its entirety. Then relatives should prove that this property was acquired in lawful ways. If they prove it, then they will receive it back, and if not, then it will go to the benefit of the state budget.[32]

The Kremlin responds that such suggestions are especially strange when they come from the Chair of the Council of Federation, referring to the 49th Article of the Constitution, where presumption of innocence applies equally to all citizens, disregarding their occupation or social status, and this certainly includes state bureaucrats.[33] Even if state bureaucrats would be stripped of the presumption of innocence, how would this action apply to their relatives who may be in possession of some shared property and yet covered by the presumption of innocence rule?

While unconstitutional, this suggestion has some rationale in its base. The media reports that around 60 percent of buyers of elite apartments in Moscow at a price of $2 million and up are bureaucrats.[34] Another source of information about bureaucrats and law enforcement officers living clearly above their means is traffic accident reports. Bureaucrats' vehicles, reported in accidents, are almost always too luxurious and expensive brands to be afforded on a modest salary. Reporting incomes annually does not help disclose the real income of bureaucrats. For instance, the billionaire MP Andrei Skoch, allegedly the richest member in the State Duma, filed an income declaration which shows that he lives off his salary and owns only a small 65.3 square meters (around 700 square feet) apartment in Belgorodskaya oblast'. The media alleges that Skoch "forgot" about his Airbus A319–115CJ that costs $50 million, while declaring his property.[35] In yet another documented case, an officer of the Ministry of the Interior in Caucasus forgot to report his nine apartments and fifteen plots of land in his income declaration.[36] The Auditing Chamber checked the income declarations of bureaucrats over the next half year.[37] Legal sanctions were considered to remind such "forgetting" civil servants of their obligations. All this work is of little interest to the public: 71 percent of the respondents in a 2010 poll say that they do not believe bureaucrats' declarations on property and income. The fact remains that housewives sometimes magically earn hundreds of times more than their husbands on civil service.

The media propels public perceptions about corruption in the state and the high level of corruptness in society. "Only nine out of every hundred people have not learned how to give bribes" reads the title in *RBK Daily*.[38] "Average bribe in Russia exceeds $10,000" reads another report.[39] Average bribes Russians pay are 250,000 rubles, says the Ministry of the Interior in its press-release in 2011.[40] From 2008 to 2012, the average size of bribes increased 33 times, reaching 300,000 rubles or $12,000.[41] Figures vary, however. The Economic Crimes Prevention Unit within the Ministry of the Interior reports the average bribe to be around $2,000.[42] In 2013, the average bribe was reported at 145,000 rubles, i.e. around $5,000, more than doubling as compared to 2012.[43] Human rights activists reported that the average bribe in Russia in 2014 has tripled, reaching $10,000.[44] In 2017, the Ministry of the Interior reported that the average bribe in

Corruption and raiding 129

Russia increased 75 percent over 2016 and exceeded $5,000.[45] In Moscow, the average bribe increased 2.5 times over 2016, reaching $35,000.[46] The Minister of the Interior said that from 2012 to 2013, cases of bribery increased 18 percent.[47] Similarly, in Moscow, cases of bribery increased 17 percent from 2016 to 2017. Corruption damage in the first ten months of 2013 is estimated at 21 billion rubles.[48] Almost 20 percent of Russians believe that corruption in law enforcement and courts is widespread.[49]

There are champions of course, for whom the size and the very notion of average bribe does not apply. And these champions do not necessarily reside in Moscow. For instance, a state bureaucrat in Tula was arrested for a bribe of 40 million rubles, i.e. around $1.5 million.[50] In order to avoid declaring their real property, assets, and income, many bureaucrats take their capital away from the country. The Ministry of the Interior estimates total illegal capital outflow from Russia at 5 trillion rubles, around $200 billion.[51] It is not clear how the police are going to trace the bureaucrats' foreign bank accounts and property, especially if all of this information is confidential by law in foreign entities and jurisdictions outside of Russia, and the self-reporting rule may not work well with dishonest state bureaucrats.

Measures taken by the authorities to fight corruption within its own apparatus are insufficient. Nevertheless, the authorities report some progress in this gargantuan task. Vice Prime Minister Shuvalov, who serves as the Head of the Board of Trust in Rosatom (Russian State Nuclear Energy Corporation), uses Rosatom as an example of an anti-corruption campaign for state corporations, saying that this state-owned corporation does not follow the principle of hiding its problems, but instead makes its data on corruption open to the public. This strategy implies certain reputational risks, but the company overall benefits from such an anti-corruption policy, based on transparency. The head of the company's property and asset security, who is also a major general of the police, Viktor Bratanov, said that during the period of 2008 to 2010 Rosatom created a complex anti-corruption system, including such elements as internal control and audit, control over purchases, and arbitration. As a result, the number of cases of making decisions regarding property without the consent of the owner decreased six times, actions in the interest of third parties declined 8.5 times, and cases that involve conflict of interest, 4.5 times.

There are 357 controllers working in this system, as compared to only seven controllers in 2007. The number of audits and controlling operations increased from 32 in 2008 to 274 in 2011. Rosatom is a federal agency which includes over 300 enterprises. The open bidding process used to purchase supplies helped to save 19.7 billion rubles in 2010. The total number of open and competitive bidding operations increased from 2,103 in 2009 to 34,879 in 2011.[52] This is of no surprise that such claims come from Shuvalov, who is likely a major Russian front-man when it comes to inviting foreign investors to Russia, and advertising and promoting Russia as a field of good business opportunities for the West. Open bidding processes, transparency, and competition among bidders are all recipes coming from the West.

130   *Corruption and raiding*

Such a change in procedures and a new system of anti-corruption measures and efforts are quite timely, if one is to take into consideration a recent scandal with Rosatom's former deputy director, Evgeni Evstratov. In July of 2011, investigators asked the court to arrest Evstratov.[53] He was suspected of embezzlement of around 50 million rubles.[54] One of the charges comes from the allegation that employees of Rosatom were downloading texts on nuclear safety from the internet and then presenting them as newly developed know-how, while the money allocated for this type of R&D was filling the pockets of those involved and members of the company's administration.[55] The total damage inflicted on the federal corporation is estimated at around 110 million rubles.

Major General of the Ministry of the Interior, Vladimir Ovchinsky, says that the mafia has infiltrated all state bureaucracies in Russia.[56] New types of especially serious crimes, such as contract killings and kidnapping with ransom demands, appeared on the scene in Russia. Physical elimination of inconvenient competitors turned out to be a much more effective form of hostile takeover of market segments, than a multi-year economic struggle through price policies and advertisement techniques. There were 348 cases of gangster operations, 32 contract killings, and 873 kidnappings officially registered in Russia in 2007. There were also 305,900 economic crimes committed in that year, of which 53,800 were of especially large scale (Russian Statistical Yearbook, 2008, p. 299). Those involved in bribery are normally sentenced to fines or receive suspended sentences. Only those state bureaucrats who are convicted in taking large or especially large bribes risk being sentenced to real terms in prison. Those who give bribes have even lesser chances to end up in prison or even pay a small fine for bribing state officials, street-level bureaucrats, or civil servants.

Russia's record for investigating and prosecuting serious crimes associated with violence is far from ideal. For many years and now even decades, some categories of serious violent crimes are resolved at the level of well below 50 or even 30 percent. In many instances, professionally prepared killings and other serious violent crimes remain unresolved. There was a common view that during the Soviet era, corruption as a form of economic crime or white collar crime and violent crimes, including murders, were not strongly connected. Zon (2008) points out in this regard that during Boris Yeltsin's rule, corruption was not a newly emerged phenomenon, but the violence associated with corruption was new to Russia. The merger of corruption and violence, along with other factors, found its reflection in the explosion of violent deaths during the 1990s: "While in 1985 there were 15,000 in the whole of the Soviet Union, in 2000 there were 31,829 for Russia alone. It was difficult to distinguish between organized crime and state bureaucracy" (Zon, 2008, p. 50). The author is referring to the rapid increase in the number of committed violent crimes during the period of the so-called rough 1990s [likhie devyanostye]. Violence and threat of violence, including order killings previously unheard of in the USSR, helped raiders to physically eliminate uncooperative owners of targeted enterprises and pieces of much valued property.

Physically liquidating the competitor through contract killings became easier, and cheaper, than using legally predetermined economic methods of struggle with

Corruption and raiding   131

uncertain outcomes. Indeed, "if there is no person, there is no problem." Businesses are based on family and clan relations. This model of business does not anticipate the high level of trust to employees, nor does it anticipate hiring managers from the outside. Thus, physical elimination of the top manager inevitably becomes a heavy blow to the entire enterprise. A replacement is hard to find, not because of rare qualifications, but because of immanent distrust and the need to choose from among the clan. The blood ties in company management limit the expansion of businesses and at the same time stimulate the business of contract killings.

Imitating an anti-corruption campaign

Bureaucrats help raiders in exchange for certain benefits. An expert of the Department of Economic Security of the Chamber of Trade and Commerce of the Russian Federation [Torgovo-promyshlennaya palata Rossijskoj Federatsii, TPP RF], Alexander Bogatikov, notes that "Raiding and corruption are two shores of the same river."[57] The growing army of state bureaucrats is in a constant search for additional sources of income. This process eases the life of raiders, if they have something to offer to state bureaucrats.

The level of corruption in Russia remains extremely high. There were 10,500 cases of corruption investigated in 2007.[58] The number of the investigated cases of corruption grows steadily. In 2009, there were 43,000 cases of corruption discovered by the authorities. Medvedev pointed out that the real number of corruption crimes in Russia is "tens of times, hundreds of times higher than discovered."[59] The leader of the Liberal Democratic Party of Russia (LDPR) [Liberal'no-demokraticheskaya partiya Rossii], Vladimir Zhirinovsky, called the newly elected Moscow City Council a "hotbed of corruption," and named Moscow mayor's office "the dirtiest criminal government in Russian history."[60] Such accusations against high-ranking state officials and politicians are not rare in Russia. Moscow government frequently becomes an object of media attacks and accusations of corruption.[61] It becomes more and more popular for politicians and some outspoken individuals to accuse certain state bureaucrats or entire bureaucratic divisions and state agencies and corporations of rampant corruption, including bribery, embezzlement, kickbacks, fraud, bid rigging, nepotism, and all kinds of financial misconduct.

When leaving presidency in 2008, Putin named corruption as the most important of all unresolved problems. The newly elected president Medvedev signed the Order "On the measures against corruption" and ordered the creation of the Presidential Anti-Corruption Council. Medvedev said that "We need to do something. We can't wait any more. Corruption turned into a systemic problem and we must confront it with systemic measures."[62] The Russian government applied the legal anti-corruption expertise to examining laws and other legal documents for potential corruption. Medvedev said that in 2009, state prosecutors identified over 36,000 laws, other legal documents, and projects of laws and legal documents which contain potential for corruption. This potential may provoke bureaucrats'

132 *Corruption and raiding*

corrupt actions. According to the president, 90 percent of these legal documents are at the local level.[63] Judging by the number of legislative and regulatory documents, identified by the anti-corruption expertise, one may think that prosecutors and legislators create even more work for themselves. If there is a potential for corruption, it will be realized.

Medvedev points to the need to modernize anti-corruption legislation, fight and prevent corruption, create stimuli for anti-corrupt behavior, and develop the standard of anti-corrupt behavior. The President also points to the need to achieve "transparency in governmental procedures of sub-contracting, as well as tenders, and a favorable business environment." Medvedev also mentions "the complex of anti-raiding measures." He suggested making the decision regarding the need for all the state officials and judges to report their wealth, as well as the creation of a new version of the code of conduct for civil servants:

> There is a list of questions, quite difficult for discussion, that nevertheless require final decision. These questions include control over the wealth of state officials and judges, conflict of interest, issues of the new version of the code of conduct for state servants.

Medvedev also says that corruption "undermines the trust of citizens in the authorities and the problems that these authorities should be working on."[64]

According to the law, adopted in Russia in 2009, the legislative documents are checked for possible loopholes that would allow corruption. In 2009, Medvedev signed the Federal law "On anti-corruption expertise of normative legal acts and projects of normative legal acts." The law was voted for by the State Duma and approved by the Council of Federation. The law creates the legal mechanism organizing and processing anti-corruption expertise. The law identifies "corruption factors," which denote certain regulations in the normative legal acts. These regulations set unreasonably wide limits for interpreting possibilities for exceptions from the generally applied rules. These regulations also include requirements that are not clearly defined. Such requirements are unreasonably cumbersome or burdensome to citizens and businesses. Thus, they create conditions for corruption to exist.[65] It appears that if there are not enough regulatory provisions, then there is a space for corruption, and if there are plenty of regulatory provisions, they are still used for corruption. It is not clear what would be a viable solution to this vicious circle.

This is not the first time that the presidential administration has activated the fight against corruption and assigned the Ministry of Justice and other ministries with the task of developing a new package of anti-corruption laws in a limited timeframe. The changes anticipate amendments to Article 104 prime of the Criminal Code. These amendments are intended to broaden the application of the confiscation of property for all corruption crimes. Changes also include amendments to Article 575 of the Civil Code, which bans bureaucrats from accepting gifts. The changes are also expected to reduce the number of officials who are subject to special investigation procedures under the Criminal Code, or so-called

Corruption and raiding   133

special subjects. According to Article 447 of the Criminal Code, immunity is granted to deputies of all levels, judges of all levels, members of the Federal audit chamber, ombudsmen, members of election commissions, candidates for deputies and the presidential office, former presidents, detectives, attorneys, and prosecutors. Deputies of the State Duma suggested stripping election commission members, detectives, attorneys, and prosecutors of immunity.[66] Zhirinovsky goes even further and suggests marking for life bureaucrats who take bribes.[67] The Chair of the Investigations Committee, Aleksandr Bastrykin, demands reintroduction of full confiscation of property in order to deal effectively with corrupt state bureaucrats.[68] Such legislative initiatives, new amendments, and changes are absolutely necessary, but at the same time they do not bring much optimism to those who oppose corruption. The authorities and the general population are equally pessimistic.

Some suggest testing bureaucrats by using provocation by bribe. The Deputy Chief of the Investigations Committee, Oleg Logunov, offers the following opinion regarding the acceptance of provocation by bribe: "I think that if an undercover police detective provokes a bureaucrat with a bribe and this bureaucrat agrees, this is an unconditional ground to fire this bureaucrat, but one cannot say about criminal responsibility in such a case."[69] Such a position is quite reasonable, but since there is no crime, there is no court-ordered restriction on the occupation of a state office. Thus, all that such undercover operations can result in is a bureaucrat moving to another office or even being reinstated in his previous position.

The Federal Services of Court Bailiffs (FSSP) [Federal'naya sluzhba sudebnyh pristavov] in Russia reports that there was an increase in economic crimes in 2009 as compared to 2008. In particular, there was a clear increase in such crimes as office fraud (40 percent increase), embezzlement or gross waste (30 percent increase), and acceptance of a bribe (34 percent increase). The Federal Bailiffs Services consider such statistics as an indication of success of anti-corruption units and services in detecting and prosecuting cases of corruption. The facts of corruption, which in earlier times would remain undiscovered, are now being detected and reported successfully. This success results in data showing the increase in the number of cases of public office abuse and corruption. In 2009, officers of the Federal Services of Bailiffs reported to their supervisors about being offered bribes from entrepreneurs. In twenty-seven of such cases, this reporting served as a ground to initiate a criminal investigation of bribe-givers. The reports were not only about small bribes offered, with the sums between 500 rubles and several thousand rubles (around $20 to few hundred dollars). There were also attempts to bribe bailiffs with bribes of up to 200,000 rubles (around $7,000).[70] For instance, in Moscow, a bailiff received an apartment from a business lady in exchange for lifting court-ordered seizure of her property.[71]

The issue of provocation by bribe was highlighted in the scholarly literature in the mid-1990s, but the attention given to this problem was very insignificant. Kotin (1996) considers the authority of state bureaucrats over the redistribution of property combined with the lack of mechanisms of control and responsibility as the major ground for corruption in Russia. The opportunistic behavior of state

134 *Corruption and raiding*

bureaucrats fuels corruption. Kotin (1996) underlines the difficulty of discovering cases of bribery and proving them in court. The author points out that acts of corruption are hidden better now than they were before. Bribe-givers and bribe-takers have become more sophisticated. Kotin (1996) agrees that the law enforcement agencies sometimes use methods not allowed by the law in order to achieve some success in their anti-corruption efforts. He also considers the provocation by bribe method.

Egorova (1997) discusses the problems that arise when the Criminal Code is applied to anti-corruption activities. In particular, she discusses the provision in the Criminal Code of the Russian Federation that makes provocation by bribe illegal. Egorova (1997) considers both bribing of a state official and commercial bribery. The author offers a detailed analysis of the elements of the crime in such cases. She also delineates provocation by bribe and the investigative technique, as they are denoted in the criminal code. President of the Moscow-based civil center "Antiproizvol" [Anti-abuse], Sergei Zamoshkin (1999), offers advice on how to behave in case one becomes a victim of provocation by bribe.

The idea of provocation by bribe as a testing device for state bureaucrats is not that bad. It is possible to test state bureaucrats by provoking them to accept a bribe, but the whole operation should be designed and described by the law. First, average bribes should be determined for every type of service bought illegally from the state officials. The size of a bribe would normally depend on the service sought by a bribe-giver and the position of the potential bribe-taker. Second, the state official may be provoked by a bribe, but the size of the offered bribe should not exceed the average value of bribes offered to similar bureaucrats for similar services or favors. If the state bureaucrat accepts the bribe, offered by an undercover detective, he/she should be dismissed from office, but not prosecuted. He/she is unfit for his/her job if he/she accepts the would-be bribe, but he/she commits no crime, because this is not a real bribe. Establishing a certain size of bribe for each level, case, service, and favor means further institutionalization of corruption.

If legalized, provocation by bribe may be applied not only to state bureaucrats and street-level civil servants, but the law enforcement officers and entire agencies as well. However, as long as the provocation by bribe remains illegal, any attempts of an anti-corruption campaign, organized by law enforcement agencies, may well end up in a criminal case against the law enforcement agencies themselves. In this regard, one example may be particularly illustrative. In February 2014, the joint task force that consisted of officers from the Federal Security Services, Investigations Committee, and Department of Internal Security of the Ministry of the Interior conducted a series of raids that included arrests and searches of offices and homes of high-ranking police officers in Moscow. The alleged perpetrators were officers from the anti-corruption bureau of the Ministry of the Interior. They were suspected in provocation by a bribe with the use of some businessman.[72]

Allegedly, arrested officers of the Head Department of Economic Security and Corruption Prevention of the Ministry of the Interior (GUEBiPK MVD) tried to

Corruption and raiding 135

frame a top state bureaucrat, provoking him to accept a bribe in exchange for protection. Later, journalists found out that the arrested officers of GUEBiPK MVD[73] tried to set up the Deputy Head of the 9th Department of the Federal Security Services, Igor Demin.[74] The 9th Department is responsible for internal security or internal investigations of the Federal Security Services. The mass media paid a lot of attention to this case. As the case had developed, it became clear that police officers used businessmen to offer Demin a bribe of $10,000 per month as a regular payment for protecting their business. Demin – or, according to competing media accounts, one of the businessmen – reported this framing to his FSB superiors. As a result, police officers were arrested and charged with the provocation by bribe via Articles 33, 304, and 286, paragraph 3 of the Criminal Code of the Russian Federation: "Organization of the provocation by bribe and abuse of public authority." As a result, two deputy heads of the Head Department of Economic Security and Corruption Prevention of the Ministry of the Interior, Colonel Lieutenant Ivan Kasaurov and Major Aleksei Bodnar, as well as several their subordinates were detained while the businessmen who offered the bribe to the FSB officer were placed under the house arrest. Demin converted from perpetrator to victim of a crime, the provocation by bribe.

As the corruption scandal grew, Putin fired the top anti-corruption police general, head of the GUEBiPK MVD, Denis Sugrobov.[75] A few days later, Major General and Deputy Head of GUEBiPK MVD, Boris Kolesnikov, was arrested, and the case resulted in arrests of at least eight high-ranking police officers from the corruption prevention unit.[76] Two high-ranking police officers from the anti-corruption unit, including General Kolesnikov and Colonel Salavat Mullayarov, were charged with provoking a bribe.[77] Finally, Putin fired Police General Kolesnikov, whose subordinates attempted to provoke a FSB officer with a bribe at Kolesnikov's request, along with a few other high-ranking police officers.[78] But that was not the end of the story. In less than two months, the key figure of this plot, General Kolesnikov, was admitted to the hospital from the detention facility with a serious head injury. He allegedly fell while in his detention cell.[79] The very next day, his boss, ex-chief anti-corruption police general, head of the GUEBiPK MVD, Denis Sugrobov, fired by Putin two month ago, was arrested while fishing.[80] In little more than a month, General Kolesnikov committed suicide while being detained in the building of Central Investigations Committee. He jumped to his death from the 6th floor, although the authorities were giving contradictory statements on whether he jumped out of the window or from the balcony.[81]

The 2014 case with the provocation by bribe is very illustrative of several interconnected phenomena that take place in the transition economy. These phenomena include corruption, bribing law enforcement officers, paying protection money to police and state security officers on a regular basis, competition between law enforcement agencies, illegal means used in such competition, selective justice, framing and extortion, state-authorized blackmail, possible state-authorized murders of "inconvenient" witnesses and perpetrators who can testify, and supremacy of the state ruler's will. Moreover, all of these are widespread practices. Above everything else, this case is the direct evidence of the exploitation of the

136 *Corruption and raiding*

corruption, coercion, and control scheme. One law enforcement agency decided to use the widespread practice of offering protection to businesses in exchange for regular bribes as a catch in order to frame and consequently influence another law enforcement agency. This competition could be for anything, including spheres of influence or a particular segment of the controlled market. Once on the hook with the documented criminal case, the targeted law enforcement agency, namely Federal Security Services, would be more cooperative with Ministry of the Interior. However, the framing operation went wrong, and as the result, those who initiated and realized this failed plot ended up in jail, or, as the case of the chief organizer, dead.

4.3 Concluding remarks

The ruling authoritarian regime that does not eliminate corruption, but on the contrary, facilitates informal and illicit state-business relations, de facto facilitates raiding. Corruption constitutes a breeding ground for raiding activities. Corporate and property raiding in Russia would be impossible without widespread corruption at all levels of state bureaucracy, starting from the very top of the bureaucratic hierarchy. Raiding is the art of taking over someone else's economic asset in such a way that the whole operation would create an impression of legitimacy and legality. State decisions that legitimize actions of raiders are rendered by state bureaucrats in corrupt ways. In some cases, these are personal business interests and stakes that state bureaucrats have in such endeavors, while in other instances these are mere bribes given by raiders. Raiders need favorable and unjust court decisions and friendly state authorities. They use abilities of state bureaucrats, courts, and corrupt law enforcement agencies to influence businesses. Raiding in Russia is to a large extent connected to the autocratic actions of state bureaucrats performed under the cover of their official duties. In essence, raiders buy discretionary powers of state bureaucrats in order to obtain certain documents and decisions that would help them to conduct hostile takeovers. Furthermore, state bureaucrats often find themselves in classic conflict of interest situations when it comes to raiding, because they own or co-own businesses.

Corruption along with other factors lies at the basis of Russian raiding, but corruption is not analogous to raiding. There are significant differences between corruption and raiding, and these differences exist not only on the fundamental level, but on the functional level as well. Corruption is invisible; everything is done in the darkness. Shady dealings do not like the light and avoid attracting attention. One can judge about corruption only based on the results that surface every once in a while or otherwise are easily viewed and may be observed by the public or those especially interested. Such visible manifestations of corruption include unaffordably high levels of consumption and a luxury lifestyle. Another way of discovering corruption is catching the bribe-taker red-handed. However, it is insufficient simply to see or identify corruption; it has to be proven. Even when state bureaucrats are caught red-handed while accepting a bribe in cash, they deny the wrongdoing and often say that they asked for a loan or decided to borrow some cash for a short term.

In comparison to corruption, raiding is visible, because raiders target material assets. A change of ownership takes place. Although bystanders do not notice the change of owners, the change of ownership is officially registered. However, as is the case of corruption, the fact of raiding has to be proven. The process of raiding is becoming seemingly more civilized and less violent just means raiding is becoming better hidden or disguised. In such cases, raiding is being done through acquisition of shares, management, real governance, and other civilized ways. It becomes even more difficult to differentiate between the lawful owner and raider. Accordingly, the process of raiding becoming more civilized will make the fight against raiding even more complicated. The increasing levels of sophistication in raiding operations make it more invisible, but there are always victims who are more than willing to report the perpetrators. Victims of raiding and victims of corruption are not the same. It is hard to prove the guilt of a bribe-taker because the bribe is the result of a consensus, and even in cases of extortion the bribe is still the result of a consensus reached between bribe-taker and bribe-giver. Raiding is different, because there is a struggle, in which one side is the winner and another one is the loser, ready to complain about the injustice to the state. However, if the state bureaucracy is utterly corrupt, the ruling regime is unlikely to react to such a complaint.

Nepotism, as a form and immanent part of corruption, plays a significant role in corporate and property raiding. Nepotism connects corruption and raiding in several ways. Nepotism and inheritance rights have long been considered as both the basis and the reason of sustainability of corrupt regimes. Those in power want to pass their accumulated fortunes to their offspring. These are fortunes accumulated at the expense of the public and the business, both of which constitute the base for extortion and embezzlement, committed by the ruling regime and particular state bureaucrats within the regime's frame. The key issue comes down to inheriting not the stream of income, illicit revenues, proceeds of corruption, access to graft, informal right to collect bribes, but the fundamental source of profit, that is, the enterprise, the company, the economic asset, the property itself.

Inheriting state office may be hard, but inheriting a state or public enterprise is simply impossible, especially in a formal, legal way. At the same time, while inheriting the state office is illegal, it is perfectly legal to inherit a private enterprise, company, or any piece of private property, including land. This seemingly axiomatic situation creates incentives for corrupt state bureaucrats to appropriate economic assets that they manage and formalize their property rights over these assets. And the best and most effective tool in securing not only the stream of bribes, but full-scale guaranteed profit participation is precisely raiding. This view of sustainability of corrupt regimes plays well with the sense of stability developed and indeed imposed by the ruling political regime. Russia's current ruling regime wants to maintain this imagery of pseudo-stability in order to guarantee the sustainability of inheritance rights. The practice of induction of the offspring

138 *Corruption and raiding*

of top politicians in the governing structures of large corporations cements the relationship between the state and business.

Large state-owned banks and other companies eagerly accept children of top Russian bureaucrats and politicians for top managerial positions. In fact, the former are not given much choice. Jointly owned companies and the private ones follow this practice as well. In this way, chief bureaucrats "outsource" their function of receiving illicit revenues, such as bribes, to their offspring and other close relatives, while companies establish close ties with the ruling political regime. As a result of such a reciprocal arrangement, state bureaucrats amass their wealth while securing themselves from formal state prosecution, while companies rely on their governmental connections in order to secure themselves from possible raiding attacks, including those led by the state. As long as this corrupt practice persists, the true anti-raiding campaigns initiated by the ruling political regime are highly unlikely.

Notes

1 Razmahova, Inna. (2008). Uchastie v reiderskih razborkah – pitatel'naya sreda dlya korruptsii [Participation in raiding is a hotbed for corruption]. *Rossijskaya gazeta*, September 3, 2008. Retrieved July 22, 2009, from www.notheft.ru/uchastie-v-rejderskih-razborkah-pitatelnaja-sreda-dlja-korrupcii

2 Krajnov, Yaroslav. (2008). Istoriya reiderstva: osobennosti natsional'nogo peredela [History of raiding: Specifics of national raiding]. *Notheft.ru*, July 17, 2008. Retrieved July 26, 2009, from www.notheft.ru/istorija-rejderstva-osobennosti-nacionalnogo-peredela

3 Reiderstvo i korruptsiya: uslugi i tseny [Raiding and corruption: Services and prices]. *Notheft.ru*, September 5, 2008. Retrieved July 22, 2009, from www.notheft.ru/rejderstvo-i-korrupcija-uslugi-i-ceny

4 Reiderstvo kak sotsial'no-ekonomicheskij i politicheskij fenomen sovremennoj Rossii: otchet o kachestvennom sotsiologicheskom issledovanii. Issledovanie "Tsentra politicheskih tehnologij" pod rukovodstvom Bunina. Moskva, 2008. [Raiding as a socioeconomic and political phenomenon of the modern Russia: A report on the qualitative sociological investigation: An investigation conducted by the Center of Political Technologies led by Bunin]. Moscow, May 2008. Retrieved June 12, 2009, from www. politcom.ru/; www.compromat.ru/main/mix1/raiderycpt.htm

5 As reported in: Russia 2016 Investment Climate Statements Report, Bureau of Economic and Business Affairs, the US Department of State. Washington, DC. July 5, 2016. Retrieved March 1, 2017, from www.state.gov/e/eb/rls/othr/ics/2016/eur/254308.htm

6 Medvedev vspomnil pro smertnuyu kazn': chinovniki navorovali iz kazny uzhe bolee trilliona [Medvedev mentioned death penalty: Bureaucrats have already embezzled from the state over one trillion]. *Newsru.com*, October 29, 2010. Retrieved October 29, 2010, from www.newsru.com/russia/29oct2010/medvedev_2.html

7 Vzyatochnikam pridetsya vyplachivat' shtrafy, stokratno prevyshayushchie summu vzyatki [Bribe-takers will have to pay fines a hundred times the size of the bribe]. *Zagolovki.ru*, February 17, 2011. Retrieved February 17, 2011, from www.zagolovki. ru/daytheme/corruption/17Feb2011

8 Prezident vvel kratnye nakazaniya za vzyatki – samye zhadnye chinovniki zaplatyat polmilliarda [President introduced multiplied punishment for bribes: The greediest bureaucrats will pay half-a-billion]. *Newsru.com*, May 4, 2011. Retrieved May 4, 2011, from www.newsru.com/russia/04may2011/kratno.html

9 Voloshin, Vladimir. (2011). Korruptsionery dadut gosudarstvu "vzyatku" v stokratnom razmere [Corrupt bureaucrats will give the state a hundred times enlarged "bribe"].

Corruption and raiding 139

Komsomol'skaya Pravda, February 16, 2011. Retrieved February 16, 2011, from http://kp.ru/daily/25639/803493/

10 Prezident vvel kratnye nakazaniya za vzyatki – samye zhadnye chinovniki zaplatyat polmilliarda [President introduced multiplied punishment for bribes: The greediest bureaucrats will pay half-a-billion]. *Newsru.com*, May 4, 2011. Retrieved May 4, 2011, from www.newsru.com/russia/04may2011/kratno.html

11 Vzyatochnikam pridetsya vyplachivat' shtrafy, stokratno prevyshayushchie summu vzyatki [Bribe-takers will have to pay fines a hundred times the size of the bribe]. *Zagolovki.ru*, February 17, 2011. Retrieved February 17, 2011, from www.zagolovki.ru/daytheme/corruption/17Feb2011

12 Ibid.

13 Syny pravitel'stva [Sons of the government]. *Newsru.com*, March 2, 2005. Retrieved March 2, 2005, from www.newsru.com/background/02mar2005/synpolka.html

14 Zhurnal Forbes: 24-letnij syn ministra oborony RF stal vitse-prezidentom Gazprombanka [Forbes magazine: 24-year-old son of the minister of defense of the RF became a vice president of Gazprombank]. *Newsru.com*, March 2, 2005. Retrieved March 2, 2005, from www.newsru.com/russia/02mar2005/piter.html

15 Zapadnaya pressa ob "igrishchah v bor'be za vlast' " v Rossii: druzej Putina v goskompaniyakh zamenyat ih synov'ya [Western media on "games in the struggle for power" in Russia: Friends of Putin in state companies will be replaced by their sons]. *Newsru.com*, May 20, 2011. Retrieved May 20, 2011, from www.newsru.com/russia/20may2011/putinschildren.html

16 Les enfants de la "nomenklatura" russe s'exercent à la lutte des places. *La Tribune*, July 18, 2011. Retrieved July 18, 2011, from www.latribune.fr/actualites/economie/international/20110718trib000636854/les-enfants-de-la-nomenklatura-russe-s-exercent-a-la-lutte-des-places-.html

17 Deti rossijskih shpionov i bankirov popolnyayut klan Putina, pishet zapadnaya pressa [Children of spies and bankers join Putin's clan]. *Newsru.com*, July 19, 2011. Retrieved July 19, 2011, from www.newsru.com/russia/19jul2011/clan.html

18 Sergei Ivanov naznachen glavoj "Alrosy" [Sergei Ivanov is appointed the head of Alrosa]. *TASS*, March 6, 2017. Retrieved March 6, 2017, from http://tass.ru/ekonomika/4073929

19 Syn Sergeya Ivanova naznachen glavoj "Alrosy" [Sergei Ivanov's son is appointed as the head of Alrosa]. *Profile*, March 6, 2017. Retrieved March 6, 2017, from www.profile.ru/economics/item/115795-syn-sergeya-ivanova-stal-gendirektorom-alrosy

20 Syn Rogozina stal vitse-prezidentom Ob'edinennoj stroitel'noj korporatsii [Rogozin's son appointed vice president of United Aircraft Corporation]. *Newsru.com*, March 14, 2017. Retrieved March 14, 2017, from www.newsru.com/russia/14mar2017/rogozin.html

21 Yuri Chajka priznal, chto bor'ba s korruptsiej v Rossii fakticheski provaiilas' [Yuri Chajka admitted that the war on corruption in Rusiia has failed]. *Newsru.com*, February 22, 2012. Retrieved February 22, 2012, from http://zagolovki.ru/daytheme/korruptsia/22Feb2012

22 Bastrykin rasskazal, kak spravit'sya s korruptsiej s pomoshch'yu "polnotsennoj konfiskatsii" [Bastrykin told how to deal with corruption with the help of true confiscation]. *Newsru.com*, March 2, 2017. Retrieved March 2, 2017, from www.newsru.com/russia/02mar2017/konf.html

23 Mironov vystupil na "Antiseligere": korruptsionerov nado sazhat' na 25 let [Mironov addressed "Antiseliger": Corrupt bureaucrats should be sentenced to 25 years]. *Newsru.com*, June 18, 2011. Retrieved June 18, 2011, from www.newsru.com/russia/18jun2011/selig.html

24 Ibid.

25 Pomoshchnikov deputatov-eserov zaderzhali za torgovlyu mandatami v budushchej dume [Aids of MPs from Spravedlivaya Rossiya were detained for trading mandates

140 *Corruption and raiding*

to the future Duma]. *Newsru.com*, July 11, 2011. Retrieved July 11, 2011, from www.newsru.com/russia/11jul2011/karamiasin.html

26 Moskovsky chinovnik, lishivshij gorod bole 250 millionov, izbezhal nakazaniya – eto bylo slishkom davno [A Moscow bureaucrat, who deprived the city of over 250,000,000 rubles, avoided the punishment; it was a long time ago]. *Newsru.com*, June 14, 2011. Retrieved June 14, 2011, from www.newsru.com/russia/14jun2011/reklama.html

27 Vedomstva Kudrina, Levitina i Golikovoj stali liderami po chislu upominanij v SMI v kontekste korruptsii [Bureaucracies of Kudrin, Levitin, and Golikova became leaders in terms of media attention in the context of corruption]. *Newsru.com*, July 14, 2011. Retrieved July 14, 2011, from www.newsru.com/russia/14jul2011/lidery.html

28 Mironov vystupil na "Antiseligere": korruptsionerov nado sazhat' na 25 let [Mironov addressed "Antiseliger": Corrupt bureaucrats should be sentenced to 25 years]. *Newsru.com*, June 18, 2011. Retrieved June 18, 2011, from www.newsru.com/russia/18jun2011/selig.html

29 Verkhovny syd otkazal aspirantu, trebovavshemu obyazat' kandidatov v prezidenty deklarirovat' svoi raskhody [Supreme court rejected a claim of a doctoral student who wanted presidential candidates to declare their expenditures]. *Newsru.com*, January 11, 2012. Retrieved January 11, 2012, from www.newsru.com/russia/11jan2012/rashody.html

30 Convention against Corruption UN. New York, 2004. Retrieved June 29, 2011, from www.unodc.org/documents/treaties/UNCAC/Publications/Convention/08-50028_R.pdf

31 V Gosdumu vnesen antikorruptsionnyj zakonoproekt o prezumptsii vinovnosti chinovnikov [The State Duma received an anti-corruption law project regarding the presumption of guilt for bureaucrats]. *Newsru.com*, December 18, 2010. Retrieved December 18, 2010, from www.newsru.com/russia/18dec2010/korru.html

32 Mironov na vstreche s Putinym predlozhil otmenit' prezumptsiyu nevinovnosti dlya chinovnikov [Mironov met with Putin and suggested to abolish presumption of innocence for corrupt bureaucrats]. *Newsru.com*, April 2, 2011. Retrieved April 2, 2011, from www.newsru.com/russia/02apr2011/mirputin.html

33 Kreml' raskritikoval Mironova, predlozhivshego otmenit' prezumptsiyu nevinovnosti dlya chinovnikov [The Kremlin criticized Mironov for suggesting to abolish the presumption of innocence for bureaucrats]. *Newsru.com*, April 3, 2011. Retrieved April 3, 2011, from www.newsru.com/russia/03apr2011/kreml.html

34 Okolo 60% pokupatelej elitnykh kvartir v Moskve ot $2 mln – chinovniki [Around 60 percent of buyers of elite apartments in Moscow at a price of $2 million and up are bureaucrats]. *Newsru.com*, November 7, 2011. Retrieved November 7, 2011, from http://realty.newsru.com/article/07nov2011/slugi_naroda

35 Deputat-milliarder podal deklaratsiyu, iz kotoroj sleduet, chto on nishchij [The billionaire MP filed income declaration, which shows that he is a beggar]. *Newsru.com*, October 1, 2010. Retrieved October 29, 2010, from www.newsru.com/finance/01oct2010/skoch.html

36 Sotrudnik MVD na Kavkaze pozabyl dolozhit' o svoih 9 kvartirah i 15 uchastkah zemli [Employee of the Ministry of the Interior in Caucasus forgot to report his 9 apartments and 15 plots of land]. *Newsru.com*, April 1, 2011. Retrieved April 1, 2011, from http://realty.newsru.com/article/01apr2011/mvd_dohody; http://genproc.gov.ru/news/news-71552/

37 Schetnaya palata za polgoda proverit dostovernost' nalogovyh deklaratsij chinovnikov [The Auditing Chamber will check the income declarations of bureaucrats over the next half-a-year]. *Newsru.com*, January 15, 2011. Retrieved January 15, 2011, from www.newsru.com/russia/15jan2011/vbn.html

38 Litvinova, Anastasiya. (2011). Tol'ko devyat' chelovek iz sta eshche ne nauchilis' davat' vzyatki [Only nine out of every hundred people have not learned how to give

Corruption and raiding 141

bribes]. *RBK Daily*, June 15, 2011. Retrieved June 15, 2011, from www.rbcdaily. ru/2011/06/15/focus/562949980430428

39 Sredni razmer vzyatki v Rossii prevysil 10 tysyach dollarov [Average bribe in Russia exceeds $10,000]. *Newsru.com*, July 24, 2011. Retrieved July 24, 2011, from www. newsru.com/finance/22jul2011/vziatka.html

40 Rossiyane dayut "na lapu" v srednem po 250 tysyach rublej, rasskazali v MVD [Average bribes Russians pay are 250,000 rubles, says MVD]. *Newsru.com*, October 18, 2011. Retrieved October 18, 2011, from www.newsru.com/russia/18oct2011/corruption.html

41 Srednij razmer vzyatki v Rossii vyros v 33 raza za chetyre goda [Size of average bribe increased 33 times over the last four years]. *Newsru.com*, August 22, 2012. Retrieved August 22, 2012, from www.newsru.com/russia/22aug2012/vziatko.html

42 V politsii vychislili razmer sredney vzyatki – ona bol'she sredney zarplaty [Police named the size of an average bribe; it exceeds average salary]. *Newsru.com*, October 25, 2012. Retrieved October 25, 2012, from www.newsru.com/russia/25oct2012/bribes.html

43 MVD: srednij razmer vzyatki v Rossii za god udvoilsya [MVD: The size of an average bribe in Russia over the last year has doubled]. *Newsru.com*, March 21, 2014. Retrieved March 21, 2014, from www.newsru.com/finance/21mar2014/rubrbery.html

44 Pravozashchitniki zayavili ob uvelichenii vtroe srednego razmera vzyatki v Rossii [Human rights activists reported that average bribe in Russia has tripled]. *Newsru. com*, September 3, 2015. Retrieved October 18, 2015, from www.newsru.com/russia/03sep2015/corrup.html

45 V MVD nazvali srednij razmer vzyatki v Rossii – za god on vyros na 75% [Ministry of the Interior reports that the average bribe in Russia increased 75 percent over the last year]. *Newsru.com*, March 16, 2017. Retrieved March 16, 2017, from www.newsru.com/russia/16mar2017/mvd.html

46 Srednyaya summa vzyatki v Moskve za proshlyj god vyrosla v 2,5 raza [Average bribe in Moscow increased 2.5 times in the past year]. *Newsru.com*, January 26, 2017. Retrieved January 26, 2017, from http://newsmsk.com/article/26jan2017/bolshedeneg2.html

47 MVD: srednij razmer vzyatki v Rossii za god udvoilsya [MVD: The size of an average bribe in Russia over the last year has doubled]. *Newsru.com*, March 21, 2014. Retrieved March 21, 2014, from www.newsru.com/finance/21mar2014/rubrbery.html

48 Ushcherb ot korruptsii za 10 mesyatsev 2013 goda sostavil 21 milliard rublej [Corruption damage in first ten months of 2013 is estimated at 21 billion rubles]. *Newsru. com*, December 9, 2013. Retrieved December 9, 2013, from www.newsru.com/russia/09dec2013/21.html

49 Rossiyane otsenili razgul korruptsii: mestnuyu vlast' obvinyayut vse chashche, GIBDD – rezhe [Russians give their thoughts on the scope of corruption: Local authorities are allegedly more frequently corrupt, while traffic patrols are less]. *Newsru.com*, October 23, 2013. Retrieved October 23, 2013, from www.newsru.com/russia/23oct2013/opros_2.html

50 Tul'skij chinovnik arestovan za vzyatku v 40 mln rublej [A bureaucrat in Tula was arrested for a bribe of 40 million rubles]. *Newsru.com*, January 7, 2011. Retrieved January 7, 2011, from www.newsru.com/russia/07jan2011/volkov.html

51 MVD otsenivaet ob'em nezakonno vyvedennyh iz Rossii za rubezh deneg v 5 trln rublej [MVD estimates total illegal capital outflow from Russia at 5 trillion rubles]. *Newsru.com*, August 15, 2011. Retrieved August 15, 2011, from www.newsru.com/finance/15aug2011/5bln_uteklo.html

52 Vitse-prem'er Shuvalov na primere "Rosatoma" pokazal goskorporatsiyam, kak borot'sya s korruptsiej [Vice Premier Shuvalov used "Rosatom" as an example of anti-corruption campaign for state corporations]. *Newsru.com*, October 4, 2011. Retrieved October 4, 2011, from www.newsru.com/russia/04oct2011/rosatom.html

142 Corruption and raiding

53 Sledstvie poprosilo sud ob areste byvshego zamdirektora Rosatoma Evstratova [Investigators asked the court to arrest former deputy director of Rosatom, Evstratov]. *Newsru. com*, July 20, 2011. Retrieved July 20, 2011, from www.newsru.com/russia/20jul2011/evstratarest.html

54 Byvshij zamgendirektora Rosatoma arestovan po podozreniyu v khishchenii poryadka 50 mln rublej [Former deputy director of Rosatom is arrested and suspected of embezzlement of around 50 million rubles]. *Newsru.com*, July 20, 2011. Retrieved July 20, 2011, from www.newsru.com/russia/20jul2011/rosatom2.html

55 Eks-zamglavy Rosatoma zaderzhan za skachivanie tekstov o yadernoj bezopasnosti iz interneta [Former deputy director of Rosatom is arrested for downloading texts on nuclear safety from the internet]. *Newsru.com*, July 20, 2011. Retrieved July 20, 2011, from www.newsru.com/russia/20jul2011/rosatom.html

56 General-major MVD Vladimir Ovchinsky: mafiya pronikla vo vse gosstruktury RF [Major General of MVD Vladimir Ovchinsky: Mafia infiltrated all state bureaucracies in the RF]. *Newsru.com*, June 29, 2011. Retrieved June 29, 2011, from www.newsru.com/crime/29jun2011/ovchinskymafiarf.html

57 Court. Raiding. *3 Kanal*, June 8, 2009. Retrieved July 29, 2009, from www.youtube.com/watch?v=VyvwC5VehQs

58 Dmitry Medvedev nachinaet kompleksnuyu bor'bu s korruptsiej [Dmitry Medvedev starts a systemic fight with corruption]. *Newsru.com*, May 19, 2008. Retrieved May 9, 2009, from www.newsru.com/russia/19may2008/corrupt.html

59 Medvedev priznal svoyu bor'bu s korruptsiej besplodnoj i predlozhil pomenyat' rossiyanam mental'nost' [Medvedev admitted that his struggle against corruption is fruitless and called on Russians to change their mentality]. *Newsru.com*, July 14, 2010. Retrieved July 14, 2010, from www.newsru.com/russia/14jul2010/medvedev.html

60 Mosgorduma, kotoruyu Zhirinovsky nazval "rassadnikom korruptsii," hochet ot nego deneg [Moscow city council wants money from Zhirinovsky for he called them the "hotbed of corruption"]. *Newsru.com*, November 11, 2009. Retrieved November 11, 2009, from www.newsru.com/russia/11nov2009/mosgordum_zhirin.html

61 Luzhkov poluchit po polmilliona rublej ot "Kommersanta" i Nemtsova. Poslednij sochinil original'noe oproverzhenie [Luzhkov will receive half a million rubles from each of the respondents, "Kommersant" and Nemtsov: The latter composed a clever response]. *Newsru.com*, November 30, 2009. Retrieved November 30, 2009, from www.newsru.com/russia/30nov2009/polmil.html

62 Medvedev nameren slomat' stereotypy rossiyan v otnoshenii suda [Medvedev is intended to break the stereotypes of Russians regarding the courts]. *Newsru.com*, May 20, 2008. Retrieved May 9, 2009, from www.newsru.com/russia/20may2008/medvedevsud.html

63 Medvedev priznal svoyu bor'bu s korruptsiej besplodnoj i predlozhil pomenyat' rossiyanam mental'nost' [Medvedev admitted that his struggle against corruption is fruitless and called on Russians to change their mentality]. *Newsru.com*, July 14, 2010. Retrieved July 14, 2010, from www.newsru.com/russia/14jul2010/medvedev.html

64 Medvedev nameren slomat' stereotypy rossiyan v otnoshenii suda [Medvedev is intended to break the stereotypes of Russians regarding the courts]. *Newsru.com*, May 20, 2008. Retrieved May 9, 2009, from www.newsru.com/russia/20may2008/medvedevsud.html

65 Zakon ob antikorruptsionnoj ekspertize podpisan prezidentom [The anti-corruption expertise is signed into law by the president]. *Notheft.ru*, July 21, 2009. Retrieved July 23, 2009, from www.notheft.ru/zakon-ob-antikorrupcionnoj-jekspertize-podpisan-prezidentom

66 Administratsiya prezidenta aktiviziruet bor'bu s korruptsiej [Presidential administration enforces the fight against corruption]. *Newsru.com*, May 21, 2010. Retrieved May 21, 2010, from www.newsru.com/finance/21may2010/korruption.html

67 U Zhirinovskogo predlagayut stavit' klejmo na chinovnikakh-vzyatochnikakh [Zhirinovsky suggests marking for life bureaucrats who take bribes]. *Newsru.ua*, July 19, 2010. Retrieved July 19, 2010, from http://rus.newsru.ua/world/19jul2010/zhirik.html

Corruption and raiding 143

68 Bastrykin rasskazal, kak spravit'sya s korruptsiej s pomoshch'yu "polnotsennoj konfiskatsii" [Bastrykin told how to deal with corruption with the help of true confiscation]. *Newsru.com*, March 2, 2017. Retrieved March 2, 2017, from www.newsru.com/russia/02mar2017/konf.html

69 MVD predlagaet sazhat' vzyatkodatelej, dazhe esli oni sami prishli v militsiyu s zayavleniem [MVD offers to sentence bribe-givers, even if they voluntarily came to the police]. *Newsru.com*, July 26, 2009. Retrieved July 26, 2009, from www.newsru.com/russia/26jul2009/nmj.html

70 Annual Report of the Federal Bailiffs' Service of the Russian Federation for 2009. *The Federal Bailiffs' Service of the Russian Federation*, February 17, 2010. Moscow. Retrieved February 17, 2010, from www.fssprus.ru/press_itogi_god.html

71 V Moskve sudebnyj pristav poluchil ot biznes-ledi kvartiru za snyatie aresta s imushchestva [In Moscow, a bailiff received an apartment from a business lady in exchange for lifting court-ordered seizure of her property]. *Newsru.com*, May 20, 2015. Retrieved May 20, 2015, from www.newsru.com/crime/20may2015/fsspbribeflatmsk.html

72 Bortsy s korruptsiej iz glavka MVD zapodozreny v provokatsii vzyatki u chinovnikov [Officers from the anti-corruption bureau are suspected in provocation of a bribe from bureaucrats]. *Newsru.com*, February 17, 2014. Retrieved February 17, 2014, from www.zagolovki.ru/daytheme/kurgan/17Feb2014

73 GUEBiPK MVD, Glavnoe upravlenie ekonomicheskoj bezopasnosti i protivodejstviya korruptsii Ministerstva vnutrennikh del [Head Department of Economic Security and Corruption Prevention of the Ministry of the Interior].

74 Arestovannye sotrudniki GUEBiPK MVD pytalis' podstavit' zamglavy upravleniya FSB, uznali zhurnalisty [Journalists found out that the arrested officers of GUEBiPK MVD tried to set up the deputy head of FSB]. *Newsru.com*, February 18, 2014. Retrieved February 18, 2014, from www.newsru.com/russia/18feb2014/demin.html

75 Putin uvolil glavnogo bortsa s korruptsiej v MVD iz-za korruptsionnogo skandala [Putin fired the major anti-corruption police general due to the corruption scandal]. *Newsru.com*, February 22, 2014. Retrieved February 22, 2014, from www.zagolovki.ru/daytheme/putin/22Feb2014

76 Zamnachal'nika GUEBiPK MVD Rossii zaderzhan po delu o "provokatsii vzyatki" [Deputy head of GUEBiPK MVD of Russia is arrested as a part of the case on provocation of bribe]. *Newsru.com*, February 25, 2014. Retrieved February 25, 2014, from www.newsru.com/russia/25feb2014/kolesnikov.html

77 Dvum vysokopostavlennym bortsam s korruptsiej iz MVD RF pred'yavleno obvinenie v provokatsii vzyatki [Two high-ranking police officers from the anti-corruption unit were charged with provoking a bribe]. *Newsru.com*, March 5, 2014. Retrieved March 5, 2014, from www.newsru.com/russia/05mar2014/salavat.html

78 Putin uvolil politsejskogo generala Kolesnikova, ch'i podchinennye pytalis' sprovotsirovat' vzyatku sotrudnika FSB [Putin fired police general Kolesnikov, whose subordinates attempted to provoke a bribe for a FSB officer]. *Newsru.com*, March 11, 2014. Retrieved March 11, 2014, from www.newsru.com/russia/11mar2014/koles.html

79 Arestovannyj za "provokatsiyu vzyatki" general MVD dostavlen iz SIZO v bol'nitsu s ser'eznoj travmoj golovy [Arrested for the provocation of a bribe MVD general is admitted to the hospital from the detention facility with a serious head injury]. *Newsru.com*, May 7, 2014. Retrieved May 7, 2014, from www.newsru.com/russia/07may2014/kolesnikov.html

80 Zaderzhan eks-glava antikorruptsionnogo upravleniya MVD – generala vzyali na rybalke [Former head of the anti-corruption bureau of MVD was arrested while fishing]. *Newsru.com*, May 8, 2014. Retrieved May 8, 2014, from www.newsru.com/russia/08may2014/sugrobov.html

81 Arestovannyj za "provokatsiyu vzyatki" general MVD pokonchil s soboj vo vremya doprosa [Arrested for the provocation of a bribe MVD general committed suicide during the interrogation]. *Newsru.com*, June 16, 2014. Retrieved June 16, 2014, from www.newsru.com/arch/russia/16jun2014/kolesnikov.html

144 *Corruption and raiding*

References

Barnes, Andrew. (2006). *Owning Russia: The Struggle over Factories, Farms, and Power.* Ithaca: Cornell University Press.

Bunin, Igor. (2008). Reiderstvo kak sotsial'no-ekonomicheskij i politicheskij fenomen sovremennoj Rossii: otchet o kachestvennom sotsiologicheskom issledovanii. Issledovanie "Tsentra politicheskih tehnologij" pod rukovodstvom Bunina. Moskva, 2008. [Raiding as a Socio-Economic and Political Phenomenon of the Modern Russia: A Report on the Qualitative Sociological Investigation: An Investigation Conducted by the Center of Political Technologies Led by Bunin]. Moscow, May 2008. Retrieved June 12, 2009, from www.politcom.ru/; www.compromat.ru/main/mix1/raiderycpt.htm

Chapaev, Roman. (2007). International Commercial Arbitration: Assessment Report on the Results of the Assessment in the CIS (Armenia, Azerbaijan, Georgia, Kazakhstan, Kyrgyz Republic, Moldova, Russia, Tajikistan, Turkmenistan, Ukraine, Uzbekistan) and Mongolia. EBRD-World Bank. Retrieved from www.ebrd.com/country/sector/law/judicial/arbitrat/arbitration.pdf

Egorova, N. (1997). Provokatsiya vzyatki libo kommercheskogo podkupa [Provocation by bribe or commercial bribery]. *Rossijskaya yustitsiya*, 8, pp. 26–28.

Glaz'ev, Sergei. (1997). *Genotsid: Rossiya i novyj mirovoj poryadok [Genocide: Russia and the New World Order]*. Moscow: Erga.

Hanson, Philip. (2011). Networks, Cronies and Business Plans: Business-State Relations in Russia. In Vadim Kononenko & Arkady Moshes (eds.). *Russia as a Network State: What Works in Russia When State Institutions Do Not?* (pp. 113–138). New York: Palgrave Macmillan.

Ivanova, K. (2009). Vliyanie kachestvennogo sostava predstavitel'nogo organa poseleniya na vozmozhnosti razvitiya munitsipal'nogo obrazovaniya [The Influence of Qualitative Structure of a Representative Body of a Settlement on the Possibilities of Municipal Body Development]. *Vestnik Povolzhskoj akademii gosudarstvennoj sluzhby*, 4(21), pp. 15–21. Saratov. Retrieved from www.pags.ru/vestnik/archive/text_pdf/21.pdf

Kotin, V. (1996). Provokatsiya vzyatki (K problem sovershenstvovaniya zakonodatel'stva) [Bribe Provocation]. *Gosudarstvo i pravo*, 3, pp. 82–88.

Kryshtanovskaya, Olga & White, Stephen. (2011). The Formation of Russia's Network Directorate. In Vadim Kononenko & Arkady Moshes (eds.). *Russia as a Network State: What Works in Russia When State Institutions Do Not?* (pp. 19–38). New York: Palgrave Macmillan.

Ledeneva, Alena. (2004a). The Genealogy of *Krugovaya Poruka*: Forced Trust as a Feature of Russian Political Culture. In: Markova, I., ed., *Trust and Democratic Transition in Post-Communist Europe*. Oxford, UK: Oxford University Press.

Ledeneva, Alena. (2004b). Underground Financing in Russia. In Janos Kornai, Bo Rothstein, and Susan Rose-Ackerman (eds.). *Creating Social Trust in Post-Socialist Transition* (pp. 71–90). New York: Palgrave Macmillan.

Ledeneva, Alena. (2011). Can Medvedev Change Sistema? Informal Networks and Public Administration in Russia. In Vadim Kononenko & Arkady Moshes (eds.). *Russia as a Network State: What Works in Russia When State Institutions Do Not?* (pp. 39–61). New York: Palgrave Macmillan.

Ortmann, Stefanie. (2011). The Russian Network State as a Great Power. In Vadim Kononenko & Arkady Moshes (eds.). *Russia as a Network State: What Works in Russia When State Institutions Do Not?* (pp. 139–163). New York: Palgrave Macmillan.

Petrov, Nikolay. (2011). Who Is Running Russia's Regions? In Vadim Kononenko & Arkady Moshes (eds.). *Russia as a Network State: What Works in Russia When State Institutions Do Not?* (pp. 81–112). New York: Palgrave Macmillan.

Corruption and raiding 145

Pistor, Katarina & Xu, Chenggang. (2004). Beyond Law Enforcement: Governing Financial Markets in China and Russia. In Janos Kornai, Bo Rothstein, & Susan Rose-Ackerman (eds.). *Creating Social Trust in Post-Socialist Transition* (pp. 167–189). New York: Palgrave Macmillan.

Power, Timothy & Taylor, Matthew. (2011). *Corruption and Democracy in Brazil: The Struggle for Accountability*. Notre Dame, IN: University of Notre Dame Press.

Rose-Ackerman, Susan & Søreide, Tina (eds.). (2011). *International Handbook of the Economics of Corruption*, Volume Two. Northampton, MA: Edward Elgar.

Russian Statistical Yearbook, 2008. Moscow: Goskomstat.

Simis, Konstantin. (1982). *USSR: The Corrupt Society*. New York: Simon & Schuster.

Vaksberg, Arkady. (1991). *The Soviet Mafia*. New York: St. Martin's Press.

Varnalij, Zakharij & Mazur, Irina. (2007). Reiderstvo v Ukraini: peredumovy ta shlyahi podolannya. *Strategichni Pryoritety*, 2(3), pp. 129–136. Retrieved April 2, 2009, from www.niss.gov.ua/book/StrPryor/3/17.pdf

Voslensky, Michael. (1984). *Nomenklatura: The Soviet Ruling Class*. Garden City, NY: Doubleday.

Wedeman, Andrew. (2012). *Double Paradox: Rapid Growth and Rising Corruption in China*. Ithaca & London: Cornell University Press.

Whitefield, Stephen. (1993). *Industrial Power and the Soviet State*. Oxford: Clarendon Press.

Yadav, Vineeta. (2011). *Political Parties, Business Groups, and Corruption in Developing Countries*. New York: Oxford University Press.

Zamoshkin, Sergei. (1999). Vzyatka. A mozhet byt' provokatsiya? [Bribe. Or may be provocation?] *Chistye ruki*, 2, pp. 82–84.

Zon, Hans van. (2008). *Russia's Development Problem: The Cult of Power*. New York: Palgrave Macmillan.

Conclusion

The phenomenon of raiding is normally considered as a direct and explicit manifestation of the ongoing struggle for economically productive or valuable assets. These assets, including enterprises, are either profitable or have a strong potential to generate profit after certain corporate procedures and manipulations, including restructuring, change of management, enlargement, or reinvestment. Raiding in the post-Soviet Russia is regarded as nothing less than the ongoing war for property. And as any other war, this war for property is detrimental to the national economy. The state is periodically declaring war on corruption and raiding, but thus far utterly unsuccessful. At the same time, the ruling authoritarian regime itself may be taking part in corporate and property raiding. A sense of permanent struggle for anything of an immediate market value is in the air. There is also a strong sense that this epic battle will never see an end. Building on the previously published scholarship combined with legal documents, policy briefs, results of interviews and surveys, and numerous media reports, this study offers the corruption, coercion, and control model as an explanatory tool for the phenomenon of post-Soviet raiding.

Suppression of corporate autonomy, the induction of state bureaucrats into corporate governing boards, the imposition of pseudo-accountability under the nontransparent financial regulations, and direct informal control are used by the central authorities and local administrations in order to control businessmen and the business activities of the companies. These are all manifestations of the corruption, coercion, and control model. Under the conditions of market transition, when laws are constantly changing and the rules are unclear or subject to wide interpretation, the emerging class of entrepreneurs and private property owners cannot feel comfortable, unless they build their business with the help of corruption and buy protection from bureaucrats. State bureaucrats are placed in conditions of financial survival while businessmen find it hard to comply with laws and regulations even if they in good faith attempt to do so. Numerous violations of confusing laws become virtually unavoidable. These violations are registered and used by state bureaucrats to blackmail businessmen. This type of blackmail comes not from criminals and racketeers, but from the ruling autocratic regime. The Russian political establishment uses this mechanism of corruption and subversion in order to advance the corruption, coercion, and control model of governance. The

Despite the large scale and scope of raiding, this socioeconomic phenomenon remains vague and not well defined. This study defines raiding as a relation that emerges between economic actors regarding alienation and appropriation of property, when alienation is done against the will or without consent of the previous owner and without proper compensation, while appropriation occurs within the layers of legality. This study understands proper compensation to be in accordance with existing market prices on a given asset. Raiding anticipates an economic damage that may exist in the form of a loss of economic asset, or in the form of interruption of a production process, or as damage to business reputation. Covering raiding actions with layers of legality, giving raiding a form of legal action, can be observed through many stages of the hostile takeover: raiders submit proper documentation in courts, even though some documents may be nothing else but fraud; storm troopers used by raiders to take over the targeted enterprise often dress in a uniform reminiscent of that of the state law enforcement agencies or even the real police uniform with all the insignia, which is clearly illegal. Raiders use the mask of legality with a special level of hypocrisy and at full capacity in order to project an image of the state-served justice, and produce some impression of legality. Even in cases of outright fraud with the fake court decisions and manipulations with the charter and registration documents, the act of appropriation is dressed in the cloth of pseudo-legality.

Corporate and property raiding in Russia is distinct from corporate raiding in the West not only with its frequently exposed violent character and latent corruption. There is yet another – fundamental – distinction that becomes clear when placed in the context of the market transition. In addition to such a fundamental determinant as corruption, raiding in Russia has an inverted character. This means that the stage of appropriation precedes alienation. At first, court decisions are made and documents for the change of owner are legalized. This initial stage of raiding symbolizes appropriation. Then comes the second stage, the alienation. Alienation can manifest itself in a violent form as a storming of the property, or a nonviolent form. The latter is what one sees in mass media reports, while the former is much less visible. As a result of this inversion, many enterprises and property have two or more owners at once. These owners claim exclusive ownership rights over the entire property, not the shared property. Each of such owners supports his/her claims with court decisions and other legal documents that give the right to manage the property, derive income from it, or to sell it in part or in full.

There is a time lag between the final realization of the acts of alienation and appropriation. The inverted character of raiding is preserved in its essence even in cases when a property is first alienated and only then appropriated. This rule holds because formally the alienation is done with a hidden intent and a clearly designed plan of the consequent appropriation. This means that de facto appropriation in raiding always precedes alienation. The delineation between the formal and the real becomes especially clear in discovering the raiding phenomenon. The formality of the initial stage of alienation is based on the real existing and preceding

148 *Conclusion*

stage of appropriation. For instance, when state bureaucrats alienate state property and remove it from state control, they a priori know how exactly they will pass the property rights to themselves or the client who ordered and paid for the whole raiding operation. It means that there is a clearly designed plan and the basis for such an appropriation.

The state in Russia is distinct with its duality, and this duality has a direct impact on the character of raiding. Dualism of the position of the post-Soviet state in Russia is determined by the trajectory of the inverted development. The inversion in this case is due to the fact that the state, which owned everything during the Soviet era, now refuses the part of a whole instead of gaining control over it. The state continues facing the issue of optimizing its presence in the economy. The state, and more specifically the ruling political regime, has yet to decide how much of the national economy should be given away to private hands through privatization, and how much should be retained in state or public ownership. Families or clans that constitute the core of the ruling political regime personify the state and express their interests through the state. This personification partially removes the controversy between privatization and the wish of the state to retain the assets. Clans that captured the state privatize state assets to their personal benefit, transferring state property to themselves on behalf of the state.

In terms of relationships with private capital and business in general, modern Russian bureaucracy demonstrates transition from the security and protection function to the redistribution function. Participation of the state bureaucracy in the process of corporate raiding marks this transition. In this regard, this study introduces economically active bureaucracy as a new term that denotes a phenomenon of post-Soviet bureaucracy. Stalinist bureaucracy enjoyed plenty of ascriptive characteristics, and not necessarily favorable ones. Nevertheless, the post-Soviet bureaucracy has overdone the Stalinist bureaucracy in just about every negative category, including corruption. The bureaucratic caste is traditionally considered as the community of civil servants working for a certain salary determined and paid by the state. Accordingly, bureaucrats as a rule have no special financial incentives to work more efficiently and effectively. In addition, bureaucrats collect bribes and other illicit benefits to the extent possible to sell functions of the state. At the same time, they have to be cautious and weigh possible risks of losing their bread-winning places and facing criminal prosecution. Economically active bureaucracy means something more than this, extending the boundaries of a usual bureaucracy while preserving its rigidity.

Post-Soviet bureaucrats are not satisfied with the salary received from the state budget and illicit benefits collected from businesses and other clients. Russian bureaucrats want to share in the profits, and this is known to be a function of the business owner, the one who owns at least a part of the production. And it is not that civil servants are forbidden to engage in private business – all those who have a business use well-known schemes to circumvent this prohibition set by the state. Not all bureaucrats have their own business, including not only street-level bureaucrats, but also high-ranking state officials. State bureaucrats are no longer satisfied with their function of protecting businesses against external aggressors

Conclusion   149

and their raiding assaults on businesses, prescribed by the ruling regime. Bureaucrats offer services to facilitate redistribution of not only access to limited resources, public goods, spheres of influence and market segments, but business assets as well. While helping raiders to capture someone else's business, state bureaucrats in fact participate in the redistribution of property, profit-generating assets, and businesses, and expect a reward from this future profit, obtained by the raiders or the new owners. Therefore, bureaucrats reach the stage and the level of profit participation. This is no longer the use of functions delegated by the state for personal purposes or personal enrichment, but an explicit economic activity.

Although Russian raiders frequently break laws and use services of post-Soviet bureaucrats rendered in exchange for bribes, they are quite different from economically active bureaucrats. They are also very different from their Western counterparts. Methods of Russian raiders oftentimes include actions punishable as crimes. The most obvious methods of raiders include document fraud, falsification of protocols of shareholder meetings, production of signatures, bribery of the state registry officers and state bureaucrats, and production of false documents. One of the popular methods of this kind is production of fraudulent court decisions, handed down in a distant region. Raiding is now traditionally being divided into three types: "black," "grey," and "white." Such a gamut apparently reflects the degree of darkness of different elements of raiding, from the most violent and illegal to almost legal or even perfectly legal. It appears that while in the West raiders act within the acceptable legal limits, in the post-Soviet space legal actions of raiders are oftentimes not considered as raiding at all. Both entrepreneurs and ordinary people suffer from raiders. Entrepreneurial activities are aimed at receiving profit. However, raiders are often interested not in the profit that a firm receives from its business activities, but in extracting profit from a hostile takeover and sale of certain valuable economic assets, be it an enterprise, real estate, a housing unit, or any other asset that has market value. Accordingly, entrepreneurs who do not own any material assets are unlikely to be targeted by raiders. At the same time, those individuals who own certain assets, such as housing or land, are potential objects of raiding attacks, even though they may not necessarily be entrepreneurs.

The widespread raiding that targets property owners and businessmen leaves the latter in a position of permanent search for protection. Concerns over security of business and property may well exceed concerns over high profitability. But the situation is even more complex, given the dual nature of the Russian state and the constant striving of the ruling political regime for its survivability. Results of surveys indicate that concerns over high tax rates differentiate Russian businessmen from their peers in Europe and Central Asia regions, upper middle income group countries, and the world. At the same time, their worries about access to finance and corruption are about the same as those of their peers in the region, the income group, and the world. It may sound confusing at first that in such a highly corrupt country as Russia, businessmen see corruption only as the third most significant obstacle for doing business. The corruption, coercion, and control model serves as a perfect explanation for this seemingly confusing ranking of priorities. High tax

150 *Conclusion*

rates combined with confusing tax legislation and contradictory provisions make it very difficult or even impossible to comply with tax laws. The noncompliance, in its turn, leads to administrative and criminal responsibility of business owners and managers. This responsibility becomes a powerful tool in the hands of corrupt state bureaucrats. By using this leverage, top-ranking state officials exploit large corporations while street-level bureaucrats attack small enterprises. Business vulnerability based on tax violations and selective justice forms the base for extortion and threats of hostile takeovers. In many instances, it is less costly for entrepreneurs to give bribes to state officials than to pay taxes to the state budget.

When family clans privatize state assets to their personal benefit, they face the need to transfer these assets to their offspring in the future. Nepotism, as a form and immanent part of corruption, plays a significant role in corporate and property raiding. Nepotism connects corruption and raiding in several ways. Nepotism and inheritance rights have long been considered as both the basis and the reason of sustainability of corrupt regimes. Those in power want to pass their accumulated fortunes to their offspring. These are fortunes accumulated at the expense of the public and the business, both of which constitute the base for extortion and embezzlement, committed by the ruling regime and particular state bureaucrats within the regime's frame. The key issue comes down to inheriting not the stream of income, illicit revenues, proceeds of corruption, access to graft, informal right to collect bribes, but the fundamental source of profit, that is, the enterprise, the company, the economic asset, the property itself.

The prospects of Russia overcoming corruption-based corporate and property raiding are rather bleak. Given the high level of corruption that characterizes law enforcement agencies, it should not be expected that these agencies will literally fight themselves – and do so effectively – in an attempt to eradicate unlawful corporate raiding, especially if officers of law enforcement agencies benefit from it directly. The solution might be in developing institutions of civil society, including those aimed at protecting private property rights of entrepreneurs. At present, however, this solution appears to be unrealistic; Russia lacks civil society, its culture and principles. It is remarkable that political instability, so typical for the former Soviet bloc, is only the fourth most significant obstacle for doing business named by entrepreneurs in Russia. Russia's ruling authoritarian regime places significant effort in creating the illusion of stability, including political stability. Here, political stability is equated to sustainability of the ruling regime. Thus, businessmen are not much concerned with political instability, focusing instead on tax rates and corruption. Furthermore, the ruling authoritarian regime suppresses any attempts at constructing civil society in the country as it perceives civil society initiatives as being threatening to the regime's sustainability.

Index

Abramovich, Roman 66
abuse of public office 5
Academy of the National Economy 71
accountability 114, 117
administrative resource 25, 46, 114
Akademiya narodnogo hozyajstva 71
alienation 31, 32, 36, 37–41, 47
Allen, David 23
Almond, George 20
amendment 72, 73, 75, 76, 122, 127
Andreski, Stanislav 20
Anechiarico, Frank 20
ANH 71
Anti-abuse 134
anti-corruption 73, 75, 114, 122, 123, 126,
    131–135
Antiproizvol 134
Anti-Raiding 2008 102
anti-raiding 47, 68, 70, 72, 75, 132
anti-raiding campaign 68, 102
anti-raiding legislation 70
anti-raiding measures 132
appraisers 76
appropriation 32, 33, 36–41, 71, 85, 147
Arbat Prestige 73, 74
Aslund, Anders 5, 6, 24
assets 12, 22, 33, 34, 45, 52, 57
Auditing Chamber 98, 128
Auerbach, Alan 28
authoritative bureaucratic hierarchy 57
average bribes 128, 134

Baev, Pavel 68
bailiffs 43, 68–70, 133
ban 69, 72
Banfield, Edward 20
bankruptcy 28, 29, 48, 71, 85, 88, 94
bankruptcy cases 71
bankruptcy law of 1998 71
Barnes, Andrew 2, 21, 44

Barzel, Yoram 30
Becker, Uwe 7
Belgorodskaya oblast' 128
Berezovsky, Boris 26, 66–67
black market 66, 121
Black, Bernard 2
blackmail 27, 50–51, 70, 89, 95, 135, 146
Bodin, Per-Arne 7
Bogatikov, Alexander 131
Bratanov, Viktor 129
Brezhnev, Leonid 121
bribe-givers 120, 122, 133–134, 137
bribery 47, 70, 90, 122, 126, 130
bribes 20, 50, 65, 87, 91, 105, 121, 131
bribe-takers 122, 123
Browder, William ix
Brück, Tilman 5
Bukato, Victor 73
Bunce, Valerie 23
bureaucracy 62–66, 77, 120, 125, 135
bureaucrats 12, 20, 26, 39, 41, 64
Buzgalin, Alexander 39
Bykov, Anatoly 64, 74

capital flight 98
causing nightmares for business 76
centralization of production 47, 52
Chajka, Yuri 126
Chapaev, Roman 117
Chavez, Hugo 59
China 13, 118–121
Chubais, Anatoly Borisovich 53
Chunling, Li 5
Church 23
civil servants 34, 65, 77, 115, 125, 128–132
clan 62, 124, 131
Coffee, John C. Jr. 28
Coleman, James 20
collective farms 45
collectors' business 70

152 *Index*

Colton, Timothy 24
commercial arbitration court 46
commercial dispute 46
commodity 76
commodity raiding 76
Communist Party of the Russian
Federation 59
competition 24, 49, 62–63, 129
complexity 28, 30, 36
confidential information 95
confiscation of property 123, 127, 132
conflict of interest 129, 132
conflict regulation 71
consolidation 49, 87
conspiracy 121
Constitution 127–128
consumer credit 70
contract killings 130–131
Convention Against Corruption 127
corporate autonomy 21, 51
corporate control 45, 116
corporate lawyers 73
corporate raiders 48, 67, 73, 86
corporate raiding 28–29, 48, 67, 75, 85
corruptibility of courts 86
corruption 3–7, 20–27, 114–118
corruption in courts 47, 52
Council of the Federation 102
court bailiffs 43, 68, 133
court decisions 32, 38, 43, 51, 84, 108, 147
court system 45–46, 52
court-ordered restriction 133
cover-up 25
creditors 94
crime 72, 99, 108
criminal activities 70
Criminal Code 72, 122–123, 126, 134–135
criminal investigations 46, 72–73, 126
criminal justice 117
criminalization 116

damage of raiding 101
Darden, Keith 20, 22, 27
De Haan, Jakob 19
Deane, Judy 2
debtors 69, 71
decentralization 3–4
default 64
defendants 69–70
delays 64
Demekhin, Aleksey 92–93
democratization 23, 40
Department for Organized Crime
Prevention 68

Department of Economic Security of the
Chamber of Trade & Commerce of the
Russian Federation 131
Department of Economic Security of the
Moscow city government 96
Deputy Head of the Prosecutor General 99
Deputy-Chief of the Investigations
Committee 133
derivative 7, 27, 86
detective 133–134
developers 41
directors of Soviet enterprises 45
discretionary power 41, 114
distribution 26, 31, 35, 77, 101
dividends 93
document fraud 88, 108
Drahokoupil, Jan 10
Drucker, Peter 28
Dugin, Aleksandr 62
Duhamel, Luc 6
Duma 31, 49, 59, 75–76, 98, 122, 126–128
Duvanova, Dinissa 47, 106
Dzarasov, Ruslan 8

Easter, Gerald 8–9
EBITDA 91
economic crime 35–36, 99–100, 130, 133
economic development 13, 39, 42, 48, 64,
89, 116, 124
economic growth 19, 59, 77, 116–117, 119
economically active bureaucracy 62–66
effective owners 33, 42, 48
effectiveness 42, 62, 102, 124
efficiency 59, 77
Egorova, Ol'ga 134
election commissions 133
electricity 90, 103, 106
embezzlement 27, 120–122, 130
embezzling funds 121
enterprise 27, 32, 37, 121, 131, 137
entrepreneurship 34–37
Ethics Committee of the State Duma 98
European appeals court 75
European Court of Human Rights 75
Evroset 76
expropriation 27, 36, 40, 59, 70
extortion 29, 44, 70, 87, 105, 120, 135

fair market price 34, 63
falsifications 26, 70
Federal Security Services 102, 134–136
Federal Services of Court Bailiffs 133
Federal Services on Financial Markets 73
Federal Tax Services 72, 74

Index 153

Federal'naya nalogovaya sluzhba 72
Federal'naya sluzhba bezopasnosti 102
Federal'naya sluzhba po finansovym
  rynkam 73
Federal'naya sluzhba sudebnyh pristavov
  133
Feniks 115
fiduciary responsibility 73
FIG 70
financial crisis 92
financial documents 75
financial-industrial group 70, 85
Finansgrup 70, 90
fine 69–70, 74, 122–123, 130
Firestone, Thomas 2, 29, 45–46
First Vice Mayor of Moscow 96
FNS 72
Foreign Intelligence Services 71
foreign investors 1, 118, 129
Fortescue, Stephen 9
fraud 32, 33, 41–42, 51, 70, 74, 86–88, 108,
  126
free market 57
Frye, Timothy 2, 3, 10
FSB 102, 135
FSFR 73
FSSP 133

gambling businesses 72
gangster operations 130
Gans-Morse, Jordan 2, 28, 29
Gaughan, Patrick 28
Gazprom 62, 75, 124
GDP 61
Gel'man, Vladimir 7
Germany 64
gift 65, 105–106, 132
Gilman, Martin 9
Giuliano, Elise 7
Glavnoe upravlenie ekonomicheskoj
  bezopasnosti i protivodejstviya korruptsii
  Ministerstva vnutrennikh del 134–135
Glaz'ev, Sergei 116
Godzimirski, Jakub 8
good governance 5, 19
Gosduma 31, 49, 59, 69, 75–76, 98, 122
greenmail 28, 37, 68, 87
Gref, German 48
Gritsenko, Andrei 39
gross waste 133
guarantees 27, 62–63
GUEBiPK MVD 134–135
Guriev, Sergei 24
Gusinsky, Vladimir 26, 75

Hanson, Philip 2, 121
Hass, Jeffrey 8–9
Hay, Colin 5
Head Department of Economic Security
  and Corruption Prevention of the
  Ministry of the Interior 66, 134–135
healthcare 91, 127
Hedlund, Stefan 7–8, 24
hierarchy 23, 25–27, 57, 64, 102
Holmberg, Sören 19
Holmes, Leslie 9
hostile takeovers 3, 6, 12, 28, 34, 42–43,
  47–49, 67
hotbed of corruption 131
housing 96, 108, 149
Huskey, Eugene 9

illegal access 46
illegal act 23
immunity 69, 133
imprisonment 23, 123
inflation 61
informal norms 121
information 62, 74, 85, 88, 93–95, 115–117
insider information 45, 52, 88
insiders 85–88
institutionalization 45, 134
institutions 23–25, 38–40, 50, 91
intellectual property 34, 93
intentional bankruptcy 85
International Foreign Trade Agency 73
Investigations Committee 98–99, 126,
  133–135
investments 62, 71, 118
Ioann Grozny 78
Ioann the IV, Grozny 78
Ivan the Terrible 60
Ivanov, Sergei 123–124
Ivanov, Vyacheslav 96
Ivanova, K. 122

Jacobs, James 20
Jakobson, Linda 7
Japan 64
joint stock companies 39, 42, 93, 102, 109
Jonson, Lena 7
judges 132–133
judicial system 46
jurisdiction 63, 69, 102, 129
Just Russia 126

Kabanov, Kirill 73
Kapliev, Andrei 126
Karatnicky, Adrian 88

154   *Index*

Karatuev, Aleksandr 64
Kazun, Anton 2, 67–68, 106, 113
KGB 14, 102, 124
Khodorkovsky, Mikhail 1, 26, 60–61, 73, 75, 126
kickbacks 11, 20, 37, 65, 122–123, 131
Kireev, Aleksei 2, 29
Kiselev, Evgeny 69
Kivinen, Markku 5
Kolganov, Andrei 38
Kommunisticheskaya partiya Rossijskoj Federatsii 78
Kononenko, Vadim 6, 64
Kotin, V. 133–134
KPRF 59
KrAZ 74
Kremlin 7, 75, 124, 127
Kryshtanovskaya, Olga 120–121
Kuchins, Andrew 24
Kupatadze, Alexander 6
Kurer, Oscar 5

land 28, 36, 85, 88, 90, 96, 121, 128, 137
law enforcement 12, 34, 51, 67–75, 101–102, 134
lawful owner 32, 37–38, 70, 120
laws 9, 23, 51, 72, 75, 108, 131
lawsuits 29, 46
lawyers 31–32, 73, 75, 85, 89
LDPR 131
Lebedev, Vyatcheslav 123
Ledeneva, Alena 36, 117, 121, 122
legal disputes 10, 86
legal gaps 46
legal loopholes 28, 31, 33, 86, 89
legal nihilism 46, 115
legality 23, 24, 32, 49, 50–51, 114
legitimacy 9, 21, 25, 50, 114
Lehmann, Hartmut 5
Liberal Democratic Party of Russia 131
Liberal'no-demokraticheskaya partiya Rossii 131
Libman, Alexander 7
Lieutenant-General Viktor Vasil'ev 98
liquidation 28
liquidity 46, 76
local authorities 20, 48, 50, 91, 95, 101, 108
localization 3–4
lockouts 118
Logunov, Oleg 133
Lowenstein, Louis 28
Lower Chamber of the Russian Parliament 31
Lundstrom, Susanna 19
Luzhkov, Yuri 42

M&A 47, 98
mafia 31, 130
Magnitsky, Sergei ix, 24
management 27–28, 30, 35–36, 73, 84, 87, 93–95
Manahov, Sergei 98
manipulations 28, 32, 42, 51
market cleaners 48
market economy 28, 38, 88, 90
market reforms 6, 40, 117, 121
market value 12, 48, 60, 90, 108
Markus, Stanislav 21, 30, 66, 70, 106
Marx, Karl 37, 63
mass privatization 3, 33, 116
Mazur, Irina 31, 47, 87, 115
McKee, David 28
means of production 3, 11, 37, 39, 44, 57, 116
Media-Most 75
Medvedev, Dmitry 1, 13, 59, 62, 76, 102, 122–126, 131–132
Medvedev, Sergei 7
Mergers and acquisitions 27–29, 36, 49, 91, 98
Meshkov, Sergei 93
military 60, 68, 70–72, 124
Ministerstvo vnutrennikh del 126
Ministry of Defense 124
Ministry of the Interior 2, 65–66, 74, 98–101, 128–130
minority holders 88
Mironov, Sergei 102, 126–127
Mishler, William 7, 25–26
mixed market type economy 1
Model Law on International Commercial Arbitration 117
monopolization 47, 52, 85
monopoly 30, 57
moratorium 122
Morris, Jeremy 6
mortgages 70
Moscow 1, 41–43, 68, 74, 76, 91, 96, 98
Moscow City Council 131
Moscow government 131
Moscow mayor 131
Moscow region 100–101
Moshes, Arkady 6, 64
Munro, Neil 7, 25–26
MVD 6, 68, 126, 134–135
Myant, Martin 10

NAK 73, 114
Namli, Elena 7
National Anti-Corruption Committee 73, 114

Index 155

nationalization 57, 59
Natsional'ny antikorruptsionny komitet 73, 114
negligence 73
Nekrasov, Vladimir 73–74
Nemtsov, Boris 142
Neutze, Jan 88
NGOs 31, 68, 106
nomenklatura 39, 121
noneconomic mechanisms 4, 57, 76
non-governmental organizations 31, 68, 106
Norilsk Nickel 59
Nornikel 78
North, Douglass 19

OBEP 68
Obydenkova, Anastassia 7
OECD 64
Ogonek 102
oil and gas industry 60–61
oligarch 9, 25, 44, 66, 126
Olson, Mancur 19
On anti-corruption expertise of normative legal acts and projects of normative legal acts, Federal law 132
On appraisals code in the RF 76
On investigation and search operations 75
On police 75
open access 107
opportunistic behavior 133
Oprichniki 78
Oprichnina 60
Order "On the measures against corruption" 131
Orenburgskaya oblast' 90
Organization for Economic Cooperation and Development 64
organized criminal groups 70, 84, 126
Ortmann, Stefanie 121
Osipian, Ararat 20, 25, 92
Otdel po bor'be s ekonomicheskimi prestupleniyami 68
outsiders 88, 98
Overland, Indra 8
oversight 20, 37, 50, 114
ownership 10, 30, 37–38, 42, 58–60, 77, 137

Padva, Genrikh 74
Panfilova, Elena 115
paratroopers 68
Pastukhov, Vladimir 75
payments 20, 50, 57, 106
Payne, Robert 23
Pei, Minxin 7–8

Perestroika 20, 125
personal connections 121
Petrov, Nikolay 121
phenomenon of raiding 11, 43, 91
piracy 32, 121
Pistor, Katharina 117
Pivovarsky, Alexander 39
plaintiff 66
planned economy 1
poison pill 47
Polese, Abel 6
police 66, 67, 69–71, 75–76, 135
Popova, Maria 6, 24
populism 91
post-Soviet space 2, 6, 29, 63, 90, 108
potential for corruption 131
Power, Timothy 117
predatory incursion 86
Presidential Anti-Corruption Council 131
prevention 66, 128, 134–135
private security firm 1, 86
private workshops 121
privatization 3–4, 10, 33–36, 44, 76, 87, 94, 115
profit sharing 92
profiteering 26–27, 122
property relations 30, 35–36, 40, 45, 72, 101, 120
property rights 3, 4, 8, 10, 21, 30, 38–39, 44–45
Prosecutor's General Office 98
protection 21, 25, 27, 29, 44–45, 71
provisions 12, 69, 104, 108, 132
provocation by bribe 13, 133–135
pseudo-accountability 3, 10, 21, 51
public sector 58–59, 77, 91, 119, 121
public services 106
Pursiainen, Christer 7–8
Putin, Vladimir 6–10, 23–25, 71, 102, 124–127, 135

racketeer 11, 21, 29, 36, 51
racketeering 29, 36–37, 44
RAGS 71
raiding 32
raiding attacks 12–13, 40, 47, 70, 84, 91, 96–98, 125
raiding movement 42, 47, 72
Rajkov, Gennady 49, 98
Rajonnoe upravlenie po bor'be s organizovannoj prestupnost'yu 68
RAN 127
rate of return 48, 72, 96
real estate 12, 45, 52, 70, 85, 90, 93–96

156 *Index*

redistribution 11, 20, 26, 33, 48, 50, 60, 66, 77–78
regulations 10, 21–22, 46, 51, 72, 132
reiderstvo 28–29
Remington, Thomas 5
replacement of management 73
re-sale 116
Research Institute 31
responsibility 12, 25, 73, 95, 99, 102, 133
restructuring 28, 43, 60, 75, 88, 94
Roberts, Sean 7
Robertson, Graeme 7
Robinson, Neil 8
Rodgers, Peter 6
Rojansky, Matthew 29
Rosatom 129–130
Rosbilding 91
Rose, Richard 7
Rose-Ackerman, Susan 4, 28, 116
Roslyak, Yuri 96
Rosoboronexport 71
Ross, Cameron 7
Rossel'khozbank 124
Rossijskaya akademiya gosudarstvennoj sluzhby 71
Rossijskaya akademiya nauk (RAN) 127
Rostovskaya oblast' 100
Rothstein, Bo 5, 19
Round, John 6
RUBOP 68
rules 21–22, 39, 51, 63, 93, 132
Rumyantseva, Anastasiya 93
Russian Academy of Sciences (RAN) 127
Russian Academy of State Services 71
Russian Ministry of Statistics 125
Russian National Anti-corruption Committee 73, 114

Sachs, Jeffrey 39
Sakwa, Richard 1, 8
Salmenniemi, Suvi 5
sanctions 128
Sberbank 48, 124
scale of raiding 96, 101
Schetnaya palata 98
searches 6, 8, 73, 76, 134
shadow economy 4, 44
Shalakov, Yuri 100
Shelley, Louise 2
Sheremet'evo International Airport 76
Shlapentokh, Vladimir 23, 25
Shuvalov, Igor 129
Shvartsman, Oleg 68, 70–71, 90–91
Simis, Konstantin 121

SK 126
Skidanova, Lilia 36, 40, 44, 67
Sledstvennyj komitet 126
Sluzhba vneshnej razvedki 71
Smith, Adam 19–20
smuggling 76
Sobolev, Anton 2
socialist property 11, 57
Sonin, Konstantin 6
Søreide, Tina 4–5, 116
Soros, George ix
Soviet Union 45, 60, 130
Spravedlivaya Rossiya 126
St. Petersburg 101
Stalinist bureaucracy 3, 121
state contracts 66, 122
State Duma 31, 49, 59, 69, 75–76, 98, 122, 126–128
Stewart, Susan 7
stock holders 68
stock market 28, 102
stock value 88
storm troopers 51, 85
storming 37, 51, 84
Strasburg Court 75
structure of property relations 1, 3
Sturm, Jan-Egbert 19
sub-contracting 132
subsidiary 73
subsidized regions 71
Sukhorukova, Svetlana 73
Supreme Court 123, 127
surprise attack 86
Sutela, Pekka 8
Sverdlovskaya oblast' 111
SVR 71
Svyaz'-Invest ix
Sychev, Pavel 30, 32

target 12, 20, 29, 31–34, 46–48, 87–96
targeted company 34, 46, 48, 76, 87–88, 94
targeted firm 87, 89
Tarkhanova, Zarina 37, 45–48
Tax Administration 71, 103
tax debts 69
tax evasion 23, 98, 122
Taylor, Brian 6, 24, 67
Taylor, Matthew 117
theft 32, 103
Tishchenko, Kirill 29
Tkachenko, N.I. 30, 47, 86, 88
Torgovo-promyshlennaya palata Rossijskoj Federatsii 131
TPP 131

Index   157

traffic police 69
transaction costs 22
transactions 46, 98, 116
transfer of property 91
transition economy 18–19, 39, 42, 135
transparency 5, 45–46, 48, 93, 114, 116, 129, 132
Transparency International, Russian Office of 115, 118
travel abroad 69
Treisman, Daniel 8
Trotsky, Lev 120
trust 5, 95, 115, 121, 131
Tsar Ioann the IV 78

undercover police detective 133
unemployment 39
Union of the Soviet Socialist Republics 41, 45, 60, 64, 121, 130
unlawful actions 32, 73
Urban, Michael 8
Uslaner, Eric 5
USSR 41, 45, 60, 64, 121, 130

Vaksberg, Arkady 121
Varnalij, Zakharij 31, 47, 87, 115
Vavilov, Andrey 9
VDV 68
velvet re-privatization 71
Venezuela 59
Vinokurov, Evgeny 7
violations 8, 11–12, 21, 51, 68, 70, 87, 93, 102, 117, 122
violence 2, 29, 30, 57, 71, 89, 102, 130
violent deaths 130
violent entrepreneurship 11, 34–37, 44
virtual reality 3
Vladivostok 96

Vneshtorgbank 73
Volkov, Vadim 2, 29, 36, 71
Voslensky, Michael 121
vouchers 3

wage arrears 94
Waite, Duncan 23
Ward, Christopher 6
Weber, Max 63–64
Wedeman, Andrew 4, 117
Western investors ix, 97
White, Stephen 7, 8, 120, 121
Whitefield, Stephen 121
Wilhelmsen, Julie 7
Williams, Aled 5
Williams, Colin 6
Wilson Rowe, Elana 7
Wincott, Daniel 5
Wolchik, Sharon 7
Woodruff, David 2, 45
workers' collective 47, 52, 94
World Bank 12, 65, 103
would-be bribe 134
wrongdoing 22, 137

Xu, Chenggang 117

Yadav, Vineeta 117
Yakovlev, Andrei 2
Yekaterinburg 100
Yeltsin, Boris 6, 23, 25, 125, 130
Yukos 8, 20, 27, 50, 60–61, 71, 74–75, 90

Zadorozhny, Grigory 39
Zamoshkin, Sergei 134
Zhdanov, Igor 22–23, 26
Zhirinovsky, Vladimir 131, 133
Zon, Hans van 71, 130